# Psychopharmacology Update

# Psychopharmacology
# Update

### edited by
### JONATHAN O. COLE M.D.
Chief, Psychopharmacology Program
McLean Hospital

**THE COLLAMORE PRESS**
D.C. Heath and Company
Lexington, Massachusetts
Toronto

*R M*
*315*
*P763*

**Library of Congress Cataloging in Publication Data**

Main entry under title:
  Psychopharmacology update.

  "A compilation of 12 papers originally written between 1976 and 1979 for
the McLean Hospital Journal's special section entitled Psychopharmacology
Update."
  1. Psychopharmacology—Addresses, essays, lectures. 2. Psychotropic
drugs—Addresses, essays, lectures. I. Cole, Jonathan O. [DNLM:
1. Psychopharmacology—Collected works. 2. Mental disorders—Drug
therapy—Collected works. WM402 P9757]
RM315.P763        615'.78        79-48064
ISBN 0-669-03695-1

Published simultaneously in Canada.

Printed in the United States of America.

International Standard Book Number: 0-669-03695-1

Library of Congress Catalog Card Number: 79-48064

*To Mrs. Evelyn Stone*
*for her skillful and warm encouragement*
*and editorial genius*
*and to my wife*
*for her tolerance and understanding.*

# Contents

Preface ix

List of Contributors xi

Part I　　　　*Drug Therapies*　1

Chapter 1　　**Lithium Therapy: A Practical Review**
*Richard I. Altesman, M.D.* and
*Jonathan O. Cole, M.D.*　3

Chapter 2　　**Tricyclic Antidepressant Blood Levels**
*Jonathan O. Cole, M.D.* and
*Paul Orsulak, Ph.D.*　19

Chapter 3　　**Drug Treatment of Anxiety**
*Jonathan O. Cole, M.D.*　29

Chapter 4　　**Beta-Blocking Drugs in Psychiatry**
*Richard Altesman, M.D.,*
*Jonathan O. Cole, M.D.,* and
*Charles H. Weingarten, M.D.*　43

Chapter 5　　**Drug Therapy of Adult Minimal Brain
Dysfunction (MBD)**
*Jonathan O. Cole, M.D.*　69

Chapter 6　　**Fenfluramine**
*Jonathan O. Cole, M.D.*　81

Chapter 7　　**Drugs and Senile Dementia**
*Roland J. Branconnier, M.A.* and
*Jonathan O. Cole, M.D.*　93

Chapter 8　　**Lecithin and Choline in Alzheimer Disease**
*Jonathan O. Cole, M.D.*　107

Chapter 9　　**L-Tryptophan: Clinical Studies**
*Jonathan O. Cole, M.D.,*
*Ernest Hartmann, M.D.,* and
*Peter Brigham, M.D.*　119

*Part II*          *Drug Side Effects*                        149

**Chapter 10**     **Tardive Dyskinesia**
                   *Jonathan O. Cole, M.D. and*
                   *George Gardos, M.D.*                      151

**Chapter 11**     **Agranulocytosis Revisited**
                   *Jonathan O. Cole, M.D.,*
                   *Harrison G. Pope, Jr., M.D. and*
                   *Chester Swett, Jr., M.D.*                 165

**Chapter 12**     **Lithium and the Kidney**
                   *Jonathan O. Cole, M.D.,*
                   *Richard I. Altesman, M.D.,*
                   *Martin Ionescu-Pioggia, A.B., and*
                   *Patricia M. Brewster, R.N., M.A.*         173

**Chapter 13**     **Memory Difficulty and Tricyclic**
                   **Antidepressants**
                   *Jonathan O. Cole, M.D. and*              189
                   *Alan F. Schatzberg, M.D.*

# Preface

This book is a compilation of thirteen papers written between 1976 and 1980 for the *McLean Hospital Journal's* special section entitled "Psychopharmacology Update." These papers had the original purpose of informing practicing psychiatrists of new developments in psychopharmacology. Because a number of my colleagues commented on the clinical usefulness of these review papers, we decided that the information should have wider distribution in a book. For this volume, I added commentaries highlighting developments since each paper was written. The volume therefore provides, as the title indicates, a comprehensive overview of important new developments in clinical psychopharmacology as it has evolved over the past five years. They balance a thoughtful analysis of clinical research data with relevant basic research information and with my ongoing clinical experience as a consultant in psychopharmacology at McLean Hospital, a 250-bed, private, Harvard-affiliated psychiatric hospital.

The areas selected for review were chosen for a variety of reasons—new research findings, special conferences I attended, drugs I have studied, or questions frequently asked of me as I talked before various medical or psychiatric groups. Chapters, therefore, range over a variety of important new developments in this rapidly evolving field. The reader will find chapters focused on new concerns in clinical psychopharmacology, such as tardive dyskinesia and the renal effects of lithium and on new treatments that are exciting because they bridge the gap between basic and clinical research, such as the use of L-tryptophan in psychiatry, the place of beta-blocking drugs like propranolol in psychiatry, and the basis for interest in the use of choline and lecithin in senile dementia. The clinician will also find helpful papers on the status of clinical laboratory tests that measure plasma levels of tricyclic antidepressants, on the clinical use of lithium, on the therapeutic implications of new diagnostic concepts, such as adult minimal brain dysfunction, and on the place of older drug therapies for elderly patients with organic dementias.

In short, I have tried to provide the practicing clinical psychiatrist with information on the utility of various modern drug treatment approaches and an understanding of the basic and clinical research data relevant to such clinical drug use in chapters written, I hope, in a clear and readable manner.

In writing these papers, I have had the help of a range of coauthors, for whose assistance I am most grateful; these include Richard Altesman, Roland Branconnier, Patricia Brewster, Peter Brigham, George Gardos, Ernest L. Hartmann, Paul J. Orsulak, Martin Ionescu-Pioggia, Harrison Pope, Alan Schatzberg, Chester Swett, and Charles Weingarten. I have worked most happily and productively with all of them at either McLean Hospital or Boston State Hospital. I would also like to thank Mrs. Pat Pershan for handling all the final manuscript preparation and Mrs. Elaine Beroz, as well as Ms. Barbara Beake and Ms. Karen-Lee Rosenthal for work on earlier stages of the various manuscripts.

# List of Contributors

*Richard I Altesman, M.D.*
Assistant Psychiatrist, McLean Hospital, Belmont, Massachusetts
Instructor, Department of Psychiatry, Harvard Medical School,
    Boston, Massachusetts

*Roland J. Branconnier, M.A.*
Research Director, Geriatric Psychopharmacology Unit, Boston State
    Hospital, Boston, Massachusetts

*Patricia Brewster, R.N., M.A.*
Research Nurse, Psychopharmacology Program, McLean Hospital,
    Belmont, Massachusetts

*Peter Brigham, M.D.*
Resident (PGYI), Psychiatry, McLean Hospital, Belmont, Massachusetts

*Jonathan O. Cole, M.D.*
Chief, Psychopharmacology Program, McLean Hospital, Belmont,
    Massachusetts
Lecturer, Department of Psychiatry, Harvard University, Boston,
    Massachusetts
Lecturer, Department of Psychiatry, Tufts Medical School, Boston,
    Massachusetts
Lecturer, Department of Psychiatry, Boston University School of Medicine,
    Boston, Massachusetts

*George Gardos, M.D.*
Director, Institute of Research and Rehabilitation, Boston State Hospital
    Boston, Massachusetts
Assistant Professor of Psychiatry, Boston University School of Medicine,
    Boston, Massachusetts

*Ernest L. Hartmann, M.D.*
Senior Psychiatrist, West-Ros-Park Mental Health Center, Hyde Park,
    Massachusetts

*Martin Ionescu-Pioggia, A.B.*
Research Associate, Psychopharmacology Department, Alcohol and Drug
    Abuse Research Center, McLean Hospital, Belmont, Massachusetts
Doctoral Candidate, Department of Psychology, University of North
    Carolina, Chapel Hill, North Carolina

*Paul J. Orsulak, Ph.D.*
Assistant Professor of Psychiatry, Harvard Medical School, Boston,
    Massachusetts

*Harrison G. Pope, M.D.*
Assistant Psychiatrist, McLean Hospital, Belmont, Massachusetts
Instructor, Department of Psychiatry, Harvard Medical School,
    Boston, Massachusetts

*Alan F. Schatzberg, M.D.*
Associate Psychiatrist, McLean Hospital, Belmont, Massachusetts
Assistant Professor of Psychiatry, Department of Psychiatry, Harvard
    Medical School, Boston, Massachusetts

*Chester Swett, M.D.*
Associate Psychiatrist, McLean Hospital, Belmont, Massachusetts
Assistant Professor of Psychiatry, Department of Psychiatry, Harvard
    Medical School, Boston, Massachusetts

*Charles Weingarten, M.D.*
Chief of Internal Medicine, McLean Hospital, Belmont, Massachusetts
Instructor in Medicine, Harvard Medical School, Boston, Massachusetts

# Part I
# Drug Therapies

# 1

# Lithium Therapy: A Practical Review

*Richard I. Altesman, M.D.*
and *Jonathan O. Cole, M.D.*

In recent years, as the clinical use of lithium carbonate has grown and research efforts have expanded, the literature on lithium has become voluminous. This chapter is not a comprehensive review of that literature. Rather, it concerns itself with some of the more salient issues and practical questions that arise concerning lithium therapy. Titles of articles and reviews for further study are listed in the references [1-5]. Also included are references on lithium's putative mechanisms of action [5-7].

Lithium is an alkali metal and exists in nature as a salt. Although its medicinal use extends back to antiquity, the use of lithium salts in modern times dates to the last 30 years. Lithium earned some notoriety because of its injudicious and uncontrolled use as a salt substitute in the 1940s [8] but has since been proved to be both safe and of considerable value in psychiatric practice. Although not approved for routine treatment of mania in the Unites States until 1970, lithium has been studied and accepted for a considerably longer period by European, British, and Australian psychiatrists. In fact, the 1949 report by John Cade on lithium's beneficial effects in several acutely manic patients [9] has been considered the beginning of modern psychopharmacology, predating the use of reserpine, the antipsychotic phenothiazines, and the antidepressant agents.

## Indications for the Use of Lithium

Lithium carbonate was initially utilized in the treatment of acutely manic patients and was first shown effective for that condition. This efficacy exists for treating both the more classic *mood* disturbances (e.g. euphoria, irritability) as well as related symptoms, such as ideas of reference, delusions, and hallucinations, which may occur in manic psychoses. The utility of lithium in the treatment of *acute mania* was initially based on uncontrolled studies [9,10] but has since been well documented in numerous double-blind controlled studies [11-15]. This efficacy should now be considered firmly established [16]. Lithium has since been shown to be of benefit in bipolar patients as a *maintenance* medication for the prevention of recurrent affective episodes, mania, and depression [17-20]. This is perhaps an even more important use of lithium, as it allows for a preventive approach

3

to treatment. This prophylactic effect has been recently reviewed in detail by Davis [2]. He points out that the effectiveness of lithium in preventing the recurrence of manic-depressive episodes has been well documented; that placebo patients are exposed to a risk of mortality and morbidity; and that other areas of lithium research still require attention. Davis therefore concludes that further studies to replicate lithium's prophylactic properties are unnecessary.

It has also been shown that lithium can be of benefit in *preventing* recurrent episodes of *unipolar depression* [2,18,21], perhaps with a greater effect for those individuals with more severe, relapsing depressions. At present, the use of lithium for the prevention of unipolar depression is less well accepted than is its use for prophylaxis in bipolar illness [22]. This may be due, in part, to the difficulty in achieving diagnostic clarity for unipolar patients and to the smaller number of such patients studied [16].

Although lithium's overall efficacy is well established, the terms "prevention" and "prophylaxis" may be misleading. Response may be incomplete or even nonexistent for some patients [22].

Lithium has been advocated by several investigators as a treatment to alleviate *existing (i.e. acute) depression* [23]. However evidence regarding this effectiveness is presently contradictory [24]. At present, lithium alone is not recommended as a treatment for existing severe depression [16].

The use of lithium in patients with disturbances referred to as "cyclothymia," "mood swing," or "emotionally unstable character disorder [25] (possible variants of affective disorder) has also been suggested. Further studies to establish lithium's effectiveness in these states and to delineate their potential relationship to bipolar illness are still necessary before conclusions can be drawn.

It appears that lithium is still in its heyday and is being advocated, sometimes as a panacea, for many diverse conditions [22]. These conditions include alcoholism [26,27], aggression [28], hypersexuality, periodic catatonia, premenstrual tension, drug addiction, organic brain syndromes, movement disorders, and various other psychiatric and medical disorders [29], bringing to mind the old aphorism: "Use a new drug while it still works." Certainly, it is important to develop treatments for additional disorders, as well as to establish a thorough understanding of lithium's spectrum of effects. After further scrutiny, some of these miscellaneous uses may show continued promise. However, until further evidence is available, the use of lithium in these varied conditions should be considered experimental and primarily of heuristic value. If lithium is employed for a condition other than primary affective illness, it is important that the clinician consider such use an empirical *trial* in the strict, experimental sense of the word.

It should be noted that since lithium is one of the medications specifically indicated for patients with recurrent affective illness [1], the accurate identification of such patients is incumbent upon the clinician if appropriate treatment is to follow. This is especially, though not exclusively, true for patients with acute psychoses. Only with the help of careful diagnosis can optimum and specific treatment plans, both pharmacologic and otherwise, be instituted [30].

**When Not to Use Lithium**

For practical purposes, there are only *relative* contraindications to lithium's use. Lithium's benefits must be weighed against the potential risk for an individual patient. In evaluating the risk, the patient's medical condition and reliability, the clinical setting, and the physician's experience must be taken into account. While not a comprehensive list, the following factors should be remembered: lithium is excreted almost entirely by the kidneys [31], and adequate *renal function* is essential for its use. Patients with certain preexisting but *stable* kidney disorders, for whom there are clear and pressing indications for lithium therapy, have been maintained on lithium with lowered doses and intensive monitoring [32]. However, such use of lithium is hazardous and not routinely recommended [1].

Particular care must be given to individuals requiring sodium-restricted diets and/or diuretic agents. Lithium is primarily reabsorbed in proximal renal tubule, with possible further reabsorption in Henle's loop. [31]. The tubular reabsorption of lithium is in competition with that of sodium [1]. With sodium depletion, as occurs in patients on sodium-restricted diets or diuretics, there will be increased lithium retention [33]. Under these circumstances, lithium levels will become elevated, with serious potential for toxicity. The use of lithium with thiazide diuretics has been reported [34] but should only be considered in selected patients whose treatment is under close scrutiny by experienced physicians.

Lithium, in therapeutic ranges, may have *cardiovascular effects* [35], although the exact incidence is unknown. Reversible T-wave changes (flattening and inversion) have been noted on electrocardiograms. To our knowledge, there is no evidence to suggest that they are of serious concern. In a study of ECG's obtained during exercise and at rest, neither ST abnormalities nor adverse effects on cardiac function by lithium were noted, but it was suggested that "ventricular arrhythmias may occur or be aggravated during lithium therapy" [36]. Occasional case reports of potentially serious conduction abnormalities have appeared, but these seem to be relatively rare phenomena. Arrhythmias with lithium toxicity are of relatively low incidence and occur as late manifestations in the course of lithium intoxication. Lithium has not been established as a direct cause of these arrhythmias [35].

Clearly, caution should be exercised in treating cardiac patients, but if given carefully and properly, lithium can be appropriately utilized [37]. It is important to recognize that other psychoactive medications used in affective illness, such as tricyclic antidepressants, may have equal or even greater cardiac effect [38,39]. The possible sequelae of not employing lithium should also be considered. The treatment of choice, if any, must be individually evaluated. (Nonpharmacologic intervention, such as electroconvulsive therapy can also be considered in the acute phase but may be insufficient if long-range maintenance treatment is necessary.)

An increased incidence in *congenital cardiac malformations* (especially Ebstein anomaly of the tricuspid valve) has been reported in newborns whose mothers were taking lithium during pregnancy [40,41]. While the actual risk to the fetus may be small, the hazard of teratogenicity cannot presently be ruled out, and lithium cannot routinely be recommended during pregnancy.[1]

Lithium has a narrow therapeutic index [1] (the ratio of the lethal dose to the effective dose), and consideration to its toxicity in *overdosage* must be given. This is especially important as lithium is prescribed for patients with affective illness—individuals with a statistically heightened risk for suicide. Some danger of lethality also exists with most other psychoactive agents. Caution must be exercised when any medication is given to potentially suicidal, impulsive, or unreliable patients.

**Prior to Initiating Lithium Therapy**

The so-called "lithium workup" is actually a simple preliminary medical screening. Its purpose is to assist in diagnosing any underlying physical illness which may be exacerbated by, or interfere with, lithium treatment and to establish a baseline of physiologic functioning for future reference. The following are suggested, but the "routine" should be tailored to the particular patient:

1. *Blood urea nitrogen (BUN) and creatinine serum levels and urinalysis* are obtained to assess kidney function and urine chemistry.
2. *A white blood count* as a baseline measure is recommended. (Leukocytosis often accompanies lithium use [42].)

---

[1]The Register of Lithium Babies, Langley Porter Neuropsychiatric Institute, San Francisco, California, requests information about *any* experience with the conception or birth of babies exposed to lithium *in utero*.

3. *Thyroid function tests* are obtained as baseline measures. (Lithium carbonate may potentiate or produce abnormal thyroid function, including goiter and/or hypothyroidism [43,44].) A thyroid-stimulating hormone (TSH) level for baseline purposes is also valuable, and repeat determinations will be sensitive measures of lithium-induced thyroid changes [45]. The thyroid function tests also rule out coincidental hypothyroidism that may be aggravated by lithium. Albeit unlikely, the possibility of underlying thyroid disease presenting with affective-like symptoms is also eliminated.

4. *Electrolytes* (particularly sodium level) may be indicated in patients for whom there is a question of electrolyte imbalance or dehydration. This is in reference to the potential for lithium retention resulting from decreased sodium.

5. *Electrocardiograms* in patients with a heightened index of suspicion for cardiac disease (including the elderly) are suggested.

6. A *fasting glucose* or blood screening profile (e.g. SMA-12) may, on occasion, be helpful.

7. A complete *medical history* is always mandated, and, as with any patient, a *physical examination* should be strongly considered.

Before starting lithium treatment, the patient should understand the reasons for its prescription. The patient should also be aware of both the expected therapeutic benefits and the possible side effects.

**Management of Lithium Therapy**

*Preparations*

Lithium is commercially available in the United States as the carbonate in 300 mg capsules and scored tablets. A liquid preparation of lithium citrate has recently become available. Sustained or slow-release forms of lithium have been developed, but these have been associated with various problems, including erratic or even rapid absorption [46], and such preparations are not available in this country.

*Dosage*

There is no standard dose in lithium treatment, as it is actually the serum lithium level which determines the amount prescribed. Wide individual differences can exist in the quantity of lithium which must be taken to achieve a particular serum level [47]. It is the serum lithium level that is important and not the number of capsules or milligrams taken to reach it. (See section on serum levels.)

*Initiating Treatment*

Lithium should be taken in divided doses to minimize intolerance and side effects attributable to transient peaks in the serum level or discomfort from direct gastric irritation. [48].

In starting nonacute treatment, one can often begin with 300 mg of lithium carbonate t.i.d. If there is special concern about the possibility of adverse effects or developing high serum levels, one should begin more conservatively with smaller amounts, especially if initiating maintenance treatment. For more acute treatment, an initial dose of 300 mg q.i.d. may be desired. The dose is then adjusted progressively to attain therapeutic levels. When first initiating lithium, increments usually need be no more than 300 mg at a time. A repeat lithium level should be obtained prior to raising the dose.

An alternate method of initiating treatment has also been suggested, based on attempting to predict the eventual dose requirements [49]. A "loading dose" is given, followed by a 24-hour serum lithium level; the starting dose is estimated from this level. This technique has potential merits but is not routinely utilized, and its ultimate value is not firmly established.

*Serum Levels*

The standard determination used in following lithium therapy is the serum level. While the relationship is inexact, it has been postulated that serum determinations reflect lithium levels in the central nervous system. Other techniques are also being investigated. The red blood cell-lithium concentration and red blood cell-plasma lithium ratio have been suggested as more accurately correlating with central nervous system (CNS) levels, side effects, and toxicity [50]. Saliva lithium levels have also been studied with the hope that they may be obtained with greater ease and practical advantage [51]. For now, serum determinations remain the accepted practice in lithium treatment.

After treatment has begun, the *frequency of levels* varies, depending on clinical needs. Levels should be obtained at least once a week initially, sometimes more frequently. Acutely ill inpatients may require more frequent levels so that the dosage may be increased more rapidly. With maintenance treatment, the frequency of obtaining levels may be gradually decreased, for example, to once per month for at least the first year. This assumes stable levels and a reliable patient. Additional levels might still be necessary should the patient's medical or psychiatric condition change. Very infrequent levels are not recommended, especially if patient acceptance or reliability has not been established.

Serum levels should be obtained 8 to 12 hours after the last dose, but *12 hours* is distinctly preferable and is the standard interval on which therapeutic levels have been based [52]. This yields consistency in following serum levels, and it is the interval at which the lithium absorption/excretion curve is the most stable. (Absorption peaks at two to four hours and usually returns to predose levels in six to eight hours.) Levels obtained after shorter intervals may not reflect steady-state lithium concentrations and cannot accurately determine if the patient's serum level is in the therapeutic range [1,52]. Serum levels are generally available rapidly and economically from almost any clinical laboratory. The therapeutic range for serum lithium levels should generally be between 0.8 and 1.2 mEq/L for maintenance treatment and from 1.0 to 1.4 mEq/L or greater for acute (often inpatient) treatment of mania [1,53]. These are only approximate guidelines. An occasional patient may do well at lower levels, others may not tolerate "average" levels, and still others may require even higher levels. (Levels greater than 1.5 mEq/L are not advised.)

*Awaiting Treatment Response*

In acute mania there may be a lag time of 7 to 14 days, or even longer, from the time adequate levels are attained to the beginning of treatment response [54]. In maintenance treatment there can be a gradual and protracted onset of prophylactic effects before affective episodes are prevented.

It has been suggested (but not confirmed) that lithium exerts a relatively specific action on manic patients, unlike the less specific antipsychotic and sedating effects of neuroleptics [13,14]. However, as there is a delayed onset of lithium's effects, antipsychotic agents are often added for more immediate management of the acutely manic patient [16]. Although the superiority of this lithium-neuroleptic combination has not been documented by well-controlled studies, the use of this combination is a commonly accepted practice.

*After Treatment Response*

When acutely manic patients improve, it has been observed that their lithium requirements may decrease and their serum levels rise despite a constant dose. Although this has not been well studied, the physician should watch for possible increases in the patient's lithium level with clinical improvement. If this occurs, the dose may need to be lowered and lithium levels followed accordingly.

If combination treatment (e.g. lithium plus an antipsychotic agent) has been used in treating mania, the dose of the antipsychotic medication should be gradually lowered. It may then be discontinued once the patient responds and relapse seems unlikely.

**Adverse Reactions**

As with most medications, lithium may produce side effects and adverse reactions. These are usually either transient or tolerable for most patients, especially with good patient education. The more noteworthy side effects are reviewed, but others can develop.

*Gastrointestinal irritation and nausea* may occur, most commonly as lithium levels are raised [55]. The symptoms will frequently decline as treatment continues. Prescribing divided doses and taking the lithium with food may decrease irritation and nausea.

A fine *hand tremor* can develop. Although a dose-related effect has been postulated, this does not always appear to be true, and the tremor may even improve spontaneously. Lowering the lithium dose may help alleviate the tremor, but caution must be exercised to avoid jeopardizing the patient's psychiatric condition by this maneuver. The beta-adrenergic blocking agent propranolol has been suggested to reduce the tremor, but results have been contradictory [56-58]. If propranolol is used, the physician must have familiarity with its systemic actions, particularly the cardiovascular and respiratory effects.

*Skin reactions*, including an acneiform follicular rash, may also be produced or exacerbated by lithium [59,60]. Standard acne vulgaris regimens can be tried, but unfortunately they are often unsuccessful.

Lithium carbonate may also produce *renal effects*. Polyuria and polydipsia are not uncommon. More rarely, lithium-induced nephrogenic diabetes insipidus may occur [61-63]. Generally these side effects have been considered benign, reversible, and usually not necessitating active intervention. With patient education and understanding, these effects have been reasonably well tolerated. Treatments for nephrogenic diabetes insipidus, including thiazide diuretics, have been suggested to counteract these lithium-induced renal symptoms [34]. Again, the combination of lithium and a diuretic may be hazardous, and its benefits are not well established.

The possible long-term renal effects of lithium are currently being examined. There have been recent initial reports of kidney lesions, including focal nephron atrophy, interstitial fibrosis, and glomerular sclerosis, in a small number of lithium-treated patients [64,65]. Some of these patients may be atypical in that it was the presence of severe renal side effects or acute intoxication that prompted their kidney biopsies. Follow-up studies on both selected and unselected patients are in progress and matched controls will need to be employed. Impaired urine concentrating ability is also observed in lithium-treated patients [66] and may parallel histological changes [67]. The incidence and consequences of such kidney changes remain unknown. Despite lengthy experience with lithium, serious kidney disease has *not* been a common occurrence. It is possible that the development of renal abnormalities may prove to be idiosyncratic, occur in only a small number of patients, have a slow progression, or be reversible. The kidney changes may also be outweighed by lithium's therapeutic benefits [68]. Conclusions at this time cannot be made. In the meantime, lithium's use should be continually reevaluated. Proper indications for its use, particularly for long-term maintenance, should exist, and both physician and patient need to remain well informed. Patients with polyuria or increased urine volume should probably be especially well scrutinized. Several authorities suggest obtaining renal function tests (e.g. creatinine clearance, urine concentrating tests) but their lack of reliability must be taken into account. Serum creatinine levels are simpler to obtain and less variable but may be insufficiently sensitive to reflect early changes; however, serum creatinines are probably warranted. If decreased concentrating ability does develop, maintaining adequate hydration can be more difficult, and the tendency for lithium intoxication may be heightened.

Another area of recent interest has been the effect of lithium on *cognition and memory*. There have been reports of mild, reversible deficits on cognitive and memory tasks in both patients and normal individuals given lithium [69,70]. According to Coppen et al., [71] the memory complaints of patients on lithium may merely reflect the increased frequency of such complaints made by patients with affective disease in general. While the clinician should be attuned to the possibility of such effects, significant confusion or impairment of cognition does not appear to be a common occurrence.

*Weight gain* has also been reported in association with lithium. Explanations postulated for this include appetite stimulation, increased caloric intake secondary to polydipsia, and altered carbohydrate metabolism [72]. Reports of increased glucose tolerance are contradictory [73]. Carefully controlled dieting has been shown to be successful [74], but adequate electrolyte and fluid intake must be maintained if lithium toxicity is to be avoided.

As mentioned above, *neuroleptics* are often added while awaiting lithium's therapeutic effects. In 1974, there was a report of four cases of neurotoxicity in patients receiving lithium and haloperidol [75]. This report has been criticized on various grounds [76], and several reviews since have failed to identify any increased danger from a lithium-haloperidol combination [77-79].

Overt lithium intoxication can develop, especially with dehydration and sodium depletion, intercurrent medical illness, decreased kidney function, or overdose. Nausea and vomiting, or diarrhea, may be early signs of impending severe toxicity, although these symptoms also occur at lower levels, especially early in treatment. Further prodromata may include lassitude, confusion, drowsiness, increased muscle tremor, and twitching. If these occur, lithium must be stopped, and a serum level obtained (taking into account the time elapsed since the last dose). Severe toxicity may present with ataxia, gross confusion, myoclonic fasciculations and twitching, vomiting, and complete lethargy progressing to impaired consciousness, seizures, and, if untreated, death [1,80,81].

Treatment depends on the degree of toxicity [82]. In some mild cases, merely stopping lithium and observing the patient closely, with repeat serum lithium levels, will suffice. Caution must be exercised, as there may be a delay between high lithium levels and the onset of toxic symptoms. Hospitalization, intensive care, and hemodialysis may prove necessary in instances of severe intoxication.

## If Lithium Appears to Fail

One must first determine if treatment has, in fact, been adequate. One possibility is that blood levels are being obtained at less than 12-hour intervals after the last lithium dose. This produces an artificial appearance of the serum level being in the therapeutic range. Inconsistent compliance may be another factor, especially if there are prolonged periods between serum level determinations. Some patients may require slightly higher levels than usual for clinical effects. In other instances, it may be premature to judge the efficacy of the trial. Merely extending the observation period may yield positive results.

If the lithium trial has in fact been adequate, other possibilities for "treatment failure" still exist. Some patients may have only a relative or partial therapeutic response [22]. The frequency, duration, and/or severity of the affective episodes may exhibit improvement, but patients may not become entirely asymptomatic. Also, it is possible that one phase of a patient's manic-depressive illness may prove less responsive to lithium (e.g. in a given patient the manic cycles may be prevented or attenuated, while the depressive ones are less affected).

A small subgroup of manic-depressive patients are referred to as having "rapid cycles" (more than four affective episodes per year). A greater than expected percentage of these individuals appear to be lithium refractory [83]. Although treatment is frustrating for patient and clinician alike, some patients will benefit only after a prolonged trial on lithium (possibly more than a year) [84]. Assuming true "lithium failure" prior to that time may deprive the patient of a potentially effective treatment.

Treatment failure is sometimes interpreted as meaning that the diagnosis of primary affective illness is incorrect. While this may be true on occasion, caution must be exercised before automatically drawing this conclusion with a given patient. Some patients may not be responsive to lithium therapy despite a correct diagnosis of manic-depressive illness. Most authorities estimate effectiveness in approximately 80% of bipolar patients [54,85]. Even though a lithium response may help support a diagnosis of primary affective illness, a lack of response does not automatically mitigate against the presence of affective disease.

## Conclusion

Clinicians are continuing to become more comfortable and familiar with lithium as experience with the substance increases and more is learned about its effects. It is hoped that both the fanfare about its supposed "wonder drug" status and the resistance to its use have now declined. Although lithium has drawbacks and limitations, it is nevertheless a significant component of modern psychopharmacologic treatment.

## Commentary

This review is still valid as written. No major new clinical uses for lithium have been clearly identified. The only major new concern, that of renal changes, is covered in chapter 5.

## References

1. Baldessarini RJ, Lipinski JF: Lithium salts: 1970-1975. Ann Int Med 83:527-533, 1975.

2. Davis JM: Overview: Maintenance therapy in psychiatry: II. Affective disorders. Am J Psychiat 133:1-12, 1976.

3. Gershon S, Shopsin B (Eds): Lithium: Its Role in Psychiatric Research and Treatment. New York, Plenum, 1973.

4. Jefferson JW, Greist JH: Primer of Lithium Therapy. Baltimore, Williams and Wilkins, 1977.

5. Johnson FN (Ed): Lithium Research and Therapy. London, New York, Academic Press, 1975.

6. Bunney WE, Murphy DL: Neurobiological considerations on the mode of action of lithium carbonate. Pharmakopsych-Neuro-Pychopharmak 9:142-147, 1976.

7. Gerbino L, Oleshansky M, Gershon S: Clinical use and mode of action of lithium. *In* Lipton MA, DiMascio A, Killam KF (Eds): Psychopharmacology: A Generation of Progress. New York, Raven, 1978, pp. 1261-1275.

8. Corcoran AC, Taylor RD, Page IH: Lithium poisoning from the use of salt substitutes. JAMA 139:685-688, 1946.

9. Cade JF: Lithium salts in treatment of psychotic excitement. MJ Australia 36:349-352, 1949.

10. Noack CH, Tantner EM: The lithium treatment of maniacal psychosis. MJ Australia 38:219, 1951.

11. Schou M, Juel-Nielsen N, et al: The treatment of manic psychoses by the administration of lithium salts. J Neurol Neurosurg Psychiat 17:250-260, 1954.

12. Goodwin F, Murphy DL, Bunney WE: Lithium carbonate treatment in depression and mania. Arch Gen Psychiat 21:486-496, 1969.

13. Prien RF, Caffey EM Jr, Klett CJ: Comparison of lithium carbonate and chlorpromazine in treatment of mania. Arch Gen Psychiat 26:146-153, 1962.

14. Shopsin B, Gershon S, et al: Psychoactive drugs in mania. Arch Gen Psychiat 32:34-42, 1975.

15. Johnson G, Gershon S, Burdock EI, et al: Comparative effects of lithium and chlorpromazine in the treatment of acute mania. Br J Psychiat 119:267-276, 1971.

16. APA Task Force: Current status of lithium therapy. Am J Psychiat 132:997-1006, 1975.

17. Angst J, Weis P, et al: Lithium prophylaxis in recurrent affective disorders. Br J Psychiat 116:604-614, 1970.

18. Baastrup PC, Poulsen KS, Schou M, et al: Prophylactic lithium: A double blind discontinuation. Lancet 2:326-330, 1970.

19. Coppen A, Noguera R, Bailey J, et al: Prophylactic lithium in affective disorders. Lancet 2:275-279, 1971.

20. Prien RF, Klett CJ, Caffey EM Jr: Lithium prophylaxis in recurrent affective illness. Am J Psychiat 131:198-203, 1974.

21. Quitkin F, Rifkin A, Klein DF, et al: On prophylaxis in unipolar affective disorders. Am J Psychiat 133:1091-1092, 1976.

22. Prien RF, Caffey EM Jr: Long-term maintenance drug therapy in recurrent affective illness: Current status and issues. Dis Nerv Sys 38:981-992, 1977.

23. Mendels J: Lithium in the treatment of depression. Am J Psychiat 133:373-378, 1976.

24. Bennie EH: Lithium in the management of acute depressive illness. *In* Johnson FN, Johnson S (Eds): Lithium in Medical Practice. Baltimore, Univ Park Press, 1978, pp 41-46.

25. Rifkin A, Quitkin F, et al: Lithium carbonate in emotionally unstable character disorder. Arch Gen Psychiat 27:519, 1972.

26. Kline NS, Wren JC, et al: Evaluation of lithium therapy in chronic and periodic alcoholism. Am J M Sc 268:15-19, 1974.

27. Merry J, Reynolds CM, Boile J, et al: Prophylactic treatment of alcoholism by lithium carbonate. Lancet 2:481-483, 1976.

28. Sheard MH, Marini JL, et al: The effect of lithium on impulsive aggressive behavior in man. Am J Psychiat 133:1409-1412, 1976.

29. Schou M: The range of clinical uses of lithium. *In* Johnson FN, Johnson S (Eds): Lithium in Medical Practice. Baltimore, Univ Park Press, 1978, pp 21-39.

30. Pope HG Jr, Lipinski JF: Diagnosis in schizophrenia and manic-depressive illness: A reassessment of the specificity of "schizophrenic" symptoms in the light of current research. (In press).

31. Thomsen K, Schou M: Renal lithium excretion in man. Am J Physiol 215:823-827, 1968.

32. McKnelley WV, Tupin J, Dunn M: Lithium in hazardous circumstances with one case of lithium toxicity. Comp Psychiat 11:279-286, 1970.

33. Petersen V, et al: Effect of prolonged thiazide treatment on renal lithium clearance. Br Med J 3:143-145, 1974.

34. Himmelhoch JM, et al: Thiazide-lithium synergy in refractory mood swings. Am J Psychiat 134:149-152, 1977.

35. Tilkian AG, Schroder JS, Kao JJ, et al: The cardiovascular effects of lithium in man. Am J Med 61:665-670, 1976.

36. Tilkian AG, Schroder JJ: Effect of lithium on cardiovascular performance. Am J Cardiol 38:701-708, 1976.

37. Ayd FJ: Cardiovascular effects of lithium in man. Internat Drug Ther Newsletter 12:17-20, 1977.

38. Bigger JT, Kantor SJ, et al: Cardiovascular effects of tricyclic antidepressant drugs. *In* Lipton MA, DiMascio A, Killam KF (Eds): Psychopharmacology: A Generation of Progress. New York, Raven, 1978, pp. 1033-1046.

39. Robinson DS, Barker E: Tricyclic antidepressant cardiotoxicity. JAMA 236:2089-2090, 1976.

40. Schou M, et al: Lithium carbonate and pregnancy. Br Med J 2:135-136, 1973.

41. Weinstein MR, Goldfield MD: Cardiovascular malformation with lithium carbonate use during pregnancy. Am J Psychiat 132:529-531, 1975.

42. Murphy DL, Goodwin FK, Bunney WE: Leukocytosis during lithium treatment. Am J Psychiat 127:1559-1561, 1971.

43. Berens SC, Wolf J: The endocrine effects of lithium. *In* Johnson FN (Ed): Lithium Research and Therapy. London, New York, Academic Press, 1975, pp. 445-464.

44.Shopsin B: Effects of lithium on thyroid function. Dis Nerv Sys 31:237, 1970.

45. Lindstedt G, et al: On the prevalence, diagnosis and management of lithium-induced hypothyroidism. Br J Psychiat 130:452-458, 1977.

46. Tyrer SP: The choice of lithium preparation and how to give it. *In* Johnson FN, Johnson S (Eds): Lithium in Medical Practice, Baltimore, Univ Park Press, 1978, pp. 395-405.

47. Frys B, Petterson U, Sedvall G: Pharmacokinetics of lithium in manic depressive patients. Acta Psychiat Scand 49:237-247, 1973.

48. Amdisen A: Variation of serum lithium concentration during the day. Acta Psychiat Scand Supp 207:55-58, 1969.

49. Cooper TB, Simpson GM: The 24-hour lithium level as a prognosticator of dosage requirements: A 2-year follow-up study. Am J Psychiat 133:440-443, 1976.

50. Lee CR, et al: The relationship of plasma to erythrocyte lithium levels in patients taking lithium carbonate. Br J Psychiat 127:596-598, 1975.

51. Verghese A, et al: Usefulness of saliva lithium estimations. Br J Psychiat 130-248-250, 1977.

52. Amdisen A: Serum lithium estimations. Br Med J 2:240, 1973.

53. Prien RF, Caffey EM Jr: Relationship between dosage and response to lithium prophylaxis in recurrent depression. Am J Psychiat 133:567-570, 1976.

54. Goodwin FK, Ebert MH; Lithium in mania. *In* Gershon S, Shopsin B (Eds): Lithium: Its Role in Psychiatric Research and Treatment. New York, Plenum, 1973, pp. 237-252.

55. Amdisen A, Schou M: Biochemsitry of depression. Lancet 1:507, 1967.

56. Kirk L, Baastrup PC, Schou M: Propranolol treatment of lithium-induced tremor. Lancet 2:1086-1087, 1973.

57. Kallet JM, et al: Beta blockade in lithium tremor. J Neurol Neurosurg Psychiat 38:719-721, 1975.

58. Lapierre YD: Control of lithium tremor with propranolol. Canad Med J 114:619, 1976.

59. Rifkin A, Kurtin SB, et al: Lithium-induced folliculitis. Am J Psychiat 130:1018-1019, 1973.

60. Yoder FW: Acneiform eruption due to lithium carbonate. Arch Dermatol 111:396-397, 1975.

61. Angrist BS, et al: Lithium induced diabetes insipidus-like syndrome. Comp Psychiat 11:141-146, 1970.

62. Forrest JN, Cohen AD, et al: On the mechanism of lithium-induced diabetes insipidus in man and the rat. J Clin Invest 53:1115-1123, 1974.

63. MacNeil S, Jenner FA: Lithium and polyuria. *In* Johnson FN (Ed): Lithium Research and Therapy. London, New York, Academic Press, 1975.

64. Hestbech J, Hansen HE, et al: Chronic renal lesions following long-term treatment with lithium. Kidney Internat 12:205-213, 1977.

65. Burrows GD, Davies B, Kincaid-Smith P: Unique tubular lesions after lithium. Lancet 1:1310, 1978.

66. Bucht G, Wahlin A: Impairment of renal concentrating capacity by lithium. Lancet 1:778, 1978.

67. Hansen HE, Hestbech J, et al: Renal function and renal pathology in patients with lithium-induced impairment of renal concentrating ability. Proc Eur Dialysis Transpl Assn 14:518-527, 1977.

68. Schou M: A note on reports of nephrotoxic effects of lithium. *In* Johnson FN, Johnson S (Eds): Lithium in Medical Practice. Baltimore, Univ Park Press, 1978, p 264.

69. Judd LL, Hubbard B, Janowsky DS, et al: The effect of lithium carbonate on the cognitive functions of normal subjects. Arch Gen Psychiat 34:355-357, 1977.

70. Kysumo KS, Vaughan M: Effects of lithium salts on memory. Brit J Psychiat 131:453-457, 1977.

71. Coppen A, et al: Lithium and memory impairment. Lancet 1:488, 1978.

72. Vendsborg PR, et al: Lithium carbonate treatment and weight gain. Acta Psychiat Scand 53:139-147, 1976.

73. Vendsborg PR, Prytz S: Glucose tolerance and serum lipids in man after long-term lithium administration. Acta Psychiat Scand 53:64-69, 1976.

74. Dempsey GM et al: Treatment of excessive weight gain in patients taking lithium. Am J Psychiat 133:1082-1084, 1976.

75. Cohen WJ, Cohen NH: Lithium carbonate, haloperidol and irreversible brain damage. JAMA 230:1283, 1974.

76. Ayd FJ: Lithium-haloperidol for mania. Internat Drug Ther Newsletter 10:29-36, 1975.

77. Baastrup PC, et al: Adverse reactions in treatment with lithium carbonate and haloperidol. JAMA 236:2645-2646, 1976.

78. Juhl RP, Tsuang MT, Perry PJ: Concomitant administration of haloperidol and lithium carbonate in acute mania. Dis Nerv Syst 38:675-676, 1977.

79. Krisha NR, Taylor MA, Abrams R: Combined haloperidol and lithium carbonate in treating manic patients. Comp Psychiat 19:119-120, 1978.

80. Horowitz LC, Fisher CU: Acute lithium toxicity. New Eng J Med 281:1369, 1969.

81. Schou M, Amdisen A, Trap-Jensen J: Lithium poisoning. Am J Psychiat 125:520-526, 1968.

82. Thomsen K: Renal lithium elimination in man and active treatment of lithium poisoning. Acta Psychiat Scand Supp 207:83-84, 1969.

83. Dunner DL, Fieve RR: Clinical factors in lithium carbonate prophylaxis failure. Arch Gen Psychiat 30:229-233, 1974.

84. Dunner DL, Vijayalakshay P, Fieve RR: Rapid cycling manic depressive patients. Comp Psychiat 18:561-566, 1977.

85. Fieve RR: Overview of therapeutic and prophylactic trials. *In* Gershon S, Shopsin B (Eds): Lithium: Its Role in Psychiatric Research and Treatment. New York, Plenum, 1973.

# 2 Tricyclic Antidepressant Blood Levels

*Jonathan O. Cole M.D.*
and *Paul Orsulak, M.D.*

For many years, the only psychotherapeutic drug for which plasma levels were routinely available was lithium carbonate. Diphenylhydantoin levels have also been in general clinical use for several years. Chemical technology, with such sophisticated techniques as mass spectrometry, gas chromatography, and radioimmunoassay, has reached a stage at which blood levels of almost any substance can be accurately measured down to a few nanograms per milliliter ($10^{-9}$ gm) or even at the picogram level ($10^{-12}$ gm). The last four investigational drugs we have been studying have all had available, workable methods for measuring plasma levels. Schildkraut and Orsulak, in their laboratory at the Massachusetts Mental Health Center, have now been determining plasma levels on several tricyclic antidepressants on a research basis for almost two years. Greenblatt's laboratory at the Massachusetts General Hospital has been able to do benzodiazepine levels for a similar period. It seems likely that practicing psychiatrists will soon have access to routine plasma-level determinations at least for the tricyclics and probably for benzodiazepine and quite possibly for several antipsychotics within the early foreseeable future.

This paper will explore the general properties of drug plasma levels and will review the evidence of the probable utility of such measures for monitoring treatment with tricyclic antidepressants, the group of active drugs best suited at this time for the treatment of depressive conditions.

## Pharmacokinetics and Plasma Levels

This area has been well reviewed for drugs in general by Greenblatt and Koch-Weser [1,2] and for antipsychotic drugs in particular by Davis et al. [3]. Both Greenblatt's and Koch-Weser's papers, although clearly and precisely written, give psychiatric readers the feeling that they have wandered into a mathematical forest, inhabited by unfriendly computers and phantasmagoric kinetic constants. The issues can, we hope, be presented in simpler form.

To work in the central nervous system, drugs have to get into the blood stream from the gastrointestinal tract or, less commonly, by intramuscular or intravenous injection. Transport into the blood stream and into the more accessible extracellular fluid spaces is affected by the rate and completeness of absorption from the gastrointestinal tract or the muscle injection site. For drugs given by mouth, metabolic destruction begins in the intestine through bacterial action, in the intestinal wall (at least for chlorpromazine [3]), and in the liver as the drug leaves the portal circulation. At the same time, the drug begins to spread into more remote tissues and may be bound to fat or other cellular material.

In pharmacokinetic terminology, the initial drug metabolism in the liver is called the "first pass-effect" and probably accounts for the marked differences that sometimes occur between the clinically effective oral and parenteral doses of the drug.

The "two compartment" model common in pharmacokinetics assumes a central compartment (plasma and more accessible intracellular fluid) into which drugs are absorbed; this compartment is in kinetic equilibrium with the peripheral compartment, which is made up of the rest of the body, including drug-binding tissues.

When a drug is given rapidly intravenously, the blood level rises sharply and then falls in a curve which has two slopes, an early one based on, chiefly, distribution within the body (from the central to the peripheral space) and a second, and more important, one based on rate of elimination (destruction, plus excretion in feces, urine, or expired air).

Each slope gives a calculable half-life, the time it takes for the plasma level to decrease by 50%. (Plasma half-life is the handiest and clearest measure of how long a drug stays in the body.)

For drugs given by mouth, the phases are overlapping, since the entry of a new drug into the central compartment, its diffusion into the peripheral compartment, and its excretion/metabolism are all going on at once.

The peak plasma level is a function of the rate of absorption, diffusion, and excretion, and of the drug dose.

The "steady-state" plasma level often is more important. In theory and in practice on a steady daily dose of a drug, in-put and out-go come into crude balance after a period of time (about five times the drug's metabolism/excretion half-life). Obviously, there are increases in plasma level after each oral dose, which then fall until the next dose is ingested, but these variations occur around a relatively stable average level. Plasma levels will vary less if the drug is ingested in small, frequent doses than in single, bedtime doses. Generally, a plasma level taken 10 to 12 hours after the last oral dose is considered as reflecting steady-state levels, at least for lithium and tricyclic antidepressants.

**Why Plasma Levels?**

Anyone experienced in managing patients on maintenance lithium therapy observes some patients with plasma levels of 0.8 mEq/L on one 300 mg capsule, while others require 8 or even 12 capsules. The relationship between dose and steady-state plasma level on the better-studied tricyclics (imipramine and nortriptyline) is equally irregular. On a standard daily dose of imipramine (3.5 mg/kg), Glassman and associates report steady-state plasma levels ranging from 50 to 1,050 ng/ml [4]. Variations in patients on a standard dose not adjusted for weight are probably even greater.

Even if plasma levels of a drug vary widely, knowing the level becomes an expensive way of making sure the patient is taking his pills, unless steady-state plasma levels are related to either clinical changes or to side effects. In theory, plasma levels should be in some kind of equilibrium with cerebrospinal fluid levels, brain levels, and with levels at a drug's possible binding sites at the appropriate synapse or enzyme where it really acts.

It is possible to conceive of drugs for which these presumptions may be false. The peak level of the drug may cause permanent changes in an enzyme which is only slowly reversed, as is probably true in the case of monoamine oxidase inhibitors [5] such changes may be only weakly related to plasma steady-state levels. The active chemical may be a metabolite of the ingested drug, and we are not measuring it at all. It is also possible that the blood-brain barrier actively transports the drug into the brain or excludes it in some complicated way, or shifting levels of tissue tolerance or hypersensitivity may make a plasma level at one point pharmacologically more or less effective than the same level a month later.

Since most drugs used in psychiatry bind to plasma protein, there is also the possibility that the percentage of free unbound drug (5 percent to 23 percent for imipramine [6]) is the important level, and total plasma level has a weaker relationship. It is quite possible that intracellular levels in our handiest cells, the red blood cells, or total blood levels would be more useful, but to date there is little evidence to suggest that these other measures would be more effective than total plasma levels. It is also possible that monitoring a known biochemical effect of a drug (platelet monoamine oxidase level for drugs like phenelzine) or a central physiological effect (changes in EEG frequency spectra) would better reflect clinical drug response.

At the clinical drug use end, there are also problems. If the patient is getting better in spite of the drug, or if the patient shows a high rate of spontaneous improvement or placebo response, plasma levels obviously will not correlate with clinical change. In fact, if the drug causes side effects that prevent improvement, and these *are* related to plasma level, the higher the plasma level the worse the patient will do.

If all clinicians are skilled in picking correct and accurate therapeutic doses of a drug, then everybody will have an optimal plasma level, except patients who are totally unresponsive to the drug. Such patients might well get much higher doses (and higher plasma levels), and again plasma level would be uncorrelated with, or even negatively correlated with, improvement.

Response to tricyclic antidepressants occurs so slowly that it is hard for the clinician to know for several days whether an optimal dose has been reached; the response lag makes rational dose adjustment difficult at best. This problem has made everyone hope that tricyclic plasma levels are really related to improvement, since at the present state of our art we are never sure whether the patient is unresponsive or the dose is too low or too high, unless the patient develops limiting side effects.

If plasma level is related to clinical response in a simple way, then, as plasma level rises, more and more patients will respond until all patients who are going to respond have done so (figure 2-1). Such a drug is said to show a roughly linear relationship between plasma level and improvement which plateaus eventually.

For some drugs, the relationship is not linear. As plasma level rises a bit, more patients respond, but above a certain level patients again do poorly. This curvilinear relationship produces a "therapeutic window," a range of plasma levels within which patients do well. Above or below the window, patients do equally badly (figure 2-2).

At present, two antidepressant drugs have been relatively well studied: imipramine and nortriptyline. Nortriptyline, the desmethyl metabolite of amitriptyline, is marketed as Aventyl. Nortriptyline was studied early in

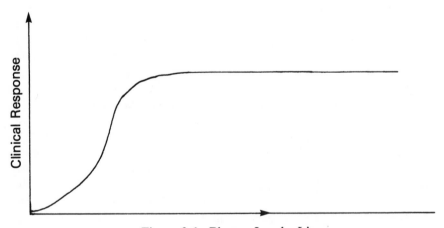

**Figure 2-1.** Plasma Level—Linear

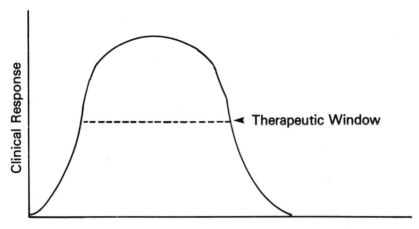

**Figure 2-2.** Plasma Level—Curvilinear

1971 because it was the first tricyclic to have a relatively simple method established to measure plasma level. Six studies have been reported [7-12]. Of these, two [11,12] did not show a relationship between plasma level and improvement; one [12] of the two managed to miss the "window" almost completely. The other four are compatible with the existence of a therapeutic window between 49 ng/ml and 140 ng/ml. Most impressive is Kragh-Sorensen's second study [7]. Here, half of a small group lowered to the presumed therapeutic range, while the other half remained at excessive levels. All patients with lowered levels improved; none of the patients remaining above 180 ng/ml improved.

Imipramine appears to show a linear relationship between plasma levels and clinical response, despite the fact that imipramine is demethylated to desipramine by the body, and patients tend to run grossly equal levels of the two active antidepressants (imipramine and desipramine) in their plasma. Four studies relating plasma levels to clinical response have been reported. Two were in small samples [13,14], and one of these [13] measured only plasma imipramine. A third [15] suggests, but does not demonstrate convincingly, that imipramine plasma level is more important than desipramine level in determining clinical improvement. All three studies are consistent with a linear relationship between plasma level and clinical improvement.

The fourth study, the work of Glassman's group [4], is the most impressive and covers the largest patient group (60 patients). Since 18 delusional, depressed patients showed negligible clinical improvement at any plasma level, 42 unipolar or bipolar depressions remained for study of the relationship of improvement to plasma level. Using 180 ng/ml as a cutoff, both bipolar and unipolar, nondelusional depressions showed significant improvement differences if their plasma level was over 180 ng/ml.

If patients were stratified into three groups by plasma level, those with steady-state levels less than 150 ng/ml showed only 29 percent improvement, a rate of improvement resembling that seen in placebo groups in controlled studies of hospitalized depressives. Those between 150 ng/ml and 225 ng/ml showed 64 percent improvement, a level often seen with imipramine therapy in the same controlled studies. Patients with levels greater than 225 ng/ml showed an impressive 93 percent improvement! All this occurred at a standard dose of 3.5 mg/kg (about 250 mg, q.d. for a 70 kg man). At this moderately high dose, one-third of the patients had inadequate (less than 150 ng/ml) plasma levels. Glassman's data suggest that females with unipolar depressions may be less responsive than males to adequate (more than 150 ng/ml) levels. The otherwise excellent report does not mention whether anticholinergic or other side effects are, or are not, related to plasma levels.

According to Gram et al. [15], clinical response to imipramine requires both a plasma level of more than 75 ng/ml for imipramine *and* a plasma level of more than 45 ng/ml for desipramine. Gram and associates found no correlation between anticholinergic side effects and blood levels in imipramine patients but did find a significant increase in hypotension in patients with total imipramine plus desipramine plasma levels greater than 400 ng/ml.

Glassman and Perel [18] documented a significant quinidine-like action for imipramine. The drug slows electrical conduction in the heart, increasing the QRS interval and other conduction time measures and tending to suppress premature atrial and ventricular contractions. Changes in the QRS interval are correlated with plasma tricyclic levels [16].

There is some evidence that various drugs may influence plasma levels of tricyclics [17]. At least for imipramine, smoking lowers plasma levels; methylphenidate and phenothiazine raise them; and sodium amobarbital (Amytal) and chloral hydrate probably lower them [18].

It is possible that we will be able to predict a patient's drug needs by measuring the plasma levels obtained after a single, standard dose. One study has demonstrated the feasibility of this for nortriptyline [19]. This technique is well worked out for lithium by Cooper et al. [20], but it is not yet in general use.

## What We Need to Know

Our present knowledge has been well reviewed by Kane et al. [21] and by Glassman and Perel [18] in greater detail than this article provides. From their reviews, it is clear that we know a good deal about imipramine and nortriptyline and that these drugs are quite different. Desipramine alone probably will behave like imipramine; Glassman estimates that 80 percent of the tricyclic drug in cerebrospinal fluid is desipramine in patients being treated with imipramine because desipramine is less bound to plasma than imipramine. However, it is possible that desipramine, like nortriptyline, will show a therapeutic window on the quasilogical basis that all desmethyl metabolites of tricyclic antidepressants should somehow be similar. Without specific clinical steady-state studies, it is not possible for one to be certain whether desipramine will have a therapeutic window or not.

There are no adequate data available on amitriptyline. Since the plasma of patients on this drug contains both the parent drug and nortriptyline, one can guess that patients who fail to respond and who have nortriptyline plasma levels over 140 ng/ml might have their doses lowered, but it is not possible to be certain that the drug works this way. The two available studies suggest that there is no amitryptyline therapeutic window but do not really prove this [22,23].

Braithwaite [22] was quoted by Biggs [24] as defining the effective range for amitriptyline as 77 to 197 ng/ml of *total* amitriptyline and nortriptyline levels. A single study suggests that protriptyline might have a level over which patients do less well [25].   Work with doxepin is almost nonexistent.

## Conclusions

On the basis of the available evidence, it appears that plasma levels of tricyclics are moving steadily from the research laboratory toward general clinical utility. Imipramine, measured as the total of plasma imipramine and desipramine, should reach a level of 150 to 250 ng/ml before the drug can be judged ineffective. For nortriptyline, a ceiling exists, and a plasma level between 50 ng/ml and 140 ng/ml seems clearly related to clinical response, with higher levels interfering with improvement. Probably, useful data on appropriate plasma levels for the other tricyclics will be developed shortly. Even at our present level of knowledge of the other drugs, it seems likely that very low levels (under 50 ng/ml) are probably inadequate, and this suggests that the dose should be raised. If plasma levels are as crucial as appears likely, older studies of these drugs will need to be repeated using plasma-level monitoring. Perhaps drug-placebo differences will be shown to be even greater than in earlier studies, and studies looking for predictors of drug response will yield clearer findings.

## Commentary

This paper was written as the methods for plasma-level determinations began to be more widely available to clinicians around the country, and it coincided with the opening of a laboratory service in Boston run by Doctors Schildkraut and Orsulak under the auspices of the Deaconess Hospital clinical laboratory. It attempted to summarize the state of the art at that time.

Surprisingly, the field of tricyclic plasma levels has stayed where this paper describes it. I know of ongoing studies attempting to relate plasma level to clinical response longitudinally, and I have seen small studies that seem to complicate the area more than they clarify it. For example, Friedel et al. [26] describe a ceiling effect for desipramine at low plasma levels in a small clean study, while I personally have treated patients with this drug who only responded at very high dosages and at plasma levels over 300 ng/ml. Perhaps there are two response levels! We also have some pilot data from Schatzberg et al. (unpublished data, 1979) suggesting that depressed patients who excrete low levels of methoxyhydroxyphenylglycol (MHPG) respond rapidly to a noradrenergic antidepressant (maprotiline), while high-MHPG patients sometimes respond more slowly and at much higher plasma levels.

In short, the whole area seems likely to become more complex in the future, and our review may oversimplify reality. Nevertheless, plasma levels remain clinically useful. If a patient has low plasma levels without side effects at a high daily tricyclic dose, the clinician can feel safer in raising the dose above the usual suggested maximum.

## References

1. Greenblatt D, Koch-Weser J: Drug therapy: clinical pharmacokinetics (Part I). New Eng J Med 293:702-705, 1975.

2. Greenblatt D, Koch-Weser J: Drug therapy: clinical pharmacokinetics (Part II). New Eng J Med 293:964-970, 1975.

3. Davis J. Erickson S, Derkimenjian H: Plasma levels of antipsychotic drugs and clinical response. *In* Psychopharmacology: A Generation of Progress: Lipton M, DiMascio A, Killam K (Eds). New York, Raven Press (in press).

4. Glassman A, Perel J, Shostak M, et al.: Clinical implications of imipramine plasma levels for depressive illness. Arch Gen Psychiat 34:197-207, 1977.

5. Simpson L, Cabot B: Monoamine oxidase inhibitors. *In* Drug Treatment of Mental Disorders: Simpson L (Ed). New York, Raven Press, 1976, pp. 147-160.

6. Glassman A.H, et al.: Plasma binding of imipramine and clinical outcome. Am J Psychiat 130:1367-1369, 1973.

7. Kragh-Sorensen P, et al.: Self-inhibiting action of nortriptyline's antidepressive effect at high plasma levels. Psychopharmacologia 45:305-312, 1976.

8. Kragh-Sorensen P, et al.: Plasma levels of nortriptyline in the treatment or endogenous depression. Acta Psychiat Scand 49:444-456, 1973.

9. Asberg M, et al.: Relationship between plasma level and therapeutic effects of nortriptyline. Br Med J 3:331-334, 1971.

10. Ziegler V, Clayton P. Taylor J, et al.: Nortriptyline plasma levels and therapeutic response. Clin Pharm Ther 20:458-463, 1976.

11. Burrows GD, et al.: Plasma concentrations of nortriptyline and clinical response in depressive illness. Lancet 2:619-623, 1972.

12. Burrows GD, et al.: A sequential trial comparing two plasma levels of nortriptyline. Aust New Zeal J Psychiat 8:21-24, 1974.

13. Walter CJS: Clinical significance of plasma imipramine levels. Proc Roy Soc Med 64:282-285, 1971.

14. Olivier-Martin R, Marzin D, Busenshutz E, et al.: Concentrations plasmatiques de l'imipramine et de la desmethylimipramine et effet anti-depresseur au cours d'un traitement controlé. Psychopharmacologia 41:187-195, 1975.

15. Gram L, Reisby N, Ibsen I, et al.: Plasma levels and antidepressant effect of imipramine. Clin Pharm Ther 19:318-324, 1976.

16. Bigger J, Giardina E, Perel J, et al.: Cardiac anti-arrhythmic effect of imipramine hydrochloride. New Eng J Med 296:206-208, 1977.

17. Spiker D, Weiss A, Chang S, et al.: Tricyclic overdose: clinical presentation and plasma levels. Clin Pharm Ther 18:939-946, 1975.

18. Glassman A, Perel J: Tricyclic blood levels and clinical outcome. *In* Psychopharmacology: A Generation of Progress: Lipton M, DiMascio A, Killam K (Eds). New York, Raven Press (in press).

19. Alexanderson B: Pharmacokinetics of nortriptyline in man after single and multiple oral doses: the predictability of steady-state plasma concentrations from single-dose plasma-level data. Eur J Clin Pharm 4:82-91, 1972.

20. Cooper TB, Simpson GM: The 24-hour lithium level as a level prognosticator of patient dose requirement: a two-year follow-up study. Am J Psychiat 133:440-443, 1976.

21. Kane J: Antidepressant drug blood levels, pharmacokinetics and clinical outcome. *In* Diagnosis and Drug Treatment of Psychiatric Disorders: Klein DF, David J (Eds). Baltimore, Williams and Wilkins, 1969.

22. Braithwaite RA, et al.: Plasma concentration of amitriptyline and clinical response. Lancet 1:1297-1300, 1972.

23.Ziegler VE, Taylor JR, Clayton PJ, et al.: Amitriptyline plasma levels and therapeutic response. Clin Pharm Ther 19:795-801, 1976.

24. Biggs J, Clayton P, Ziegler V: Tricyclic plasma levels and adverse effects. Paper presented May 2 1977 at the 130th Annual Meeting of American Psychiatric Association, Toronto, Canada.

25. Whyte S, MacDonald A, Naylor G, et al.: Plasma concentrations of protriptyline and clinical effects in depressed women. Br J Psychiat 128:384-390, 1976.

26. Friedel R, Vieth R, Bloom V, and Bielski R: Desipramine plasma levels and clinical response in depressed outpatients. Commun Psychopharmacol 3:81-88, 1979.

# 3

# Drug Treatment of Anxiety

*Jonathan O. Cole, M.D.*

Anxiety is a universal phenomenon. When severe or protracted, or when it interferes significantly with functioning, it leads patients to seek help. Although primary-care physicians appear to see far more patients with anxiety than do psychiatrists—they certainly prescribe most of the antianxiety drugs used in this country and may often see the simpler and more drug-responsive forms of anxiety—psychiatrists handle many anxious patients and often use drug therapy either as a main treatment modality or as an adjunct to psychotherapy [1].

The purpose of this paper is to review current knowledge about the pharmacotherapy of anxiety, with emphasis on the range of drugs available and their differences in terms of efficacy, side effects, and pharmacokinetics.

## What is Anxiety?

As studied in the antianxiety drug literature, anxiety is a melange of conditions and symptoms including anxiety, nervousness, or tension as subjective complaints, often complicated by irritability, depression, and insomnia. Anxious patients also usually show one or more of a range of somatic manifestations of anxiety, such as tremor, palpitations, frequent urination, sweating, bowel complaints, fatigue, and muscle pain. Sometimes these complaints are associated with clearly psychiatric symptoms, such as pathological or unreasonable fears, phobias, obsessive preoccupation with abnormal ideas, or compulsions to repeat actions over and over to relieve anxiety. Less commonly, patients will have clear, brief panic attacks—episodes of acute, severe anxiety and fear lasting 5 to 30 minutes with relatively less anxiety as time goes on [2].

Obviously, symptoms of anxiety occur in a variety of clinical contexts. Anxiety in a schizophrenic patient generally requires the use of an antipsychotic drug, although occasional schizophrenic patients with anticipatory anxiety can be helped a bit by adding a benzodiazepine to antipsychotic medication. Patients with significant depression generally do better on a tricyclic antidepressant than on a benzodiazepine. A recent collaborative study comparing amitriptyline alone, chlordiazepoxide alone, and a combination of both and a placebo showed that the combination had some advantages in reducing dysphoria during the first week of drug therapy; by the third or fourth week, the combination was no better than the tricyclic alone and both were clearly superior to benzodiazepine alone [3]. This supports our recent review of the literature comparing the efficacy of tricyclics and benzodiazepines in depression and in mixed anxiety and depression, which showed that tricyclic antidepressants are generally superior or equal to benzodiazepines in controlled studies [4].

For patients who present with pure or predominant anxiety symptoms, there is a further distinction that is worth making. Patients with episodic, brief severe panic attacks are probably manifesting a different condition from patients with only chronic anxiety, but many patients with prolonged exposure to panic attacks develop both chronic anticipatory anxiety and phobic symptoms, such as fear of being alone or of being in closed spaces or open spaces. In such patients, tricyclic antidepressants, and probably monoamine oxidase inhibitors, suppress the panic attacks nicely but may not relieve the chronic anxiety [5]. The latter may require the use of a benzodiazepine and/or behavioral approaches to restore functioning. Imipramine is the drug best studied in this condition; occasional panic patients respond to remarkably small doses of imipramine (10 mg/day or even less) and develop marked side effects on higher doses [6]. Most patients with panic attacks require higher dosages (150 to 200 mg/day). Klein, the major investigator in this area, recommends that two specific symptoms, the presence of clear panic attacks or the presence of clear anhedonia (inability to enjoy anything), make antidepressants the drugs of choice independent of the nature or extent of coexistent anxiety or neurotic symptoms.

**Drug Therapy versus Psychotherapy**

For anxiety symptoms that do not fall into any of the above categories, antianxiety drugs are often quite helpful [7]. There is an argument going on in the lay press and in some corners of the mental health field that contends that anxiety should not be relieved by drugs. Rather, patients should either solve their own problems and suffer it out, or they should receive psychotherapy (or counseling, casework, or pastoral guidance) so they can really understand and solve their problems, not "suppress it all with a drug." It is impossible to tell how valid this argument is. Most psychiatrists will, in fact, involve anxious patients in some form of psychotherapy, brief or prolonged, supportive, dynamic, or behaviorally oriented, with or without drug therapy. Unfortunately, there is little or no evidence on the relative efficacies of drugs and psychotherapies either in the short or long run.

Studies comparing drugs and psychotherapy in anxious outpatients have been few in number (I know of only two using ordinary dynamic or supportive psychotherapy [8,9]) and neither showed psychotherapy to be particularly effective. Studies comparing behavior therapies, such as systematic desensitization with drugs, tend to show that the combination is superior to either treatment alone, but most published studies are concerned with phobias and use monoamine oxidase inhibitors or tricyclic antidepressants as the drug studied. Only two studies involve combinations of a benzodiazepine (diazepam) and a behavioral approach. Both show the combination to be better than behavior therapy without drugs. One shows that the behavior therapy (flooding) has the greatest effect when the diazepam effect is wearing off, not when the patient is more sedated [10].

Psychotherapy versus drug therapy in depression is better studied. There, the answer is relatively clear. Drugs reduce symptoms; psychotherapy improves interpersonal adjustment [11]. It may well be that the same difference holds for anxious patients.

**Drugs for Use in Anxiety**

*Sedative Hypnotics*

Hollister has divided drugs used in the treatment of anxiety into the sedative hypnotics and the automatic sedatives [12]. His first group, the sedative hypnotics, includes all antianxiety drugs that are relatively pure antianxiety or sedative agents and that lack major autonomic side effects. Although the benzodiazepines are the most widely known and widely used members of this class, alcohol, the barbiturates, chloral hydrate, meprobamate, paraldehyde, and methaqualone all qualify. They all produce some sedation and anxiety relief at lower dosages and can produce sleep at higher dosages.

These drugs share some common pharmacological properties. They all tend to disinhibit behavior in animals and human beings. The effect is clearer and more reliable in animals. A rat that has learned to fear pressing a lever to get food when a special light is on (because it is likely to get a painful shock) will cheerfully press the lever anyway when on any of several hypnosedative drugs [13]. On a different system of animal-behavior testing, these drugs at low doses will increase exploratory activity [14]. By inference, they may be especially useful in overinhibited, anxious neurotic patients and may have undesirable disinhibiting effects in alcoholics who become overactive and troublesome when drunk.

Although this unique property of the benzodiazepines has been related to changes in serotonin metabolism, current research suggests that the key central action of these drugs is gabanergic (i.e. increased activity of synapses that use gamma-aminobutyric acid (GABA) as a neurotransmitter). The exact way in which drugs like diazepam achieve this is unclear at present. The effect seems neither to be a direct effect of the drug on gabanergic synapses nor a direct effect on GABA synthesis or metabolism. Diazepam has its stimulant effect on gabanergic activity only in the presence of GABA itself [15]. Earlier theories that diazepam and related drugs acted on glycine receptors seem unsupported. Gabanergic stimulation probably has secondary ramifications into serotonergic, cholingeric, and dopaminergic systems. An early increase in noradrenaline turnover in the brain caused by benzodiazepines does not persist on chronic administration. The exact mechanism by which increased gabanergic activity yields reduced anxiety is not clear, but the fact that most gabanergic systems are inhibitory may be relevant.

It is interesting to note that the barbiturates, but not meprobamate, are also gabanergic [15]. Conceivably, meprobamate may be different enough to be worth a trial in anxious patients who fail to respond to, or who are made worse by benzodiazepine. Meprobamate's other advantages include availability in cheaper generic forms; its disadvantages, as compared with the benzodiazepines, include greater risk of successful suicide and greater risk of physical dependence at doses only a bit higher than the therapeutic range.

All the hypnosedatives also share the ability to produce both phsyical dependence and withdrawal symptoms, including convulsions and delirium tremens, if they are given long enough and in high enough dosages [7]. For drugs like pentobarbital, this dosage is about 600 mg/day for one to two months. With the benzodiazepines, the minimum dependence-producing dosage for human beings has never been worked out. It is also hard to tell if patients who are on diazepam doses of 40 to 60 mg/day and find it very difficult to lower their daily dose are physically dependent or only psychologically dependent. True, serious physical abstinence syndromes are very rare with the benzodiazepines [16], but one sees a fair number of patients who claim to have developed tolerance to diazepam. ("It used to work, Doc, but now the same dose doesn't help any more.")

All the sedative hypnotics can relieve anxiety and produce sedation. Since sedation can bring with it behavioral toxicity—unsteady gait, poor driving, careless errors on tasks requiring focused attention—the aim of new drug development has been to create drugs that provide maximum anxiety relief without causing sedation or psychomotor inefficiency. The benzodiazepines in general are better in this regard than the barbiturates or meprobamate [7,16]. They are also more effective than are the older drugs when compared with placebo in anxious patients.

The benzodiazepines have two other major advantages over the barbiturates: first, it is very difficult to kill yourself with an overdose of a benzodiazepine alone. However, when the benzodiazepines are combined with other drugs, successful suicides do occur. Second, the benzodiazepines do not induce hepatic microsomal enzymes and thus do not speed the metabolism of other drugs. They, in fact, mix well with other psychiatric drugs [12].

One particular adverse effect of diazepam requires special comment. In studies of *nonanxious* volunteers, diazepam has been shown to increase hostility and irritability. It did not do so in *anxious* volunteers. Oxazepam was studied in the same way and did not have this effect [17]. Cases have been reported in which anxious patients on diazepam noted the emergence of suicidal ideation for the first time [18]. Both effects may merely be an expression of the disinhibiting effects of hypnosedative drugs. I believe these effects to be quite rare in practice, but it is well to keep an eye out for them. In a similar vein, one old study in which I was peripherally involved showed that "more good things happen" to patients on chlordiazepoxide than to patients on placebo; the drug patients described some of their "good" events as involving helpful confrontations with wives or bosses [19]. (We never asked the wives or bosses whether the confrontations seemed "good" to them. A little disinhibition may be helpful; a lot may be troublesome!)

## The Autonomic Sedatives

In contrast, the autonomic sedatives produce both sedation and anxiety reduction without apparent risk of disinhibition. The sedation produced is generally not viewed as particularly pleasurable by drug abusers. These autonomic sedative drugs are usually marketed for some other purpose—as antihistamines, antidepressants, or antipsychotics. They generally have anticholinergic and often adrenergic properties and, at some dosages, can cause dry mouth, blurred vision, trouble passing water, hypotension, or tachycardia.

Drugs like diphenhydramine and hydroxyzine are probably a bit less effective than the benzodiazepines and are therefore less useful. The tricyclic antidepressants (e.g. doxepin, imipramine) are quite useful in mixed anxiety and depression but have never been adequately studied in anxious patients without depression [4]; they can affect cardiac function adversely in patients with partial heart block. The antipsychotic drugs (e.g. thioridazine, trifluoperazine, haloperidol) probably are effective in controlling anxiety when used in low doses [16], doses at which their neurological side effects are unlikely to occur. Unfortunately, the risk of tardive dyskinesia [20] with these drugs is real—I have seen eight patients who were not schizophrenic but who developed dyskinesia on one or more antipsychotic drugs given for the treatment of anxiety or depression.

This syndrome, often manifested by chewing, tongue and lip movements and/or choreiform movements of the fingers and toes, can progress to gross athetoid body and limb movements and facial grimacing. Luckily, in most cases, it will fade gradually if it is caught early and all antipsychotic drugs are stopped. Nevertheless, it makes low-dose antipsychotic drug use in anxious nonschizophrenics undesirable without special justification. There are a few patients who either are not helped by the benzodiazepines or abuse them but who do well on an antipsychotic. In this case, such use is legitimate, but patients should be carefully monitored for early signs of dyskinesia—finger or tongue movements often appear first.

*Propranolol*

Propranolol and other beta-adrenergic blocking drugs have been reported to have some beneficial effect in anxiety states, particularly by suppressing presumed peripheral manifestations of anxiety such as tachycardia, palpitations, tremulousness, diaphoresis, hyperventilation, and dizziness. Although these drugs are sometimes superior to placebo in controlled clinical trials, they are generally less effective than diazepam. Although occasional patients may respond to drugs like propranolol by reduction in anxiety symptoms, the general utility of these drugs in anxiety symptoms has not been adequately demonstrated [21].

**The Treatment of Anxiety Symptoms
with the Benzodiazepines**

In treating anxious patients with the benzodiazepines, the main initial idea is to relieve the patients' symptoms adequately without causing either excessive drowsiness or incoordination. Differences between the existing benzodiazepines, all of which have adequately documented evidence of efficacy, become important in this context. The important differences lie in the metabolism and pharmacokinetics of the available agents [22]. Chlordiazepoxide and diazepam both have long half-lives and yield active metabolites, including desmethyldiazepam and oxazepam. Chlorazepate and prazepam are pro-drugs, being transformed in the body to desmethyldiazepam, a particularly long-acting active metabolite of diazepam. Thus, this group of drugs can be expected to accumulate gradually in the body and to reach steady state (the point at which plasma levels, of both the parent drug and its active metabolites, are no longer rising) after approximately one to two weeks. This effect has both assets and liabilities. On the positive side, it suggests that the drugs could well be given only once a day and that, given a constant dose, gradually increasing antianxiety effect might continue to become manifest over several days. It also seems likely that the antianxiety effect might continue to persist for several days after the drug has been stopped. It also explains the three- to five-day delay between stopping the drug and the emergence of severe symptoms of physical dependence, such as convulsions or delirium tremens. This long-lasting property also makes these drugs useful in the treatment of withdrawal symptoms in alcoholics [23].

On the negative side, behavioral toxicity, such as drowsiness or ataxia, may sneak up on both patient and doctor several days after both believe that a safe, useful daily dosage has been achieved. In elderly patients, and in patients with markedly impaired liver function, the half-life of diazepam is at least doubled, suggesting that cumulative undesirable effects may be still further delayed [24]. In addition, there is some evidence that in cirrhotic patients, diazepam has adverse effects on brain function even at plasma levels that are safe in healthy adults.

Oxazepam and lorazepam are shorter acting, oxazepam being the shortest acting available benzodiazepine [22]. Neither drug has an active metabolite, and both drugs are detoxified by glucuronide formation while the longer-acting drugs are demethylated. In the elderly or cirrhotic patient, glucuronide formation remains essentially normal, while demethylation is impaired [24]. Oxazepam is almost certainly the benzodiazepine of choice in patients with a serious liver disease. It may also be a more useful and less behaviorally toxic drug in the elderly, though this proposition has not been proven. I have seen elderly patients who became ataxic and confused on diazepam or flurazepam who tolerated oxazepam well. Intramuscular diazepam and chlordiazepoxide tend to bind at the injection site and are less useful in acute anxiety than oral forms of the drug [22]. This does not appear to be true of lorazepam given intramuscularly (this preparation is not yet commercially available for prescription use).

The other implication of the differences in drug half-life and metabolism between various benzodiazepines is that oxazepam and probably lorazepam should be given b.i.d. or t.i.d., while the longer-acting drugs could be given at bedtime only, though many anxious patients have a subjective need for more frequent dosage schedules.

Although diazepam has a longer half-life than oxazepam, it is more rapidly absorbed and produces an earlier and clearer subjectively discernible drug effect that could probably contribute to its popularity with drug-abuse-prone individuals [21,25]. Chlordiazepoxide also rapidly peaks in the blood, while oxazepam and lorazepam have a slower onset of action as do azepate and chlorazepate.

What do the available pharmacokinetic data tell us?

(1) Drugs like diazepam have a long, cumulative effect because they produce steady state in 10 to 20 days. Patients who initially do not benefit adequately may get more effect over time. Studies relating steady-state plasma level to clinical response are few and conflicting, but plasma levels over 500 ng/liter are probably in the therapeutic range.

Diazepam also has a rapid-onset peak effect after single and oral doses which may make it the best-liked benzodiazepine for patients wanting immediate relief of acute, severe anxiety. Chlordiazepoxide probably is similar in this regard. This peak effect may also increase the drug's abuse liability.

(2) Chlorazepate and prazepam are slower in initial onset but have long half-lives, should produce increasing symptom relief over time, and may also accumulate.

(3) Oxazepam and lorazepam have a less dramatic acute peak effect but reach steady state more rapidly, after two to three days, making dose titration easier and more flexible. While their shorter duration of action makes b.i.d. or t.i.d. rather than bedtime dosages desirable and makes their effects more likely to wear off rapidly in chronically anxious patients, the drugs are safer in the elderly and in patients with liver disease and should be less abusable in drug-abuse-prone individuals. Using diazepam only at bedtime in chronically anxious patients might also reduce abuse.

On the other hand, an argument can be made for using the benzodiazepines as p.r.n. medications for patients to take when something increases their anxiety. Winstead and associates have shown that, in psychiatric inpatients, less diazepam is used when it is available p.r.n. than when it is given on a regular basis [26]. For patients with mainly situational anxieties, p.r.n. use may be desirable. Even when regular use is indicated, patients should be warned about oversedation; some obedient, compliant, anxious patients will continue to oversedate themselves and not feel comfortable about adjusting the dose themselves or calling their physician to complain.

Because of their rapid onset of action, diazepam or chloridazepoxide seem the drugs of choice when anxiety occurs occasionally and is being treated like a headache. When the slower-onset drugs are being used for patients with more enduring anxiety symptoms, the patient should be instructed not to expect instant relief; when relief does not occur early in therapy, the dose should be titrated upward until either symptom relief or sedative side effects occur. The relatively modest effects obtained in Rickel's studies might be bettered with more careful dose tritration. A recent double-blind crossover study comparing chlordiazepoxide and placebo showed striking drug-placebo differences, presumably because the best dose for each patient was determined before the crossover study was carried out [27].

**Response to the Benzodiazepines**

The degree of improvement obtained by the benzodiazepines is often quite satisfactory to all concerned. However, Rickels' data suggest that patients even markedly improved on the benzodiazepines sometimes are still more symptomatic than "normal" general practice patients. Such markedly improved patients constitute about 40 percent of benzodiazepine-treated patients in outpatient clinical trials [16].

Rickels has done the largest number of well-analyzed studies of the benzodiazepines in outpatient settings [16]. His data show that the largest drug-placebo differences (i.e. the biggest drug effect) occur on subjective and on somatic symptoms of anxiety. Effects on other self-report rating-scale factors are less impressive. The other, less responsive, areas measured are depression, interpersonal difficulties, and obsessive-compulsive symptoms. This last factor includes items concerned with difficulty in thinking, concentrating, and getting things done, as well as more clearly compulsive items such as having to recheck things or redo them several times to make sure they are done right.

The characteristics of patients who do well on diazepam and chlordiazepoxide in Rickels' studies have been examined in a number of ways. Those which stand up well across studies sound, in fact, quite reasonable:

(1) If the doctor is comfortable with the patient, comfortable prescribing drugs, and believes the drugs will help the patient, the patient is likely to do well. Similarly, if the patient is married, employed, well educated, has insight into his or her emotional problems but expects drug therapy, things go well.

(2) If the patient is not too chronic, has not been overexposed to drugs or has done well on past antianxiety drugs, and has become anxious in a context of stress, he or she does better. Premenopausal women do better as do patients without concurrent medical illnesses. Sedative side effects at two weeks on a drug, probably an indicator of adequate drug dose, also predict improvement.

(3) Patients with a diagnosis of anxiety state or mixed anxiety-depression do best. Higher initial levels of subjective anxiety predict good response, while higher levels of depression, interpersonal sensitivity or obsessive-compulsive symptoms are prognostically bad.

In short, patients with relatively pure anxiety symptoms, with good pre-illness adjustment and health, who want drug therapy and get it from doctors who are comfortable with both the particular patient and the drug to be used do well.

**Problems with the Benzodiazepines**

Although the benzodiazepines are safer and more effective than the older antianxiety drugs, they are also much more expensive. Where cost is a real problem, generic meprobamate may be a reasonable alternative if the physician recognizes that meprobamate can be used successfully in suicide attempts and that the dosage inducing physical dependence is relatively low, making a dosage level of 1,600 mg/day the safe maximum. Chlordiazepoxide is also now available in generic forms.

Another potential problem is the clinical efficacy of long-term use of the benzodiazepines; the available double-blind controlled clinical trials only document efficacy for four to six weeks. Some patients certainly feel helped by the benzodiazepines for months or years, though occasional patients feel the drugs are less effective with prolonged use.

The problem of benzodiazepine abuse is rather like a vague skeleton that may or may not be hiding in a closet whose door has never been opened; people only peek in through the cracks. The available literature is sparse, spotty, and hard to interpret. Three short notes report significant diazepam abuse in methadone maintenance patients [28,29] and in other drug-abuse-prone individuals [30]. One paper describes some patients who are unable to terminate chronic use of medically prescribed diazepam [31] and one note mentions a case of excessive oxazepam use [32]. A recent survey of drug use by college seniors found 7% of 710 seniors report regular nonmedical use of minor tranquilizers; another 15% report using such drugs "many times" for nonmedical purposes [33]. I have seen a small number of patients who have difficulty stopping diazepam use and one patient in the last four years with withdrawal convulsions after heavy diazepam use. Both phenomena certainly occur, however rarely, and should serve to warn physicians against prolonged or excessive use of the benzodiazepines.

**Conclusion**

Among the drugs available for the treatment of anxiety symptoms uncomplicated by other major psychiatric syndromes, the benzodiazepines are the safest and most effective. The barbiturates, meprobamate, and other sedative hypnotics have a greater risk of both physical dependence and of lethal overdose. The autonomic sedatives such as diphenhydramine and hydroxyzine are less effective, while the antipsychotics at low dose carry a risk of tardive dyskinesia. Antidepressants are more effective in treating recurrent panic attacks with secondary phobias.

Among the benzodiazepines, oxazepam and lorazepam have shorter half-lives and a simpler metabolism. On the other hand, diazepam and chlordiazepoxide produce the most rapid peak blood levels, although their longer half-lives may lead to prolonged drug accumulation.

The clinical response to the benzodiazepines is generally favorable, though often less than doctor or patient might desire. The utility and efficacy of the benzodiazepines in long-term therapy (over two months) is unstudied and unclear.

Although the benzodiazepines can cause physical dependence and can be abused, such problems are poorly documented and appear to be relatively rare, given the extensive and widespread use of the agents by physicians of all sorts and specialties. The interaction of benzodiazepines with various forms of psychotherapy is little studied but is probably favorable.

**Commentary**

This seems to be a perennially popular topic for symposia at medical and psychiatric meetings. The present paper evolved after my participation in several such continuing medical education programs. In rereading it, I find it still represents my best assessment of this popular but controversial area.

The new basic research development in this area is the identification of benzodiazepine receptors on neurones in the central nervous system [34]. These are separate from the GABA receptors described in the preceding chapter. Their real role in relation to anxiety remains to be clarified. One must assume that neither God nor Darwin purposefully anticipated the invention of diazepam; the receptors presumably play some different role under nondrug conditions.

At the clinical level, little new is occurring. More benzodiazepines continue to emerge. Perhaps the most interesting is triazolam [35] a short-acting hypnotic that may be as safe and effective as flurazepam but with less tendency to cause a morning hangover. Also of interest may be buspirone, as investigational, nonsedative, antianxiety drug that is not a benzodiazepine and that may be less likely to interfere with psychomotor performance [36].

I have been impressed clinically with the problems caused by chlordiazepoxide and diazepam in at least one patient with cirrhosis. On two occasions, after brief periods of alcohol consumption, the patient was admitted to a hospital and was placed on the hospital's standard alcohol detoxification regimen, which involved regular doses of either chlordiazepoxide or diazepam. In both instances, the patient went from a psychiatrically clear and sensible state on the first day to an obtunded, confused, disoriented state by the third day, and on one admission, the patient fell while groggy and fractured an arm. In neither admission did the hospital staff appear to consider that hepatic cirrhosis constituted a reason for using the benzodiazepines with great care. My guess is that on both admissions the patient would have fared far better on no medication at all or on a low dose of oxazepam at bedtime. Our geriatric unit has shifted from diazepam to oxazepam for the treatment of anxiety or agitation in the elderly; in the absence of any formal study, the shift seems to have been beneficial.

**References**

1. Perry HJ, Balter MB, Mellinger GD, et al: National patterns of psychotherapeutic drug use. Arch Gen Psychiat 28:769-783, 1973.

2. Shader R, Greenblatt D: The psychopharmacologic treatment of anxiety states. *In* Shader R (Ed): Manual of Psychiatric Therapeutics. Boston, Little Brown, 1975.

3. Freighner J, Brauzer B, Gelenberg A, et al: Limbitrol treatment of depression. Psychopharmacologia (in press).

4. Schatzberg A, Cole JO: Benzodiazepines in depressive disorders. Arch Gen Psychiat (in press).

5. Klein DF: Delineation of two drug-responsive anxiety syndromes. Psychopharmacologia 5:397-408, 1964.

6. Zitrin C, Klein DF, Woerner M: Behavior therapy, supportive therapy, imipramine and phobias. Arch Gen Psychiat 35:307-320, 1978,

7. Cole JO, David JM: Antianxiety drugs. *In* Freedman DX, Dyrud J (Eds): American Handbook of Psychiatry, Vol V. New York, Basic 1975.

8. Brill N, Koelger R, Epstein L: Controlled study of psychiatric outpatient treatment. Arch Gen Psychiat 10:581-594, 1964.

9. Lorr M, McNair D, Weinstein G: Early effects of chlordiazepoxide used with psychotherapy. J Psychiat Res 1:257-270, 1963.

10. Greenberg I, Altman J, Cole J: Combination of drugs with behavior therapy. *In* Greenblatt M (Ed): Drugs in Combination with Other Therapies. New York, Grune and Stratton, 1975.

11. Klerman G: Combining drugs and psychotherapy in the treatment of depression. *In* Cole J, Schatzberg A, Frazier SH (Eds): Depression: Biology, Dynamics and Treatment. New York, Plenum, 1978.

12. Hollister LE: Clinical Use of Psychotherapeutic Drugs. Springfield, Ill, Thomas, 1973.

13. Cook L, Sepinwall J: Behavioral analysis of the effects and mechanisms of action of benzodiazepines. *In* Costa E, Greengard P (Eds): Mechanisms of Action of Benzodiazepines. New York, Raven, 1975.

14. Irwin S: A rational framework for the development, evaluation and use of psychoactive drugs. Am J Psychiat 124:1-19, 1968.

15. Hafely W: Behavioral and neuropharmacological aspects of drugs used in anxiety and related states. *In* Lipton M, DiMascio AD, Killam K (Eds): Psychopharmacology: A Generation of Progress. New York, Raven, 1978.

16. Rickels K: Use of antianxiety agents in anxious outpatients. Psychopharmacology 58:1-18, 1978.

17. DiMascio A: The effects of benzodiazepine on aggression: reduced or increased? Psychopharmacologia 30:95-102, 1973.

18. Hall R, Jaffe J: Aberrant response to diazepam: a new syndrome. Am J Psychiat 129:738-740, 1972.

19. Lipman RS, Hammer HMM, Bernardes JF, et al: Patient report of significant life situation events. Dis Nerv Syst 26:586-590, 1965.

20. Cole JO, Gardos G: Tardive dyskinesia. McLean Hosp J 3:155-166, 1977.

21. Greenblatt DJ, Shader RI: Pharmacotherapy of anxiety with benzodiazepines and B-adrenergic blockers. *In* Lipton M, DiMascio AD, Killam K (Eds): Psychopharmacology: A Generation of Progress, New York, Raven, 1978, pp 1381-1390.

22. Greenblatt DJ, Shader RI: Pharmacokinetic understanding of antianxiety drug therapy. Southern Med J 71:2-9, 1978.

23. Cole JO, Ryback R: Pharmacological therapy. *In* Tarter R, Sugerman A (Eds): Alcoholism, Reading, Mass, Addison-Wesley, 1976, pp 687-734.

24. Hoyumpa AM Jr: Disposition and elimination of minor tranquilizers in the aged and in patients with liver disease. Southern Med J 71:23-28, 1978.

25. Bliding A: Effects of different rates of absorption of two benzodiazepines on subjective and objective parameters: significance for clinical use and risk of abuse. Eur J Clin Pharmacol 7:201-211, 1974.

26. Winstead D, Anderson A, Blackwell B, et al: Diazepam on demand. Arch Gen Psychiat 30:349-353, 1974.

27. Kellner R, Rada R, Anderson T, et al: The effects of chlordiazepoxide on self-rated distress and well being. Psychopharmacology (in press).

28. Wiersum J: Psychotropic drugs in addiction. JAMA 227:79, 1974.

29. Woody G, O'Brien C, Greensten R: Misuse and abuse of diazepam. Internat J Addict 10:843-848, 1975.

30. Patch V: The dangers of diazepam, a street drug. New Eng J Med 290:807, 1974.

31. Maletzky B, Klotter J: Addiction to diazepam. Internat J Addict 11:95-115, 1976.

32. Hanna S: A case of oxazepam dependence. Br J Psychiat 120:443-445, 1972.

33. Pope H, Pioggia-Ionescu M: (Personal communication).

34. Braestrup C, Squires R: Brain specific benzodiazepine receptors. Br J Psychiatry 133:249-260, 1978.

35. Liebowitz M, Sunshine A: Long-term hypnotic efficacy and safety of triazolam and flurazepam. J Clin Pharmacol 18: 302-309, 1978.

36. Goldberg H, Finnerty R: The comparative efficacy of buspirone and diazepam in the treatment of anxiety. Am J Psychiatry 136:1187-1188, 1979.

# 4

# Beta-Blocking Drugs in Psychiatry

*Jonathan O. Cole, M.D.*
*Richard I. Altesman, M.D.*
*Charles H. Weingarten, M.D.*

Within the autonomic nervous system, two main types of adrenergic receptors have been identified by differential response to agonist (activating) drugs and to antagonist (blocking) drugs. Alpha-adrenergic receptors are most responsive to norepinephrine and are blocked by phentolamine and phenoxybenzamine. When stimulated, these receptors cause vasoconstriction, mydriasis, and contraction of sphincters in the stomach and bladder. Beta-receptors, on the other hand, are most sensitive to isoproterenol and are blocked by a variety of newer drugs, including propranolol. Stimulation of beta-receptors causes vasodilation, relaxation of the bronchi, relaxation of stomach and bladder sphincters, and a general increase in heart rate and in conduction velocity and contractility of the heart. Beta-receptor stimulation also causes release of glucose from glycogen in the liver and a rise in free fatty acids in the plasma [1,2].

Beta-receptors are now subdivided into $\beta_1$ receptors, which chiefly activate the heart, and $\beta_2$ receptors, which control the other varied effects noted above. This may be of importance, since some beta-blocking drugs act principally on $\beta_1$ receptors, while others have a broader spectrum of activity [1].

Of possible special relevance to the potential utility of beta-blocking drugs in psychiatry is the existence of beta-adrenergic receptors in the central nervous system. These are, however, more difficult to study than the peripheral receptors. There is evidence that specific beta-receptors exist in the central nervous system, both from binding studies involving radioactive ligands [3] and from studies of the effects of locally applied beta-blocking drugs [4].

None of this work appears to be at a level where specific brain-behavior relationships affected by beta-blocking drugs have any clear relevance for clinical psychopharmacology. This area is complicated by the fact that various beta-blocking drugs differ in the extent to which they cross the blood-brain barrier and to which they possess membrane-stabilizing effects, local anesthetic effects, and mild agonist (stimulant) activity at the receptor site [5,6]. In the latter case, a "stimulant" beta-blocker can occupy the receptor and prevent its overactivation by isoproterenol or locally released neurotransmitters while still mildly stimulating the receptor itself [6].

This kind of mixed agonist-antagonist activity is also seen in the opiate analgesics of which pentazocine (Talwin) is a good example.

It seems reasonable that anxiety has something to do with sympathetic nervous system overactivity. Many patients who describe themselves as anxious have chronic autonomic physiological symptoms, such as palpitations, tremor, sweaty palms, frequent urination, diarrhea or constipation, dizziness, headache or discomfort in the chest or stomach, nausea, vomiting, or muscle spasms or pains. In some patients, these somatic symptoms are prominent; in others, they are minimal or absent, and the anxiety is mainly a subjective mood manifestation variously described as nervousness, worry, fear, panic, etc. [7]. In addition to these subjective complaints, some patients are phobic—that is, they experience anxiety only in the presence of, or in anticipation of, certain feared objects or situations. Some also have obsessions or compulsions that seem to bear some complex relationship to anxiety. Some patients have episodic panic states or anxiety attacks, often unrelated to external events, which almost always last less than an hour and are usually accompanied by marked physical symptoms. The St. Louis criteria for anxiety neurosis [8] specify that, to fit this diagnostic category, patients must have:

1. chronic subjective anxiety,
2. discrete anxiety attacks of extreme fearfulness,
3. a variety of somatic symptoms during the attack.

The diversity of "anxiety-related" symptoms and the fact that, although some anxious patients have discrete panic attacks, most have chronic anxiety that may wax and wane in response to external situations, makes one wonder whether anxiety is in fact a single phenomenon physiologically or biochemically. Attempts to detect physiological measures of anxiety have had only limited success. Many measures, such as sweat-gland activity (assessed as skin conductance), pulse rate, blood pressure, pulse volume in the fingers, tremor, respiratory efficiency, muscle tension, alpha-wave frequency in the EEG, and adrenocortical function all show some relationship to subjective anxiety at some time in some subjects. Each of these measures probably correlates with anxiety only over a part of the possible full range of anxiety experience possible in man [7].

It would be ideal if, in our search for better antianxiety drugs, the specific neurohumoral substance that causes one or more types of clinical anxiety had been identified; drugs that block its actions would then be "good" antianxiety drugs. Unfortunately, the best current candidate for this role, adrenaline, does not reliably produce anxiety symptoms in normal subjects [9,10]. An excellent study by Schachter and Singer [11] suggests that adrenaline has a variety of mood effects that are a function of the situation—it can increase pleasure and anger as well as anxiety. The subjective effects of noradrenaline are even less clear than those of adrenaline. It can increase anxiety, but its effects are mainly those of vasoconstriction [2]. Isoproterenol, the most potent available beta-adrenergic stimulant, can precipitate panic attacks in patients prone to these attacks but has only mild effects in normal subjects [12]. Lactic-acid infusion shares this property of precipitating panic attacks only in attack-prone patients, but the mechanism by which this is accomplished remains obscure [8,9]. Yohimbine, a complex, autonomically active drug, also has been shown to elicit anxiety symptoms in man that are more typical of clinical anxiety than those produced by epinephrine [10]. Even this is not very helpful because yohimbine acts as an alpha-adrenergic stimulant, dropping blood pressure and heart rate in anesthetized animals while having exactly the opposite effects by unknown mechanisms in alert animals and in man. This whole area has never been systematically explored. Since many of the substances noted do not cross the blood-brain barrier, studies of anxiety-producing drugs in man may only be able to elicit peripheral, somatic symptoms of anxiety. In chronic clinical anxiety, there are almost certainly both central nervous system and autonomic nervous system dysfunctions, and central anxiety may be mediated by different neurotransmitters than are those involved in the presumably secondary peripheral manifestations. Obviously, the old dichotomy between the James-Lange theory that anxiety is "only" the perception of bodily sensations and the view of Cannon that anxiety is only a central state remains unresolved [5].

This dichotomy is reflected again and again in the literature on the use of beta-blocking drugs in the treatment of various types of anxiety. Do drugs like propranolol act in anxious patients only by blocking peripheral beta-adrenergic symptoms of anxiety, or do these drugs also have important direct central effects?

## Beta-Blockers in Anxiety

There is some agreement [5,6,13] that beta-blockers are effective in patients who present themselves to internists with functional cardiac complaints. In fact, the use of these drugs in anxiety grew out of observations in cardiac patients that beta-blockers not only improved cardiac function but also decreased the patients' accompanyng anxiety. Propranolol and several other beta-blocking drugs marketed in foreign countries slow heart rate, improve angina pectoris by reducing myocardial oxygen requirement, and reduce blood pressure. These drugs decrease myocardial irritability and can benefit a range of cardiac arrhythmias, including the blocking of extrasystoles.

Patients with functional cardiovascular complaints, including chest pain, dyspnea on exertion, palpitations, dizziness, decreased effort tolerance, fatigue, headache, sweating, nervousness, and tremors have received a variety of medical diagnoses, such as cardiac neurosis, neurocirculatory asthenia, or hyperventilation syndrome. Greenblatt and Shader refer to this group of conditions as "psychocardiac disorders [13]." Patients with such symptoms often respond dramatically to beta-blocking drugs. Frohlich describes a similar group of patients as having a "hyperdynamic beta adrenergic circulatory state," and documents this by showing that such patients are made acutely worse (he describes the response as "hysteria" but he probably precipitated panic attacks) by intravenous administration of the beta agonist, isoproterenol; comparable doses of this drug had no effect in patients with essential hypertension or in normal controls [14]. Easton and Sherman describe similar responses to isoproterenol in four patients with histories of sudden attacks of severe anxiety accompanied by somatic symptoms of the sort described above [12]. Both studies report that propranolol effectively blocked both cardiac symptoms and anxiety. It appears that beta-blockers are generally useful in psychocardiac disorders, both in patients with chronic symptoms and in those with episodic attacks of cardiac symptoms. It is interesting that Suzman, one of the early psychiatrists working with propranolol, in describing a large series of patients successfully treated with this drug, notes that half the patients came to him complaining primarily of somatic symptoms, not anxiety [15]. It is possible that patients with cardiovascular symptoms, but no diagnosed cardiac disease, do in fact have an organically based cardiac dysfunction, such as tachycardia, cardiac irritability, or angina that responds to a beta-blocker. The treatment of anxious patients in psychiatric settings, mainly outpatient clinics, has been more extensively studied, but the results are less clear. There are 13 published studies comparing beta-blockers to placebo in anxious patients. Tyrer and Lader compared sotalol, a cardiospecific beta-blocker, with placebo in the treatment-resistant anxious clinic patients in a crossover design, with patients staying two weeks on each treatment [16]. Each patient was evaluated both by investigators and by self-report at the end of a four-week study experience, and a global judgment was made as to which treatment (sotalol or placebo) was superior. The trial was halted after 14 patients because a prespecified statistical criterion was reached showing no significant difference between the treatments. The physician judgments, however, strongly favored sotalol over placebo. Using a similar crossover design with sequential analysis, Granville-Grossman and Turner compared one-week trials of 80 mg of propranolol and placebo [17]. In this study, the clinicians' judgments reached statistical significance, favoring propranolol after 16 patients had been studied. Nine of the patients also subjectively favored propranolol, while six felt the two treatments to be equivalent. Analyses of differences in symptom response detected drug-placebo differences for somatic anxiety symptoms but not for psychic symptoms. Using the same format, Bonn et al. compared two-week trials of 400 mg of practolol (another cardiospecific beta-blocker) and placebo [18]. In this study, sequential analysis based on clinicians' preferences showed the drug to be superior after only 8 patients had been studied, while patient preferences significantly favored practolol after 15 had completed the trial. Inspection of changes in individual symptoms again suggested that somatic anxiety symptoms showed more drug-related improvement than did psychic symptoms.

On the basis of the data from the above studies, Tyrer and Lader carried out a more-complex, three-treatment crossover study utilizing six patients with mainly somatic anxiety symptoms and six with mainly psychic symptoms. Comparing the effects of diazepam (6 to 18 mg/day), propranolol (120 to 360 mg/day) and placebo, the authors found diazepam to be the drug most preferred by patients in both groups, while propranolol was superior to placebo only in the somatically anxious patients [19].

Kellner et al. reported a double-blind crossover trial in 22 anxious outpatients, comparing a week on propranolol on patient-adjusted dosages of 40 to 80 mg/day with a comparable week on placebo [20]. Although almost all 35 measures showed better response to propranolol than to placebo, the difference reached statistical significance only in two clusters of items assessing somatic symptoms and psychic anxiety. Tanna et al. carried out a more complex crossover design in which 28 anxious patients meeting strict criteria for anxiety neurosis (both chronic symptoms and clear anxiety attacks [8]) received placebo, 40 mg/day of propranolol and 120 mg/day of propranolol for one week each [21]. Three symptoms—fatigue, shakiness, and initial insomnia—were improved more by 120 mg/day of propranolol than by placebo and, as in the Kellner study, propranolol at the higher dose looked a bit better than placebo on most measures.

Bonn and Turner have tried to test the possibility that propranolol may act by mechanisms other than beta-adrenergic blockade [22]. Since propranolol is racemic and d-propranolol is a much weaker beta-blocker than l-propranolol, they studied 160 mg/day of d-propranolol versus placebo in a 10-patient double-blind crossover design with all patients having a week on each treatment. No drug-placebo differences were observed.

Surprisingly, only two conventional double-blind, random assignment, independent treatment group, noncrossover studies of beta-blockers in anxious outpatients have been conducted. Burrows et al. compared oxprenolol (240 mg/day), diazepam (15 mg/day) and placebo in groups of about 20 patients, each for a three-week trial [23]. All three patient groups improved. Both active drugs were superior to placebo only in the third and final week of the study. There was a trend favoring diazepam over oxprenolol in global improvement ratings by the investigators, but patient self-reports did not reflect this difference. Johnson et al. compared the same doses of the same drugs for three weeks. Thirteen diazepam, 11 oxprenolol, and 5 placebo patients completed the trial; the study was planned to have only half as many patients on placebo as on the other drugs [24]. Physicians' ratings showed diazepam to be significantly superior to both oxprenolol and placebo after the first week. By the end of the third week, diazepam was still superior to placebo with oxprenolol being intermediate but not significantly different from either placebo or diazepam. Patients' ratings showed diazepam to be superior to placebo and oxprenolol after one week. After three weeks, patients with psychic anxiety symptoms were better on diazepam than on placebo with oxprenolol falling in between, while patients with somatic anxiety did equally well on all three treatments.

Gaind et al. studied oxprenolol and placebo in the behavior therapy of phobias. As part of the treatment, phobic patients were given repeated periods of exposure to the feared objects. Oxprenolol (16 mg/day) and placebo were given before alternating treatment sessions [25]. Patients were less anxious during sessions after oxprenolol, but patients scored lower on fear and avoidance scores after the session was over if they had been pretreated with placebo. Thus, oxprenolol seemed to make behavior therapy more pleasant but less effective.

In a second study of propranolol versus placebo in the behavior therapy of agoraphobics involving repeated exposure in vivo to stressful situations, patients received either propranolol only or placebo only. Propranolol, given in a single 40 mg dose 90 minutes before exposure, positively hindered clinical response [26]. Placebo patients were statistically more improved than propranolol patients over the month after treatment. One problem in this design was that the antianxiety effects of propranolol were evident at the beginning of the five-hour exposure sessions but wore off, leaving propranolol patients more and more anxious as the therapy sessions ended. One uncontrolled study of propranolol in 10 patients with panic states, and/or agoraphobia, using rather low dosages (20 to 60 mg/day), found good relief of panic attacks without agoraphobia (three patients) but no effect in three agoraphobics [27]. Two depressed patients with panic attacks had the attacks but not the depression relieved by propranolol.

One other study deserves mention. Suzman reports on 40 patients (in his practice) with anxiety treated by propranolol in individually adjusted dosages of 40 to 320 mg/day for periods of weeks to months [28]. When these improved patients were shifted to placebo single-blind, 88% relapsed—many within a couple of days.

Wheatley compared propranolol (90 mg/day) with chlordiazepoxide (30 mg/day) in 105 anxious patients treated by a large number of general practitioners. The study was double-blind, noncrossover, and six weeks in duration [29]. In general, the two treatments were not significantly different on either physician or patient measures, including improvement in tremor and tachycardia. There was a modest trend in favor of chlordiazepoxide (35% of the patients on chlordiazepoxide were symptom-free at six weeks versus 29% of the propranolol patients). The drug differences were most marked for depression and sleep disturbance; for these particular symptoms, chlordiazepoxide was significantly superior to propranolol. McMillin reported a small study in 12 anxious patients stressed by events in Northern Ireland. He compared 15 mg/day of diazepam with 240 mg/day of oxprenolol, each for one week in a crossover study [30]. Patients improved on both treatments. Although no significant differences were found, diazepam was judged a bit better for insomnia while oxprenolol seemed to improve concentration more.

Becker compared clinical outcome in anxious patients randomly assigned to either propranolol or oxprenolol, both at 240 mg/day [31]. The two beta-blockers were both quite effective in anxiety, tension, insomnia, impaired concentration, and depression. Propranolol effected a more rapid improvement in palpitations but had slightly more side effects.

After considering the results of the 16 controlled or partially controlled studies noted above, it appears that beta-blocking drugs may have a weak antianxiety effect, being a bit better than placebo but probably less effective than modest doses of standard benzodiazepines. Lader's general proposition that beta-blockers are more effective in somatic anxiety than in psychic anxiety is sometimes, but by no means always, borne out by the data [7]. The other hypothesis, that beta-blockers may be particularly effective in preventing recurrent panic attacks, has not really been tested. The one controlled study which required patients to have panic attacks did not, in fact, examine this symptom for drug-placebo differences [22]. Most studies do not separate out symptoms likely to result from beta-adrenergic overactivity (e.g., tremor, palpitations, chest pain) from other anxiety symptoms (e.g., insomnia, concentration difficulty, nausea) so that the possible specificity of beta blockade has not really been adequately tested. Most studies also used rather short drug trials of one or two weeks, rather small samples of 10 to 25 patients, and they did not titrate the dose upward. The two studies evaluating propranolol as an adjunct to the behavior therapy of phobias showed the drug to be actually worse than placebo [25,26].

Some interesting, although for the most part untested, ideas are raised in the available literature. Perhaps intravenous administration of the beta agonist isoproterenol would identify patients who are made more anxious by this drug and who would respond uniquely to drugs like propranolol. The effective propranolol dose might be determined in advance by finding the dose necessary to decrease pulse rate to about 60 beats/minute for each patient. The hyperventilation stress used by Suzman, although it can cause changes in the electrocardiogram, could be generally useful; he titrated the propranolol dose upward until this procedure no longer caused subjective distress [15]. Most of the negative or weakly positive controlled studies of beta-blockers in anxiety suffer from arbitrary dose requirements that may leave patients inadequately blockaded.

Since controlled studies reflect a relatively restricted segment of the real world, it is interesting to consider the opinions of two psychiatrists who have published their experiences with extensive use of beta-blockers in psychiatric practice. Hawkings, in England, used oxprenolol and propranolol in 104 patients, motivated in part by problems of sedative drug dependency in his area [32]. He found oxprenolol and propranolol quite similar in dose, side effects and efficacy. He classified his patients into mental anxiety, physical anxiety, anxiety with depression, and phobic anxiety. Fifteen percent of his 104 original patients could not tolerate beta-blockers because of side effects, such as fatigue, dizziness, nausea, bradycardia, or hypotension. His best results occurred in patients not on other medications when treatment began (83% improvement) and in patients in his somatic anxiety group (84% improvement). Both improvement rates exclude patients dropping out because of side effects. With patients who were previously on the benzodiazepines or other sedatives, he found that stopping the sedative before starting a beta-blocker usually worked out badly, while adding the beta-blocker first and then tapering the benzodiazepines gradually worked much better. Overall, Hawkings' improvement rate, excluding side-effect dropouts, was 75 percent. His median propranolol dose was 120 mg/day; his maximum dose was 320 mg/day.

Suzman, in South Africa, treated 513 anxious patients with propranolol, usually in dosages between 80 mg/day and 320 mg/day, but sometimes up to dosages as high as 1,200 mg/day [15]. The majority of his patients had predominantly somatic symptoms and, in half, the diagnosis of anxiety state had not been made by the referring physician because of the prominent body complaints. The other half had mostly failed on benzodiazepines and some had been made irritable or agitated by these drugs. Suzman used a stress test (hyperventilation while standing) to induce anxiety symptoms and tachycardia, presumably by inducing increased adrenergic activity. Sometimes, electrocardiographic changes (ST segment depression and/or T-wave inversion) occur during this test. This stress test is used during therapy to assess the extent and adequacy of beta blockade. Suzman found that symptoms of fatigue, muscle weakness, tremor, palpitation, headache, and muscle pain as well as gastrointestinal and genitourinary symptoms were "almost invariably" relieved or improved. Preexisting tendencies to hyperventilate under stress were subdued, thereby removing secondary effects of hyperventilation, such as dizziness, fainting, impaired concentration, weeping, and feelings of apprehension and unreality. Panic states, irritability, agitation, and insomnia improved as did the general social functioning of the patients. Two-thirds of the patients with coexisting depression improved on propranolol alone; the others required added antidepressants. Patients with predominantly psychic complaints often did not respond well at ordinary dosages (probably the author means under 160 to 320 mg/day) but did well on even higher dosage levels.

Many patients required prolonged treatment to stay symptom-free, but often gradually tapered their daily dosage downward. None of the patients required progressively higher dosage. Seventy-six patients were shifted to placebo single-blind. Some relapsed within a few hours, while others had a gradual return of symptoms over days or weeks, with somatic symptoms usually returning first. Occasionally, patients developed "bizarre subjective symptoms." Bronchospasm and peripheral vasospasm also occurred occasionally. No numerical data on improvement rates were presented.

Thus, the general impression gained from both the Hawkings and the Suzman reports is that beta-blockers used in higher dosages for longer periods than were employed in the currently available controlled studies may result in more impressive clinical responses, particularly in patients with prominent somatic complaints.

In addition to the above studies in conventional clinical anxiety states, beta-blockers have also been employed in less usual situations—examination "nerves," stage fright, bowling, and stressful dental procedures. Brewer compared propranolol and placebo in a study using single doses given to university students just before a psychology examination. The dose of propranolol was determined as that needed to slow a student's pulse rate to 55 to 65 beats/minute [33]. The study showed no impairment of test performance due to the drug and some benefit in more anxious students. In a somewhat more elaborate study, Krishnan randomly assigned 32 students with preexamination anxiety to either oxprenolol 80 mg/day or diazepam 4 mg/day [34]. There were no clear differences between the drugs on symptom relief. Diazepam subjects believed they had done better on their examinations. However, using professors' predictions of probable examination grades, five of the 15 oxprenolol students did better than predicted, while only two did less well; of the 17 diazepam students, none did better and six did worse than predicted. In a crossover study comparing single doses of 40 mg oxprenolol and placebo in music students' initial public performances, oxprenolol, particularly on the first performance, improved experts' judgments of the quality of the students' musicianship [35]. Decrease in tremor probably contributed most to this improvement. Oxprenolol also decreased pulse rate. A study comparing oxprenolol 80 mg, diazepam 5 mg and placebo in a crossover study in anxious dental patients undergoing three unpleasant dental procedures showed no clear effect on either subjective reports of anxiety or on ratings of anxiety by the dentists [36]. There was a trend for oxprenolol to be a bit better than diazepam, which was, in turn, better than placebo on subjective measures.

Eisdorfer et al. studied the effects of 10 mg of propranolol versus placebo on serial rote-learning of word lists in elderly male volunteer subjects [37]. Propranolol subjects made significantly fewer errors. Pulse rate and plasma-free fatty acid (FFA) increases observed in the placebo group were blocked by propranolol; effects on skin conductance were not significant. The results were interpreted as suggesting that propranolol decreased the interference of test-related autonomic arousal with psychological functioning.

Studies in other forms of experimentally induced anxiety have been less conclusive. Tyrer and Lader compared single doses of diazepam (5 mg), racemic propranolol (120 mg), and d-propranolol (120 mg), and placebo in normal subjects stressed by electric shocks, shocks plus isoproterenol inhalation, and exposure to individually appropriate phobic stimuli [38]. Only diazepam lessened the subjective anxiety response to these stresses. The d-propranolol, which is a much weaker beta-blocker than the usual racemic form, was able to reduce pulse rate. Gottschalk et al. used a brief stressful interview and compared the effects of 60 mg of propranolol and placebo on anxiety, as indirectly measured by content analysis of a five-minute speech sample and by plasma-free fatty acids (FFA) [39]. The speech sample showed less anxiety on propranolol than on placebo only *before* the stress interview, not after it. FFA response did not differentiate significantly between the two treatments. Using hypnotically induced psychological stress, Cleghorn et al. compared 0.3 mg/kg of propranolol intravenously with saline [40]. Anxiety was measured by the same indirect measures used by Gottschalk's group. Here, propranolol decreased FFA response but had no effect on verbal anxiety measures. Nakano et al. used mirror drawing and the Stroop color-word test to induce stress [41]. Propranolol (40 mg) decreased changes in heart rate compared with placebo but had no differential effects on either subjective anxiety or on performance.

In short, artificial stress situations seem even less useful than "real" stress situations in demonstrating that propranolol may have antianxiety effects [16].

## Tremor

Several types of tremor are encountered in psychiatric practice. These include tremor associated with marked anxiety, parkinsonian tremor associated with either spontaneous or drug-induced parkinsonism, essential or familial tremor as an incidental finding, senile tremor, tremor associated with lithium therapy, and tremor associated with withdrawal from alcohol and other sedative drugs. Informal observations of patients with tremor who received propranolol for cardiac conditions suggested that tremor could be suppressed by beta-blockers. This general impression is probably correct, but the published evidence is spotty. It is well reviewed by Corbett [42].

There is evidence that the tremor induced by beta-agonists (e.g., isoproterenol and, presumably, by internally produced epinephrine) is mediated by peripheral beta-receptors. At least, intra-arterially administered propranolol can suppress isoproterenol-induced tremor in the injected arm without affecting the tremor in the other arm. However, intra-arterial propranolol does not suppress essential tremor acutely, and oral propranolol may take a day or more to relieve essential or familial tremor [43]. Of the five controlled studies, four involving propranolol in dosages of 60 to 240 mg/day and one involving oxprenolol at unclear dosage, two are clearly positive [44,45], two weakly positive [42,46], and one negative [47]. Studies in parkinsonian tremor are generally negative, although two show some beneficial effects in controlled studies [42,48].

There are only four studies formally reporting on the use of propranolol in lithium tremor. One controlled study by Kellett et al. is entirely negative, perhaps because only single doses of propranolol and placebo are compared over a three-hour study period [49]. A second placebo controlled crossover study by Kirk et al., using dosages of 30 to 80 mg/day for one-week periods, showed a significant preference for propranolol over placebo in ten lithium-treated patients bothered by tremor [50]. The uncontrolled studies are uniformly positive [51,52]. In a recorded discussion, Rafaelson notes that he had obtained excellent to moderate effects from propranolol in two-thirds of his large series of patients with lithium tremor [53].

One paper reporting a double-blind crossover study in senile tremor finds only two of nine patients to be clearly better on propranolol than on placebo, but one of these was dramatically improved [54]. A recent study also shows that intravenous propranolol will suppress induced clonus in paraplegic patients [55].

Despite the mixed evidence, propranolol appears effective enough to warrant trial in essential tremor and in lithium tremor, though in the latter situation the risks and benefits of reducing lithium dosage should also be considered. The drug is probably also useful in anxious patients embarrassed or upset by tremor that appears only in stressful situations; the study of propranolol in musicians giving auditions suggests that this effect can be real [33]. Tremor is less common than other parkinsonian signs in patients on antipsychotic drugs, and antiparkinsonian drugs are the logical treatment of choice, but propranolol could be tried in severe tremor resistant to more conventional drugs. When propranolol is used to reduce tremor, dosage should be titrated gradually upward toward maximum approved levels. This should be done if symptom relief does not occur at lower dosages and side effects do not occur. A reduction in pulse rate toward 60 beats per minute when the patient is at rest suggests that adequate peripheral blockade of beta-receptors has occurred.

### Alcoholism and Drug Abuse

Alcohol withdrawal is accompanied by symptoms, including tremor, tachycardia, anxiety, and tension, that suggest adrenergic activity. It is therefore not remarkable that several studies of beta-blockers have been carried out for this condition. In the long-term management of "dry" alcoholics, the pharmacological treatment of persistent anxiety is a problem, since the benzodiazepine drugs can also cause psychological and physical dependence and can reactivate drinking in some alcoholics. Beta-blockers might well be a particularly useful addition to the limited group of non-dependence-inducing antianxiety drugs available for use in anxious alcoholics.

Although earlier studies in animals had suggested that propranolol might actually block the central depressant effects of acute doses of ethanol, studies of interactions between alcohol and propranolol in man have been inconclusive and complex in their findings [56]. The earliest study of propranolol in alcohol withdrawal focused on circulatory changes during alcohol withdrawal and showed that propranolol returned such changes toward normal [57]; it was coincidentally noted that patients in this study receiving propranolol also became more relaxed. The same group ran a double-blind controlled study comparing propranolol, 160 mg/day, with placebo in 44 male alcoholics undergoing withdrawal [58]. Unfortunately, all patients received chlormethiazole, a mild sedative used in alcohol withdrawal in Scandinavia, and often diazepam. Given this weakening of the study, propranolol still caused a significantly greater reduction in tension symptoms, by self-report, than did placebo during the first eight days of treatment. There was a trend for depressive symptoms also to decrease more on the active drug. In a third study, by Carlsson et al., propranolol (120 mg/day) was compared with diazepam (30 mg/day) in a four-week double-blind, random-assignment crossover study, using alcoholics who had completed detoxification (one to three weeks after admission to the hospital) [59]. Comparisons of symptom reduction on 13 symptom or mood measures favored propranolol, although only 5 of the 26 possible contrasts reached statistical significance. Four of these occurred during the second phase (i.e., patients who had received diazepam first and propranolol second showing lower symptom scores than those receiving propranolol first and diazepam second). Gallant et al. compared propranolol in increasing dosages from 40 to 120 mg/day over four weeks with placebo in detoxified drug-free hospitalized alcoholics with anxiety and tension [60]. Neither a 35-item self-report form nor a 14-item interview rating scale completed by a psychiatrist differentiated drug from placebo. Most patients improved in this inpatient treatment setting, but global improvement ratings made by the "blind" psychiatrist significantly favored the drug. Three of 10 patients on placebo compared with 9 of 10 propranolol patients improved substantially, reminding one of similar discrepancies between patient and observer ratings in the studies of anxious outpatients by Lader's group.

In a similar study by Ladewig et al., recently admitted patients undergoing alcohol withdrawal were randomly assigned to oxprenolol, 160 mg/day, or placebo [61]. After the first week, when withdrawal symptoms were most manifest, no drug-placebo difference was observed on either physician ratings or self-report scales. However, by day 22, oxprenolol was significantly superior to placebo on a composite total distress score utilizing data from all four rating instruments. Only one item—difficulty in concentrating—was able by itself to significantly discriminate between drug and placebo, being more improved on oxprenolol. An informal clinical report of the use of propranolol in about 50 presumably outpatient alcoholics claims that the drug is useful in dosages of 40 to 80 mg/day in controlling anxiety and tremor [62]. Propranolol is said to enable the patient to reduce the use of other drugs such as diazepam. The authors note that the drug is particularly helpful in alcoholics with essential tremor who have been using alcohol to suppress the tremor. There is also a suggestion from one case report that propranolol is good for hangover [63].

Investigators at the Addiction Research Center in Toronto have shown that intra-arterial propranolol suppresses tremor about 10 minutes after injection in patients undergoing alcohol withdrawal bilaterally, suggesting a central locus of action [64,65]. The same group compared five treatments in alcohol withdrawal, with only six patients in each treatment group:

1. chlordiazepoxide, 25 mg every six hours (q.6h),
2. propranolol, 40 mg q.6h,
3. propranolol, 10 mg q.6h,
4. propranolol, 10 mg and chlordiazepoxide, 25 mg, q.6h,
5. placebo over the six-day withdrawal period.

The degree of beta-blockade was determined by giving intravenous isoproterenol and calculating the dose required to increase heart rate by 25 beats/minute [66]. All four drug treatments were better than placebo in reducing tremor amplitude on day 2 and day 4 of the study. On day 6 only, the higher dosage of propranolol was superior to placebo on this measure. Changes in subjective symptoms were less clear with all drug groups except on day 2 where the drug combination was superior to placebo, while on day

4 and day 6 only low-dose propranolol and chlordiazepoxide alone were superior to placebo. All active drugs significantly decreased urinary excretion of fatty adrenaline and noradrenaline on day 4 and day 6 of the study.

In a Finnish study, propranolol (120 mg/day) was compared to placebo in a double-blind crossover study in which 18 patients had three days on each treatment during withdrawal. All patients received chlormethiazole and some received diazepam [67]. No drug-placebo differences were found, probably partially because all patients showed a marked decrease in tremor over the study period.

There were preliminary reports by Grosz that low doses of propranolol blocked the euphoriant effect of street heroin, reduced craving for opiates, and even precipitated withdrawal symptoms [68,69]. Better controlled studies by Resnick et al., using known heroin doses, were essentially negative [70,71]. Propranolol did not ameliorate withdrawal symptoms and had only a negligible effect in slightly reducing the intensity of the heroin-induced high in drug-free addicts. Hollister and Prusmack, studying propranolol in opiate withdrawal treated with methadone, found a slight positive effect only in patients with mild withdrawal symptoms [72] and no evidence of any antagonistic effect to opiates. This area is well reviewed by Freedman [56].

Rappolt et al. report that intravenous propranolol (1 mg/minute up to 8 mg total) blocks the tachycardia, anxiety, and hypertension caused by overdoses of cocaine without reversing the subjective "high" or the emetic effects of cocaine [73]. This effect seems pharmacologically reasonable.

Linken reports that recurrent anxiety in patients who developed such persistent symptoms after LSD abuse is also relieved by propranolol alone (one case) or when added to chlorpromazine and diazepam, drugs that had not been effective in the absence of propranolol (two cases) [74].

In summary, propranolol appears to have some promise in the treatment of alcohol withdrawal symptoms and also as a less abuse-prone drug therapy for resisting anxiety in detoxified alcoholics. It probably can antagonize the cardiovascular effects of stimulant drugs and may be useful generally for the treatment of anxiety in drug-abuse-prone individuals for whom the benzodiazepines or meprobamate are contraindicated.

**Schizophrenia**

The most startling and unpredictable potential use for beta-blockers in psychiatry is in the treatment of schizophrenia. This area was initiated fortuitously by Atsmon et al. in Jerusalem. A severely ill, psychotic patient with an acute attack of intermittent porphyria was given propranolol to block adrenergic overactivity. After three days, at a dose of 100 mg q.6h, the patient's pulse and blood pressure dropped and her mental symptoms cleared dramatically. A relative of this patient, who eventually proved not to have porphyria, was treated for an acute postpartum psychosis with similar exellent results [75]. As of 1976, Atsmon's group had treated 44 patients with various psychiatric diagnoses with propranolol [76]. Dosage was raised rapidly to 1,000 mg/day on the second day; thereafter, increases were on the order of 400 mg/day. Pulse and blood pressure were closely watched. Often, when pulse dropped to 60 beats/minute and blood pressure to 90/60 mm Hg., psychotic symptoms would clear "remarkably." Sometimes beta-blockade would slip, and the final maintenance dose would have to be a bit higher than the dose that initially depressed cardiac function and controlled psychosis. Patients who were clearly improved by high-dose propranolol would usually relapse within 12 to 48 hours if the drug was stopped. Seven of 11 acute schizophrenics, 3 of 15 chronic schizophrenics, 5 of 8 postpartum psychoses, and 3 of 5 manic psychoses were reported to be markedly improved. Some patients with chronic or recurrent illnesses have been stable on high-dose propranolol for two to six years.

Some patients on the Atsmon regimen developed acute hypertension despite continuing slow pulse rate. This side effect was blocked by intravenous phentolamine (Regitine) but often was associated with eventual poor clinical response. Other early signs of toxicity included vomiting, diarrhea, fatigue, vivid dreams, hypnagogic hallucinations, impaired coordination, slurred speech, and toxic psychosis. All these side effects remitted rapidly after the drug was stopped. One patient developed premature ventricular contractions, and one developed mild congestive failure.

This work has been systematically extended by Yorkston and his associates at Friern Hospital in London. They initially used the Atsmon dosage regimen but encountered hypertensive crises, marked ataxia, confusional states, and visual hallucinations [77]. They therefore shifted to using an initial test dose of 20 mg of propranolol. If this was well-tolerated, the drug was administered twice a day and dosage was increased by 40 or 80 mg/day. Patients were closely monitored: a drop in pulse below 50 to 60 beats/minute or blood pressure below 90/60 mm Hg. called for a decrease in dosage. Patients were carefully watched for early toxic signs, which included pallor, cyanosis, ataxia, incoordination, slurred speech, dizziness, or visual hallucinations. These symptoms rapidly cleared when the drug was stopped for a day or so. Nausea, vomiting, and abdominal discomfort occurred early in the study but were minimized by giving the drug after meals. Yorkston et al. have published a useful and detailed guide for managing propranolol in schizophrenic patients [78,79].

Fifty-five patients with "florid schizophrenic symptoms" were treated with propranolol alone or in combination with antipsychotics in an open study [80]. Patients had to have at least moderate schizophrenic symptoms on the Brief Psychiatric Rating Scale. Twenty-eight of the 55 patients showed dramatic remission of schizophrenic symptoms, 17 on propranolol alone and 11 on propranolol plus an antipsychotic drug, usually trifluoperazine. Twenty-one other patients showed moderate to marked improvement. Although best results were obtained in patients who had been ill less than one year, 15 of 38 patients who had been ill from one to 30 years remitted "completely." Patients in Yorkston's series usually improved gradually, becoming calmer, less irritable, and more coherent, with hallucinations stopping before secondary delusions; the latter often only remitted after many weeks. In a few patients, all schizophrenic symptoms disappeared abruptly. The propranolol dosage at which remission occurred on propranolol alone ranged from 160 to 3,000 mg/day, with the median being 1,250 mg/day. The median eventual maintenance dose was 500 mg/day in patients also receiving antipsychotics, the median effective dose was lower, 820 mg/day. The time to remission ranged from three days to a year, with a median of eight weeks. Follow-up was in progress, ranging from 10 days to 20 months at the time of publication. Toxic effects of moderate to severe intensity, though transient, occurred in 14 of the 55 patients. No long-term toxic effects had been observed. Relapse usually occurred rapidly if medication was stopped, often within three days; once a full relapse occurred, the symptoms were quite resistant to reinstitution of treatment.

The group has now completed a double-blind controlled study of propranolol versus placebo in 14 chronic schizophrenics who remained on stable antipsychotic drug dosage [81,82]. Even with this small sample size and a rather short duration (12 weeks), there were significant differences favoring propranolol on thought-disorder items, non-thought-disorder schizophrenic symptoms, global psychiatric ratings, and some nurses' ratings. The largest differences were found at the end of the 12-week study, but some measures also reached significance by the eighth week. Side effects were minimal; the only patients for whom the double-blind code had to be broken because of side effects became quite pale and hypotensive and turned out to be on chlorpromazine and placebo. The mean antipsychotic drug dosage used was 954 mg/day in chlorpromazine equivalents. The mean propranolol dosage was 500 mg/day at the end of the trial. It should be noted that patients receiving propranolol had somewhat later ages of onset, shorter hospital stays, and length of current illness than the placebo patients. These differences were not statistically significant.

Gardos et al. had completed an earlier and less-positive study of high-dose propranolol in eight chronically hospitalized schizophrenic patients (average duration of illness 16.5 years): dosage of propranolol was increased by 120 mg/week to 720 mg/day [83]. Two patients were given 2,560 mg/day and 2,880 mg/day, respectively. The study duration was six to ten weeks. No antipsychotic effects were noted, although four patients appeared less anxious than they had on placebo. Two patients were dropped from the study because of hypotensive episodes. One patient died suddenly of hemorrhage from an unsuspected and asymptomatic duodenal ulcer while on 2,800 mg/day.

Ridges et al. reported improvement in four of ten chronic schizophrenics using Yorkston's general methods [84]. However, improvement occurred earlier and at lower dosages (320 to 640 mg/day). Propranolol, in contrast to conventional antipsychotics, appears not to increase prolactin levels in blood [85]. A French group, Auriol et al., report very briefly on improvement obtained with low doses of pindolol (7.5 to 45 mg q.d.) in 30 psychotic patients [86]. They observed disinhibition and "euphorization," increased interest, and increased verbal behavior. "Delire," meaning delusions, disappeared in postpartum psychoses and involutional melancholia. A marked oral dyskinesia of some severity was produced in one patient but was rapidly controlled by levomepromazine. Insomnia and hypnagogic or visual hallucinations were also observed as side effects.

In contrast to this slightly hypomanic response to pindolol, Volk et al. observed particularly good responses to oxprenolol only in manic or schizoaffective patients with manic symptoms. This trial used high dosages (720 to 3,360 mg/day) in short trials of 9 to 20 days [87]. Good results with no side effects were observed in four patients and good results with some perspiration and extrasystoles in one other. Clinical improvement came on rather abruptly after 7 to 10 days of treatment. Two schizophrenic patients failed to respond, and one patient with agitated depression reacted to low doses of oxprenolol with pulse-slowing, blood-pressure rise, pallor, and sweating and was not treated further. The improvements seen in the manic patients were judged impressive and without the unpleasant side effects usually associated with neuroleptic therapy. Dose was raised in this study more slowly than in Atsmon's work but faster than in Yorkston's regimen. A second German group, Rackensperger et al., treated five, acute, previously untreated psychotic patients, three with propranolol and two with oxprenolol, using rapid dose escalation [88]. Two patients showed a marked rise in blood pressure, four showed marked insomnia, while two became delirious or delusional. One patient showed some reduction in manic symptoms but was not generally improved. Patients were treated for brief periods with high doses. A Dutch study involving only two patients was also negative [89], while a small (10 patient) partially controlled open study comparing chlorpromazine and propranolol in postpartum psychosis found the propranolol group to respond significantly more rapidly and more completely (as judged by days in hospital and global ratings of improvement on discharge). The patients were hospitalized relatively soon after delivery (means of two weeks in the propranolol group and one month in the chlorpromazine group) [90]. From data presented, the patients appear to have been agitated, delusional, and confused, with little depression.

Propranolol is obviously a drug urgently requiring further controlled study in acute and chronic schizophrenia and in other acute psychoses, such as mania and postpartum psychosis. Atsmon's crash program of rapid dose escalation seems too toxic for general use, but Yorkston's very gradually increasing dose regimen sounds relatively safe. Nevertheless, use of this high-dose procedure is still highly experimental and clearly demands good medical supervision in formal studies cleared with the FDA and local investigational review boards. Whether the positive effects reported are due to beta-blockage in the brain or are due to some other action of the drug is unclear. Certainly, the doses required are well above those required for full peripheral blockade of beta-receptors. Nevertheless, many psychotic patients are currently either unresponsive or inadequately responsive to existing neuroleptic drugs. The marked improvement reported in some previously treatment-resistant patients is impressive. The one positive controlled study [81], one comparative study [90], and the rapid relapse of patients a couple of days after stopping propranolol [78], all argue in favor of a real pharmacological effect of high-dose propranolol in schizophrenia.

## Pharmacokinetics, Pharmacology, and Side Effects

Propranolol is a relatively short-acting drug with a half-life of two to three hours in patients without severe liver disease. Beta-blockade usually lasts 8 to 12 hours after a single dose, making at least twice-daily dosage administration necessary. Propranolol crosses the blood-brain barrier rapidly. It has an active hydroxy-metabolite, but the contribution of the metabolite to the actions of propranolol is not clear [91].

Some potential problems with propranolol grow obviously from its pharmacology. It markedly decreases adrenergic influences on heart action; in healthy subjects, this causes either asymptomatic heart slowing and blood-pressure reduction or, rarely, dizziness and symptomatic hypotension. In patients with moderate or severe heart disease, shock or death have occurred, though very infrequently. Obviously, psychiatrists should use propranolol with caution in cardiac patients. Medical consultation is advisable in complicated cases. Propranolol also may aggravate hypoglycemic reactions in insulin-dependent diabetics, in part by blocking the patient's usual autonomic reactions to hypoglycemia, reactions that the patient uses as cues to assess his need for glucose [91]. Asthma can be precipitated in patients with a past history of this disorder; propranolol may slightly reduce airflow in nonasthmatics and should be used with caution in patients with obstructive pulmonary disease. Propranolol also aggravates Raynaud disease and may cause cold extremities in some patients by increasing peripheral vasoconstriction. It is possible that newer cardiospecific beta-blockers will be safer in asthmatics.

In two surveys of adverse reactions to oral propranolol, one in 1,500 patients [92] and the other in 797 patients [93], a variety of side effects are reported. Gastrointestinal disturbances, including nausea and vomiting, occurred in 11% of patients in the smaller series, which were drawn from published reports, but in only 1% of the larger, drug-company-sponsored series. These effects were minimized by giving the drug with meals. Dizziness or lightheadedness and fatigue combined were relatively common (3% in one series, 7% in the other). In the smaller series, cold extremities occurred in 5% and sleep disturbances in 4% of the patients. Mental depression occurred only rarely in either series, although Waal, in a study of propranolol in hypertension, found depression in half his patients treated for more than three months or with higher dosages [94]. However, the British manufacturer had received reports on only 11 cases of drug-related depression after about 60,000 patients had received the drug [95]. The significance of this is not clear but may resemble the reserpine-related depressions seen primarily in hypertensive patients. Depression is not emphasized at all as a side effect in propranolol studies involving psychiatric patients. However, visual or hypnagogic hallucinations, as well as organic confusional states, do occur, though rarely, in patients on propranolol [96-98]. Impotence has also been reported. One virtue of propranolol is that its short duration of action permits drug-related side effects to remit within 24 hours after the drug is stopped. Intravenous isoproterenol or parenteral atropine can also be used to treat severe side effects. It is possible that overdoses taken with suicidal intent will be relatively well tolerated in physically healthy patients [99]. In our local experience, diarrhea, insomnia, and nausea are the more common side effects; dosages up to 320 mg/day are often well tolerated.

In general, then, if patients with asthma (past or present), obstructive lung disease, Raynaud disease, diabetes, and cardiac disease are avoided, and other side effects, including increased depression and visual hallucinations, are watched for, propranolol seems generally safe to use in psychiatric patients in dosages under the 320 mg/day ceiling suggested in the package insert. Because some cardiac patients have had infarcts when high-dose propranolol was stopped abruptly, the drug should always be discontinued by gradual tapering. One beta-blocker, practolol, was taken off the market because of the occurrence of lupus erythematosis-like phenomena, skin and eye lesions, but propranolol seems free of these problems to date [91,100].

## Conclusion

Propranolol is an intriguing drug. It shows promise in a surprising range of psychiatric situations but has been proven conclusively to be effective in none of them. In all areas, except the work in schizophrenia, it is possible that better tailoring of dosage to assure adequate peripheral blockade of beta-receptors might have made drug-placebo comparisons more clinically and statistically impressive. This is particularly true of the several studies of the drug (or related drugs) in anxiety states and in tremor. On the basis of current evidence, the best one can say is that propranolol may be helpful in some anxious patients, particularly those with cardiovascular and related beta-adrenergic autonomic symptoms. Perhaps higher doses or longer periods of administration would make the drug more useful in some patients.

In tremor, both essential and secondary to lithium, propranolol also could be of value, again at adequate doses. In alcoholic withdrawal, the available studies look promising, but without further clinical research, it is hard to be sure whether propranolol or related drugs will prove useful either early in withdrawal or as a "safe" nonsedative antianxiety agent in anxious, "dry" alcoholics.

In schizophrenia, Yorkston's work looks very promising. We certainly need a new, safe, and potent drug which will control schizophrenic (or manic) symptoms without blocking dopamine receptors and placing patients at risk for tardive dyskinesia. Even if the drug only produces symptom reduction when added to antipsychotics in patients remaining chronically psychotic, this would be a substantial contribution. Further controlled and uncontrolled studies using Yorkston's well-described and apparently well-tolerated treatment regimen are needed.

At dosages under 320 mg/day, the drug appears to be well tolerated in many cardiac patients. It is contraindicated in patients with histories of asthma, obstructive pulmonary disease, or Raynaud disease.

Assuming propranolol has desirable central, as well as peripheral, autonomic effects, it would be very helpful if the central effects were better studied and understood. The beta-blockers may prove to be useful additions to the pharmacological armamentarium of psychiatrists, but it is still too early to tell whether their promise in the areas described in this review will be validated by the necessary controlled clinical trials.

## Commentary

This paper was written in response to the many questions about propranolol use in anxiety that were submitted from the audience during a McLean

Hospital seminar on anxiety and its treatment. In the course of the literature review, we became much more aware of other work with beta-blockers in tremor, alcoholism, and schizophrenia. Hence the review was expanded to cover the wider area.

Little new information on beta-blockers has come to my attention since the paper was written. I have used propranolol in three patients with chronic schizophrenia who did not respond to prolonged adequate treatment with several antipsychotic drugs. I added the propranolol to the previous dose of piperazine phenothiazine in all cases and was unable to increase the daily propranolol dosage beyond 400 mg/day because of bradycardia or postural hypotension. Two of the patients appear to be better—less bizarre behavior, less thought-disorder, and calmer—but in neither case is the change dramatic. A pilot open study is continuing. I have heard, informally, of negative small pilot studies in two research units and somewhat positive studies at two others. Yorkston's group continues to report positive results. The situation has not changed appreciably from that described in the paper.

### References

1. Lefkowitz RJ: B-adrenergic receptors: Recognition and regulations. New Eng J Med 295:323-328, 1976.

2. Koelle GB: Neurohumoral transmission and the autonomic nervous system. *In* Goodman L, Gilman A (Eds): The Pharmacological Basis of Therapeutics. New York, Macmillan, 1975, pp 404-444.

3. Lefkowitz RJ: Identification and regulation of adrenergic receptors. *In* Lipton M, DiMascio A, Killam K (Eds): Psychopharmacology: A Generation of Progress. New York, Raven, 1978, pp 389-395.

4. Koella W: Anatomical, physiological and pharmacological findings relevant to the central nervous effects of beta-blockers. *In* Kielholz P (Ed): Beta-blockers and the Central Nervous System. Baltimore, Univ Park Press, 1976, pp 21-34.

5. Shader R, Good M, Greenblatt D: Anxiety states and beta-adrenergic blockade. *In* Klein D, Gittleman-Klein R (Eds): Progress in Psychiatric Drug Treatment. Vol 2. New York, Brunner/Mazel, 1976, pp 500-528.

6. Jefferson JW: Beta-adrenergic receptor blocking drugs in psychiatry. Arch Gen Psychiat 31:681-691, 1974.

7. Lader M: Anxiety: some psychophysiologic aspects. McLean Hosp J 4:3-15, 1978.

8. Pitts F, McClure J: Lactate metabolism in anxiety neurosis. New Eng J Med 277:1329-1336, 1967.

9. Ackerman S, Sachar E: The lactate theory of anxiety: a review and reevaluation. Psychosomat Med 36:69-81, 1974.

10. Garfield S, Gershon S, Slettin I, et al: Chemically induced anxiety. Internat J Neuropsychiat 3:426-432, 1967.

11. Schachter S, Singer J: Cognitive social and physiological determinants of emotional states. Psychol Rev 69:379-390, 1962.

12. Easton JD, Sherman D: Somatic anxiety attacks and propranolol. Arch Neurol 33:689-691, 1976.

13. Greenblatt D, Shader R: On the psychopharmacology of beta-blockade. Curr Ther Res 14:615-625, 1972.

14. Frohlich ED, Tarazi RC, Dustan HP: Hyperdynamic B-adrenergic circulatory state. Arch Int Med 123:1-7, 1969.

15. Suzman MM: Propranolol in the treatment of anxiety. Postgrad Med J 52 (Suppl 4):168-174, 1976.

16. Tyrer PJ, Lader MH: Effects of beta adrenergic blockade with sotalol in chronic anxiety. Clin Pharmacol Ther 14:418-426, 1973.

17. Granville-Grossman KL, Turner P: The effect of propranolol on anxiety. Lancet 1:788-790, 1966.

18. Bonn JA, Turner P, Hicks DC: Beta-adrenergic-receptor blockade with practolol in treatment of anxiety. Lancet 1:814-815, 1972.

19. Tyrer PJ, Lader MH: Response to propranolol and diazepam in somatic and psychic anxiety. Br Med J 2:14-16, 1974.

20. Kellner R, Collins AC, Shulman RS, et al: The short-term antianxiety effects of propranolol Hcl. J Clin Pharmacol 14:301-304, 1974.

21. Tanna V, Penningroth R, Woolson R: Propranolol in the treatment of anxiety neurosis. Comp Psychiat 18:319-326, 1977.

22. Bonn JA, Turner P: D-propranolol and anxiety. Lancet 1:1355-1356, 1971.

23. Burrows G, Davies B, Fail L, et al: A placebo controlled trial of diazepam and oxprenolol for anxiety. Psychopharmacology 50:177-179, 1976.

24. Johnson G, Singh B, Leeman M: Controlled evaluation of the beta adrenoreceptor blocking drug oxprenolol in anxiety. Med J Australia 1:909-912, 1976.

25. Gaind R, Suri A, Thompson J: Use of beta blockers as an adjunct in behavioral techniques. Scottish Med J 20:284-286, 1975.

26. Hafner J, Milton F: The influence of propranolol as the exposure in vivo of agoraphobics. Psychol Med 7:419-425, 1977.

27. Heiser J, DeFrancisco D: The treatment of pathological panic states with propranolol. Am J Psychiat 133:1389-1394, 1976.

28. Suzman MM: The use of beta-adrenergic blockade with propranolol in anxiety states. Postgrad Med J 47:104-108, 1971.

29. Wheatley D: Comparative effects of propranolol and chlordiazepoxide in anxiety states. Br J Psychiat 115:1411-1412, 1969.

30. McMillan WP: Oxprenolol in the treatment of anxiety due to environmental stress. Am J Psychiat 132:965-966, 1975.

31. Becker AL: Oxprenolol and propranolol in anxiety states: a double-blind comparative study. So African Med J 50:627-629, 1976.

32. Hawkings J: Clinical experience with beta-blockers in consultant psychiatric practice. Scottish Med J 20:294-298, 1975.

33. Brewer C: Beneficial effect of beta-adrenergic blockade on "exam nerves." Lancet 2:435, 1972.

34. Krishnan G: Oxprenolol in the treatment of examination nerves. Scottish Med J 20:288-289, 1975.

35. James I, Pearson R, Griffith D, et al: Effect of oxprenolol on stage-fright in musicians. Lancet 2:952-954, 1977.

36. Pichot P, Olivier-Martin R, Poggioli J: Anxiety in the course of dental operations—a study on the effect exerted by a beta-blocker. *In* Kielholz P (Ed): Beta-blockers and the Central Nervous System. Baltimore, Univ Park Press, 1976, pp 59-70.

37. Eisdorfer C, Nowlin J, Wilkie F: Improvement of learning in the aged by modification of autonomic nervous system activity. Science 170:1327-1329, 1970.

38. Tyrer PJ, Lader MH: Physiological and psychological effects of ± -propranolol, + -propranolol and diazepam in induced anxiety. Br J Clin Pharmacol 1:379-385, 1974.

39. Gottschalk LA, Stone WN, Gleser GC: Peripheral versus central mechanisms accounting for antianxiety effects of propranolol. Psychosomat Med 36:47-56, 1974.

40. Cleghorn JM, Peterfy G, Pinter EJ, et al: Verbal anxiety and the beta adrenergic receptors: A facilitating mechanism? J Nerv Ment Dis 151:266-272, 1970.

41. Nakano S, Gillespie H, Hollister L: Propranolol in experimentally-induced stress. Psychopharmacology (in press).

42. Corbett J: Efficacy of oxprenolol in the treatment of essential and parkinsonian tremor—a description of two controlled trials and a review of the literature. *In* Kielholz P (Ed): Beta-blockers and the Central Nervous System. Baltimore, Univ Park Press, 1976, pp 200-217.

43. Young RR, Growdon JH, Shahani BT: Beta-adrenergic mechanisms in action tremor. New Eng J Med 293:950-953, 1975.

44. Winkler GF, Young RR: Efficacy of chronic propranolol therapy in action tremors of the familial, senile or essential varieties. New Eng J Med 290:984-988, 1974.

45. Murray TJ: Treatment of essential tremor with propranolol. Can Med Assn J 107:984-986, 1972.

46. Dupont E, Hansen HJ, Dalby MA: Treatment of benign essential tremor with propranolol. Acta Neurol Scand 49:75-84, 1973.

47. Balla J: Treatment of essential tremor with propranolol. Lancet 1:205, 1973.

48. Owen D, Marsden C: Effect of adrenergic beta-blockade on parkinsonian tremor. Lancet 2:1959, 1965.

49. Kellett J, Metcalfe M, Bailey A, et al: Beta blockade in lithium tremor. J Neurol Neurosurg Psychiat 38:719-721, 1975.

50. Kirk L, Baastrup P, Schou M: Propranolol treatment of lithium-induced tremor. Lancet 2:1086-1087, 1973.

51. Floru L: Klinische Behandlungsversuche des lithiumbedingten tremors durch einen B-rezeptoroneantagonisten (propranolol). Intern Pharmacopsychiatry 6:197-222, 1971.

52. Lapierre Y: Control of lithium tremor with propranolol. Can Med Assn J 114:619-620, 1976.

53. Rafaelson O: Discussion. *In* Kielholz P (Ed): Beta-blockers and the Central Nervous System. Baltimore, Univ Park Press, 1976, pp 231-234.

54. Thompson M: Oxprenolol in senile tremor. *In* Kielholz P (Ed): Beta-blockers and the Central Nervous System. In Baltimore, Univ Park Press, 1976, pp 218-221.

55. Mai J, Pederson E: Clonus depression by propranolol. Acta Neurol Scand 53:395-398, 1976.

56. Freedman A: Beta-blockers in the treatment of alcoholism and opiate addiction. *In* Kielholz P (Ed): Beta-blockers and the Central Nervous System. Baltimore, Univ Park Press, 1976, pp 141-148.

57. Carlsson C: Haemodynamic effects of adrenergic beta-receptor blockade in the withdrawal phase of alcoholism. Internat J Clin Pharmacol 3:61-63, 1969.

58. Carlsson C, Johansson T: The psychological effects of propranolol in the abstinence phase of chronic alcoholics. Br J Psychiat 119:605-606, 1971.

59. Carlsson C, Fast B: A comparison of the effects of propranolol and diazepam in alcoholics. Br J Addict 71:321-326, 1976.

60. Gallant D, Swanson W, Guerrero-Figueroa R: A controlled evaluation of propranolol in chronic alcoholic patients presenting the symptomatology of anxiety and tension. J Clin Pharmacol 13:41-43, 1973.

61. Ladewig D, Levin P, Gastpar M, et al: The use of beta-blockers in the management of withdrawal symptoms. *In* Kielholz P (Ed): Beta-blockers and the Central Nervous System. Baltimore, Univ Park Press, 1976, pp 149-157.

62. Drew L, Moon J: Inderal (propranolol) in the treatment of alcoholism. Med J Australia 2:282-285, 1973.

63. Tyrer P: Propranolol in alcohol addiction. Lancet 2:707, 1972.

64. Zilm D, Sellers E, Macleod S, et al: Propranolol effect on tremor in alcohol withdrawal. Ann Int Med 83:234-236, 1975.

65. Zilm D, Sellers E, Macleod S: Effect of propranolol on tremor of alcohol withdrawal. New Eng J Med 294:785-788, 1976.

66. Sellers E, Zilm D, Degani N: Comparative efficacy of propranolol and chlordiazepoxide in alcohol withdrawal. J Studies Alcohol 38: 2096-2108, 1977.

67. Teravainen H, Larsen A: Effect of propranolol on acute withdrawal tremor in alcoholic patients. J Neurol Neurosurg Psychiat 39:607-612, 1976.

68. Grosz H: Narcotic withdrawal symptoms in heroin users treated with propranolol. Lancet 2:564-566, 1972.

69. Grosz H: Effect of propranolol on active users of heroin. Lancet 2:612, 1973.

70. Grosz H: Successful treatment of a heroin addict with propranolol. J Indiana Med Assn 65:505-509, 1972.

71. Resnick R, Kestenbaum R, Schwartz L, et al: Evaluation of propranolol in opiate dependence. Arch Gen Psychiat 33:993-997, 1976.

72. Hollister L, Prusmack J: Propranolol in withdrawal from opiates. Arch Gen Psychiat 31:695-699, 1974.

73. Rappolt R, Gay G, Inaba D: Propranolol in the treatment of cardiopressor effects of cocaine. New Eng J Med 295:448, 1976.

74. Linken A: Propranolol for L.S.D.-induced anxiety states. Lancet 1:1039-1040, 1971.

75. Atsmon A, Blum I, Wijsenbeek H, et al: The short-term effects of adrenergic-blocking agents in a small group of psychotic patients. Psychiat Neurol Neurochir 74:251-258, 1971.

76. Atsmon A, Blum I: The discovery. *In* Roberts E, Amacher P (Eds): Propranolol and Schizophrenia. New York, Liss, 1978, pp 5-38.

77. Yorkston N, Zaki S, Malik M, et al: Propranolol in the control of schizophrenic symptoms. Br Med J 4:633-635, 1974.

78. Yorkston N, Zaki S, Havard C: Some practical aspects of using propranolol in the treatment of schizophrenia. *In* Robert E, Amacher P (Eds): Propranolol and Schizophrenia. New York, Liss, 1978, pp 83-97.

79. Yorkston N, Zaki S, Themen J, et al: Safeguards in the treatment of schizophrenia with propranolol. Postgrad Med J 52 (Suppl 4):175-180, 1976.

80. Yorkston N, Zaki S, Havard C: Propranolol in the treatment of schizophrenia: an uncontrolled study with 55 adults. *In* Roberts E, Amacher P (Eds): Propranolol and Schizophrenia. New York, Liss, 1978, pp 39-67.

81. Yorkston N, Gruzelier J, Zaki S, et al: Propranolol as an adjunct to the treatment of schizophrenia. *In* Roberts E, Amacher P (Eds): Propranolol and Schizophrenia. New York, Liss, 1978, pp 69-82.

82. Yorkston N, Gruzelier J, Zaki S, et al: Propranolol as an adjunct in the treatment of schizophrenia. Lancet 2:575-578, 1977.

83. Gardos G, Cole J, Volicer L, et al: A dose-response study of propranolol in chronic schizophrenics. Curr Ther Res 15:314-323, 1973.

84. Ridges A, Lawton K, Harper P, et al: Propranolol in schizophrenia. Lancet 1:986, 1977.

85. Hanssen T, Heyden T, Sundberg I, et al: Decrease in serum prolactin after propranolol in schizophrenia. Lancet 1:101-102, 1978.

86. Auriol B, Palandjian N, Bord M, et al: Beta-blockers in psychiatry. Nouv Press Med 1:1439, 1972.

87. Volk W, Bier W, Braun J, et al: Treatment of excited psychoses with a beta-receptor blocker (oxprenolol) in high dosages. Nervenartzt 43:491-492, 1972.

88. Rackensperger W, Gauppe R, Mattke D, et al: Treatment of acute schizophrenic psychoses with beta-receptor blockers. Arch Psychiat Nervenkrank 219:29-36, 1974.

89. Stam F: Experiences with propranolol use in schizophrenia. Nederl Tidsch Psychiat 13:424, 1971.

90. Steiner M, Latz A, Blum I, et al: Propranolol versus chlorpromazine in the treatment of psychoses associated with childbearing. Psychiat Neuro Neurchirurg 76:421-426, 1973.

91. Petrie J, Galloway D, Jeffers T, et al: Adverse reactions to beta-blocking drugs: A review. Postgrad Med J 52:63-69, 1976.

92. Stephen SA: Unwanted effects of propranolol. Am J Cardiol 18:463-472, 1966.

93. Greenblatt DJ, Koch-Weser J: Adverse reactions to beta-adrenergic receptor blocking drugs: A report from the Boston Collaborative Drug Surveillance Program. Drugs 7:118-129, 1974.

94. Waal HJ: Propranolol-induced depression. Br Med J 2:50, 1967.

95. Fitzgerald JD: Propranolol-induced depression. Br Med J 2:372-373, 1967.

96. Shopsin B, Hirsch J, Gershon S: Visual hallucinations and propranolol. Biol Psychiat 10:105-107, 1975.

97. Topliss D, Bond R: Acute brain syndrome after propranolol treatment. Lancet 2:1133-1134, 1977.

98. Helson L, Duque L: Acute brain syndrome after propranolol. Lancet 1:98, 1978.

99. Boakes A, Boerree B: Suicidal attempts with beta-adrenoceptor blocking agents. Br Med J 4:675, 1973.

100. Editorial. Long-term safety of receptor-blocking drugs. Lancet 2:1242-1243, 1978.

# 5 Drug Therapy of Adult Minimal Brain Dysfunction (MBD)

*Jonathan O. Cole, M.D.*

Minimal brain dysfunction (MBD) is currently a widely used name for a behavior disorder in children characterized by hyperactivity, distractibility, poor attention and concentration, impulsivity, emotional lability, and poor response to discipline [1]. Soft neurologic signs such as poor fine-motor coordination, enuresis, and learning disability are often associated with this condition. The syndrome has also been called hyperkinesis or hyperactivity and, in the current version of the DSM III, is called attentional deficit disorder [2]. There is excellent evidence that in children this syndrome is generally responsive to stimulants such as methylphenidate, dextroamphetamine (d-amphetamine), and magnesium pemoline (pemoline).

A recent controlled study by Wender's group [3], as well as older clinical reports by Huessy [4], Arnold [5], Oettinger [6], and Hill [7] suggest that adults with symptoms and behaviors resembling childhood MBD and, generally, with a history consistent with the presence of such problems during their childhood will often show clinical improvement on stimulant drugs or tricyclic antidepressants. Such patients often also qualify for other diagnostic labels under research diagnostic criteria [8], ranging from anxiety neurosis to sociopathy.

Thus far, one can plot a reasonable extension of a syndrome well recognized in latency-aged children into continuing problems in adult life. Several follow-up studies [10-14] have generally found persisting adjustment problems that range from mild employment and marital problems [14] through sociopathy and schizophrenia [13]. Klein's group has found that some adolescent and adult patients diagnosed as having a "emotionally unstable character disorder" also show a history of hyperkinetic syndrome in childhood [15].

At this point, the problem becomes complicated by the use of the term MBD in describing other groups of adult patients who have shown some degree of "neurological" impairment, including soft neurological signs, organic deficits on neuropsychological testing, abnormal electroencephalograms (EEGs), and a degree of impulsivity and episodic, brief, unpredictable increases in psychopathology. When Bellak [16] advances this broader concept and speaks of MBD schizophrenics, MBD depressions, and, heaven forbid, MBD borderline states, the mind begins to boggle. Bellak would also include here Monroe episodic dyscontrol syndrome, which is found both in ordinary psychiatric patients and recidivist criminal offenders [17], and which serves to extend the concept into temporal lobe epilepsy and less clear epileptoid states.

The purpose of this paper is to try to digest this expanding concept, or expanding group of concepts, and to reflect on possible pharmacotherapeutic approaches to various pieces of the puzzle. Although all this may be a bit premature, many of the patients found in the various groups do not respond well to conventional drug therapies and may deserve cautious trials on other kinds of drugs.

This paper will be divided into sections on (1) simple adult MBD (i.e., attentional deficit state), (2) MBD in schizophrenia, and (3) other psychiatric states with MBD. In all of these, the term MBD should be taken as having little or no precise meaning—after all, the brains of patients with psychotic depression or catatonic excitement do not function very well either—but only as a suggestion that some clinicians have believed that some of the patients involved might have something wrong with their brains.


**Simple Adult MBD**

The search for adults sharing the same kinds of symptoms and behaviors manifested by children with MBD was encouraged by a series of clinical observations growing out of studies of childhood MBD. Such children sometimes had parents who not only had MBD-like symptoms in childhood but who were still troubled by impulsivity, restlessness, and short attention-span. This led to genetic studies of the families of MBD patients and revealed a greater than expected prevalance of adult MBD and also of alcoholism, sociopathy, and Briquet syndrome (hysteria) [18-21]. These studies, which left the nature-nurture problem unresolved, have been followed by studies of the biological and adoptive parents of adopted MBD children [22-23], which clearly show the genetic relationship between alcoholism, hysteria, and sociopathy in biological parents and the occurrence of the hyperkinetic syndrome in their biological but adopted children. The extent to which such parents were hyperkinetic as children and the extent to which MBD symptoms predispose to alcoholism or sociopathy in adulthood are still largely unanswered.

Nevertheless, MBD in childhood is a condition with a genetic component and with a rapid dramatic response to stimulant drugs, which suggests that a biological deficit is being directly rectified. If adults with comparably persistent, subjective and behavioral problems would respond equally well, this could be a major advance in therapeutics, particularly since non-psychotic outpatients with impulsivity, irritability, and shifting degrees of anxiety and low self-esteem would currently be most likely to receive some form of psychotherapy, possibly aided by a pinch of a benzodiazepine.

Wood and associates [3] have located a group of adult patients in out-patient clinics in Salt Lake City who had prominent complaints of impulsivity, irritability, inattentiveness, restlessness, and emotional lability in the absence of schizophrenia, primary affective disorder, organic brain syndrome, or mental retardation. All patients included in the study had high scores on a self-report form listing 21 symptoms or behaviors thought to reflect an extension of childhood MBD symptoms into adulthood (e.g., difficulty sitting still, restlessness, on the go, getting excited easily, acting impulsively, difficulty concentrating, temper outbursts, short-tempered, easily irritated). The parents of most of the patients were available and completed a rating sheet designed for parents of MBD children; they used the scale to describe the patient's behavior as it was between ages six and ten. The majority of the patients, as described by their parents, fell in the 95th percentile on this measure, placing them clearly among the group of children usually responsive to stimulant drugs, at least in retrospect.

Eleven of the 15 patients were involved in a double-blind crossover study involving two weeks on methylphenidate in doses up to 60 mg/day and two weeks on placebo. Patients were assessed on five dimensions under both conditions and were found to be significantly less nervous, energetic, and hot-tempered and significantly more able to concentrate when on methylphenidate than on placebo. Interestingly, the drug-placebo difference on sadness did not reach significance; patients were only slightly happier on methylphenidate, making it unlikely that the drug induced the sort of euphoria seen in stimulant abusers.

All 15 patients initially selected received further drug therapy. Overall, 53% responded well to methylphenidate, 33% to pemoline, and 8% to imipramine. No patient showed any tendency to abuse methylphenidate. The improvement due to the drugs was characterized, over a period of time, by less anxiety, less irritability and anger, more stable mood, and less impulsivity. Marital adjustment, child abuse, and drug and alcohol abuse were each improved in a few patients. Two female patients were able to reach sexual climax for the first time while on the drug. Drug effects of stimulants in this population have, to date, been stable and persistent without any evidence of the development of tolerance. It should also be noted that 9 of the 15 patients were female. This was in marked contrast to the excess of males with MBD usually seen in child guidance clinics [1]. This may reflect either the known fact that women use medical facilities more often than men or, possibly, that male adults with MBD may be more likely to be seen in correctional or alcoholic programs.

Huessy [24] reported on the drug therapy responses of 64 patients whom he judged to have adult MBD as indicated by the symptoms of impulsivity, emotional overreaction, poor self-image, emotional lability, and learning problems. This patient group includes private patients, clinical out-patients, and patients at a local therapeutic community; his patients predominantly showed complaints of impulsivity, depression, anxiety, aggressive outbursts, and temper tantrums. In contrast to Wood's group, who have never been in a psychiatric hospital, 51 of Huessy's 64 patients had been hospitalized in the past and 34 had received a schizophrenic diagnosis at one time or another. Huessy generally began treatment with these patients by using imipramine or amitriptyline, obtaining improvement rates of about 45% on both drugs. Patients who failed on these drugs were then tried on d-amphetamine or methyphenidate, with an over 50% improvement rate on these drugs in patients who had failed on tricylics. Seven out of 13 patients tried on diphenylhydantoin, presumably after failing on both tricyclics and stimulants, also improved.

A colleague of Huessy's compared tricyclic antidepressant response in 12 depressed patients with MBD symptoms with the response of 12 depressed patients without MBD symptoms but otherwise matched in age, sex, and socioeconomic status. He noted an "almost immediate" clinical response to tricyclics in the MBD depressions in contrast to the more usual slower response in the ordinary depressions.

Huessy notes that some of his adult MBD patients have only been stable in the past when on diet pills, or they have reacted to the illicit use of stimulants with productive energy, rather than with euphoria. He finds some patients, though "better" on drugs, either use them only in times of stress or stop taking them for a variety of reasons despite, or perhaps because of, the return of impulsivity and acting-out behavior. It should be noted that Huessy's patients are far less "pure" than those of Wood and some remained on antipsychotic medication while also receiving stimulants or antidepressants.

It seems clear that some adult MBD's have a stable, beneficial response to stimulants. Some patients find the short-acting drugs like d-amphetamine and methylphenidate a problem in that a single dose may elicit improvement for only two to three hours. Pemoline (Cylert), a longer acting drug, may have a more consistent effect in such cases. Dosages used in adults, surprisingly, are almost identical to those used in children (i.e. 10 to 40 mg/day of d-amphetamine, 20 to 80 mg/day of methylphenidate and 18.75 to 150 mg/day of pemoline). Wender generally starts at a single tablet a day and increases the dosage every three days until improvement or unpleasant stimulation occurs.

Given the overall potential for abuse liability of stimulants—though it does not seem to be a problem in well-selected, well-monitored adult MBD patients—it would be nice if tricyclic antidepressants were equally effective. They are not generally as useful as stimulants in children with MBD.

Huessy [24], as well as Marin and Greenspan [25], report favorable results in adults, while Wender notes that in his carefully selected population, patients tend to develop tolerance to the tricyclics after a few weeks or months [26]. The issue is far from settled and awaits a formal clinical trial.

Huessy's preliminary finding that some adult MBD patients respond to diphenylhydantoin may somehow overlap with Stephens [27] study showing diphenylhydantoin to be more effective than placebo in irritable, angry (but high ego strength) anxiety neurotics.

## MBD and Schizophrenia

The existence and, if it occurs, nature of MBD in schizophrenia lacks the relative clarity and precision of the extension of childhood-typical MBD into adulthood. It touches on a number of somewhat unrelated issues:

(1) Do MBD children grow up to become schizophrenics and retain MBD characteristics complicating their schizophrenia? It seems reasonably clear that the kinds of bizarre, asocial, awkward behaviors seen by Klein's "childhood asocial" schizophrenics [15] as children are quite different from the behaviors of hyperkinetic children. On the other hand, in studies of the adopted offspring of schizophrenic parents, it has recently become evident that the natural parent stands a much greater likelihood of being an alcoholic, a sociopath, or a hysteric than is true in the rest of the population [28]. Such assortative mating would, as noted above, increase the likelihood that the offspring were at risk for both MBD and schizophrenia and therefore for the joint occurrence of the two disorders.

(2) Schizophrenic patients often show "soft" (i.e. nonlocalizing) neurologic signs such as motor overflow, right-left confusion, adiadochocinesia, and foot tapping. These have been described in a proportion of patients with schizophrenic diagnosis [29,30], and Quitkin et al. note that these neurologic signs occur principally in childhood asocial schizophrenics [31]. Bellak [16] discusses patients whom he believes to have MBD schizophrenia to be characterized by impulsiveness, low stimulus barriers (overreaction to sensory input), sociopathy, few hallucinations, but the presence of concreteness and a tendency to elope from psychiatric institutions. Such patients may also have had bouts of high fever in infancy. These patients sometimes also show signs of organicity on neuropsychological testing and have difficulties in spatial orientation and body image. According to Bellak, such schizophrenics may respond poorly to phenothiazine alone and may do better if imipramine is added (at times augmented by diphenylhydantoin or diazepam). No data on patient response to these drug interventions are presented.

Davies and Neil have carried out two studies relating EEG abnormalities in schizophrenia to clinical status and drug response. In the first study [32], schizophrenics already receiving antipsychotic drug therapy received daytime EEGs and were classified as (1) normal, (2) showing slow waves, and (3) showing paroxysmal abnormalities with or without slow waves. Patients with paroxysmal EEGs were quite different from those with normal EEGs on the bases of diagnosis (paroxysmal patients were more often latent, catatonic, or schizoaffective), of symptomatology (paroxysmal patients showed less flattened affect and more emotional lability, more irritability, poorer impulse control, more confusion and clouding of consciousness, more nonauditory hallucinations, more depersonalization, and more episodic symptoms), of history (paroxysmal patients showed more adverse physical conditions in birth and childhood and more symptoms of MBD in childhood), and of neurological signs (paroxysmal patients had more soft and hard neurological signs). Paroxysmal EEG schizophrenics had significantly more medication changes while in the Yale-New Haven unit, despite equivalent lengths of stay, due either to failure to improve on phenothiazine or to aggravation of symptoms by phenothiazine.

In the second study carried out at Western Psychiatric Institute [33] with 83 patients (meeting RDC criteria for schizophrenia or schizoaffective psychosis and lacking seizure disorders or other clear neurological disease), 19% had paroxysmal EEGs when drug-free and another 14% developed paroxysmal features after receiving antipsychotic medication for 10 to 14 days. The two paroxysmal groups combined show a number of differences from the 45% with normal EEGs before and during drug therapy. The combined group closely resembled those found in the earlier study in symptom differences and history of premorbid evidence of prenatal difficulties, clumsiness, and hyperkinesis as well as in inferior response to antipsychotic drugs. Davies and Neil [34] have the impression that in schizophrenics with paroxysmal EEGs, lowering the dose of the antipsychotic drug and adding an anticonvulsant (diphenylhydantoin is used in New Haven and carbamazepine in Pittsburgh) is helpful in some patients. A controlled study of the value of diphenylhydantoin in such patients is in progress.

Given the above observations and reports, including Huessy's, what should a clinician do? Patients with schizophrenia or psychotic states resembling schizophrenia sometimes also show various features that make one suspect an organic component to the behavior disorder. To the more usual ones of EEG abnormality and history of brain trauma or encephalitis should certainly be added organicity on neuropsychological testing. Possibly psychiatrists should learn how to test for soft neurological signs, although the predictive value of such signs in terms of treatment response is unclear. Probably childhood histories of short attention-span, distractability, impulsivity, and other common symptoms of childhood MBD should be attended to. The possibility that schizoaffective patients present atypical manic-depressive states should also be seriously considered.

On this basis, schizoaffective patients, if excited, deserve a trial on lithium carbonate and, if depressed, deserve a trial on a tricyclic antidepressant or, if that fails, a monoamine oxidase inhibitor. Although Klein [35] has shown that imipramine alone is better than placebo in many schizophrenics and only makes patients with childhood asocial schizophrenia worse, probably tricyclics will be added to a modest dose of antipsychotic medication. Atypical psychoses with a history of childhood MBD and current symptoms resembling exaggerated adult MBD of the sort described by Wood et al. [3] could receive a trial on stimulants alone with the physician being prepared to back off rapidly if the behavior worsens. In more typical schizophrenics with a history of, or current, MBD symptoms, one might emulate Huessy and add a tricyclic first to the antipsychotic drug, following this with a stimulant drug if the antidepressant is not helpful.

Both diphenylhydantoin and carbamazepine can be tried sequentially in addition to lower doses of antipsychotics in clear schizophrenics with paroxysmal EEGs and other features described by Davies and Neil. All of the approaches are not validated by well-controlled clinical trials but may be an improvement over simply persevering in the use of antipsychotics alone in patients who fail to show any appreciable response to such conventional therapy for several weeks at adequate dosages.

**Other Psychiatric States with MBD**

Both Bellak [16] and Huessy [24] suggest that borderline patients may also have MBD. Given the amorphous and unreliable ways in which this popular but idiosyncratic diagnosis is used, [36] I hope that adult MBD becomes a reliable and useful diagnosis for a subgroup of patients usually deposited in the borderline wastebasket. Borderline state is currently a diagnosis in search of a therapy, while adult MBD may well have clear therapeutic implications. Klein's group finds, within the personality disorders, a group of emotionally unstable character disorders (EUCD) who show frequent and unpredictable mood swings, some impulsivity, and frequent soft neurological signs and who respond to lithium carbonate in a controlled clinical trial [37]. This may constitute another subgroup often called "borderline" that may or may not overlap with adult MBD as used by Wender's group [3]. The EUCDs respond to imipramine with increased irritability and anger [15]; it is unknown if they respond to stimulants favorably.

Monroe's work with patients with "episodic dyscontrol" identifies a group of patients [17] who often have a history of brain insults during birth and childhood, as well as symptoms in common with simple adult MBD, such as impulsivity, mood lability, irritability and angry outbursts, school behavior problems, and learning disability. To this he adds the occurrence of epileptoid states with auras, partial memory loss, confusion, loss of control, violent behavior, feelings of intense panic, and dysphoria. He reports that such patients often show soft neurological signs and EEG abnormalities. After completing a crossover study of Mysoline and placebo which showed little difference between treatments on preselected measures, Monroe found that a number of his subjects could correctly identify their period on Mysoline, and he described the drug as delaying responses to outside stimuli and allowing the subjects to think out their reactions, rather than responding impulsively in their usual fashion [38]. Lithium [39] has been described as having a similar effect on violence-prone prisoners and psychiatric patients. Again, it is unknown whether Monroe's patients would or would not respond to stimulants. At a distance, his patients sound as if they may have aspects of simple adult MBD compounded by epileptic-like episodic states of dyscontrol. Monroe's patients have, in recent times, included a well-studied group of recidivist violent offenders. One study of adult MBD, reporting a good response to d-amphetamine [7], was also carried out in a prison setting.

**Discussion**

The term MBD has emerged from child psychiatry and is extending into a wide range of adult psychiatric conditions. The term itself not only varies in the way it is used by various investigators but is also rather unpopular with both physicians and patients because of its implications of incurable organic brain damage. *DSM-III* has avoided the term for children by substituting attentional deficit disorder, and Cantwell has proposed that we call the childhood disorder Hoffman disease, after the German pediatrician who invented "Der Struwelpeter" [20], an illustrated tale of a horrible, hyperkinetic, rebellious child who appears to have suffered from what might now be called MBD. Adult Hoffman disease may or may not be a better term than attentional deficit disorder-residual state, which would be the only way to diagnose Wender's adult MBD patients in *DSM-III* but a better, less labeling term is clearly needed.

With or without a name, Wender's adult MBD group appears to be achieving a degree of clarity sufficient for it to be reliably diagnosed and for studies of the treatment response of such patients to be carried out. He is currently completing a controlled trial of pemoline in such patients. If his findings on methylphenidate can be confirmed by others on patients meeting his criteria, we may have both a new disease and a useful treatment for it. This may also help save stimulant drugs from total extinction by governmental forces interested in fighting drug abuse by administrative action.

The utility of tricyclic antidepressants in simple adult MBD, in atypical schizophrenics with histories of childhood MBD, and/or paroxysmal EEGs, or other evidence of organic brain dysfunction, deserves careful study, as does the role of both lithium and of various anticonvulsants in simple adult MBD, MBD schizophrenics, and Monroe's episodic dyscontrol patients. Since hysteria, at least that portion defined as Briquet syndrome, alcoholism, and sociopathy are all genetically linked to childhood MBD, the possibility that some of the drugs mentioned above might be useful in some such patients is not totally ridiculous.

In summary, the concept of adult MBD is intriguing, but work must be done to define clinical criteria for diagnosing various possible types within the rather amorphous larger concept. It also needs careful clinical observation in looking for relationships between specific subtypes and clinical drug response followed by carefully controlled clinical trials validating uncontrolled clinical observations. At worst, the material reviewed above suggests some unconventional treatment options for patients unresponsive to standard drug and psychological therapies.

## Commentary

Little new has occurred in this area though a few clinical trials are in progress. Information from the conference on which this paper was partially based has now appeared in book form [40].   I have seen six patients since the paper was written who appeared to have adult MBD symptoms in the sense that they have difficulty with sustained attention plus various other symptoms, such as hyperactivity and/or impulsivity, mood lability, or hypersensitivity to criticism. Three of these patients responded well to stimulants while two did best on antipsychotics; one is just being started on lithium, having failed on both stimulants and antipsychotics. It is my impression that the presence of marked anger and/or paranoid features, despite a history of childhood hyperactivity, makes stimulants less likely to be helpful, but it is very difficult to be sure on the basis of only six variegated cases of a disorder.

## References

1. Wender PH: Minimal Brain Dysfunction in Children. New York, Wiley-Interscience, 1971.

2. Diagnostic and Statistical Manual III (Draft), Task Force on Nomenclature and Statistics. American Psychiatric Association, Washington, D.C., 1977.

3. Wood DR, Reimherr FW, Wender PH, et al: Diagnosis and treatment of minimal brain dysfunction in adults. Arch Gen Psychiat 33:1453-1462, 1977.

4. Huessy HR: The adult hyperkinetic. Am J Psychiat 131:724-725, 1974.

5. Arnold L, Strobl D, Weisenberg A: Hyperkinetic adult: Study of the "paradoxical" amphetamine response. JAMA 222:693-694, 1972.

6. Oettinger L: Proceedings of the workshop on evaluating long-term effects of stimulant drug treatment. Chevy Chase, Md.: Psychopharmacology Research Branch, NIMH, pp 150-176, 1972.

7. Hill D: Amphetamine in psychopathic states. Br J Addict 44:50-54, 1944.

8. Spitzer R, Endicott J, Robins E: Research diagnostic criteria for a selected group of functional disorders. New York, Biometrics Research, 1975.

9. Weiss G, Hechtman L, Perlman T, et al: (Personal Communication).

10. Huessy HR, Metoyer M, Townsend M: Eight to ten year follow-up of 84 children treated for behavioral disturbance in rural Vermont. Acta Paedopsychiat 40:230-235, 1974.

11. Menkes MH, Rowe JS, Menkes JH: A 25 year follow-up study on the hyperkinetic child with MBD. Pediatrics 39:393-399, 1967.

12. Morris HH, Escoll PJ, Wexler R: Aggressive behaviors of childhood—A follow-up study. Am J Psychiat 112:991-997, 1956.

13. O'Neal P, Robbins LM: The relation of childhood behavior problems to adult psychiatric status: A 30 year follow-up study of 150 patients. Am J Psychiat 114:961-969, 1958.

14. Borland BL, Heckman HC: Hyperactive boys and their brothers. A 25-year follow-up study. Arch Gen Psychiat 33:669-675, 1976.

15. Quitkin F, Klein D: Two behavioral syndromes in young adults related to possible minimal brain dysfunction. J Psychiat Res 7:131-142, 1969.

16. Bellak L: Psychiatric states in adults with minimal brain dysfunction. Psychiat Ann 7:575-589, 1977.

17. Monroe R: Episodic Behavioral Disorder: A Psychodynamic and Neurophysiologic Analysis. Cambridge, MA., Harvard Univ Press, 1970.

18. Stewart M, Pitts F, Craig A, et al: The hyperactive child syndrome. Am Orthopsychiat 36:861-867, 1966.

19. Mendelson W, Johnson J, Stewart M: Hyperactive children as teenagers: A follow-up study. J Nerv Ment Dis 153:273-279, 1971.

20. Cantwell D: Psychiatric illness in the families of hyperactive children. Arch Gen Psychiat 27:414-417, 1972.

21. Morrison J, Stewart M: A family study of the hyperactive child syndrome. Biological Psychiat 3:189-195, 1971.

22. Morrison JR, Stewart M: The psychiatric status of the legal families of adopted hyperactive children. Arch Gen Psychiat 28:888-891, 1973.

23. Cantwell DP: Genetic studies of hyperactive children: Psychiatric illness in biologic and adopting parents. *In* Fieve RR, Rosenthal D, Brill H (Eds): Genetic Research in Psychiatry, Baltimore, John Hopkins Univ Press, 1975, pp 259-272.

24. Huessy H: Clinical explorations in adult MBD. Paper presented at the Conference on MBD in Adults, Scottsdale, Arizona, March 3-4, 1978.

25. Mann HB, Greenspan SI: The identification and treatment of adult brain dysfunction. Am J Psychiat 133:1013-1017, 1976.

26. Wender P: Discussion. Conference on MBD in Adults, Scottsdale, Arizona, March 3-4, 1978.

27. Stephens J, Shaffer J: A controlled study of the effects of diphenylhydantoin on anxiety, irritability, and anger in neurotic outpatients. Psychopharmacologia 17:169-181, 1970.

28. Rosenthal D: Discussion of the concept of schizophrenic disorders. *In* Fieve R, Rosenthal D, Brill H (Eds): Genetic Research in Psychiatry. Baltimore, Johns Hopkins Univ Press, 1975, pp. 199-208.

29. Tucker GJ, Campion EW, Silberfard PM: Sensormotor functions and cognitive disturbance in psychiatric patients. Am J Psychiat 132:17-21, 1975.

30. Rochford JM, Detre T, Tucker GJ, et al: Neuropsychological impairments in functional psychiatric diseases. Arch Gen Psychiat 22:114-119, 1970.

31. Quitkin F, Rifkin A, Klein D: Neurologic soft signs in schizophrenia and character disorders. Arch Gen Psychiat 33:845-847, 1976.

32. Davies R, Neil J, Himmelhoch J: Cerebral dysrhythmia in schizophrenics receiving phenothiazines: Clinical correlates. Clin Electroencephalography 6:103-115, 1975.

33. Neil J, Merikanga SJ, Davies R, et al: Validity and clinical utility of neuroleptic-facilitated electroencephalography in psychotic patients. (In press).

34. Davies R, Neil J: Cerebral dysrhythmias in schizophrenics: Clinical correlates. Paper presented at the Conference on MBD in Adults, Scottsdale, Arizona, March 3-4, 1978.

35. Klein, D: Psychiatric diagnosis and a typology of drug effects. Psychopharmacologia 13:359-386, 1968.

36. Perry J, Klerman G: The borderline patient. Arch Gen Psychiat 35:141-152, 1978.

37. Rifkin A, Quitkin F, et al: Lithium carbonate in emotionally unstable character disorders. Arch Gen Psychiat 27:519-523, 1972.

38. Monroe R: MBD and episodic dyscontrol. Paper presented at the Conference on MBD in Adults, Scottsdale, Arizona, March 3-4, 1978.

39. Shader R, Jackson A, Dodes L: The antiaggressive effects of lithium in man. Psychopharmacologia 40:17-24, 1974.

40. Bellak, L (Ed): Psychiatric aspects of minimal brain dysfunction. New York, Grune and Stratton, 1979.

# 6 Fenfluramine

*Jonathan O. Cole, M.D.*

Fenfluramine was selected as a topic for *Psychopharmacology Update* because of my experiences in proposing this drug as a "safer" appetite suppressant to other psychiatrists whose patients wanted an anorexigenic agent but who could not or who should not take an amphetamine-like drug. I must have mentioned fenfluramine (Pondimin) to at least 25 generally well-informed psychiatrists in Massachusetts, none of whom had even heard of it! Fenfluramine may not be the solution to all the obesity problems of mankind, but it is a reasonably safe, marketed drug which is as effective as d-amphetamine in weight reduction and is generally perceived by patients as sedative or neutral rather than stimulant. Fenfluramine has a number of interesting features, both practical and theoretical, which make it a drug about which psychiatrists should be informed.

## Origin

Fenfluramine is one of many attempts to manipulate the amphetamine molecule to find a component which has appetite suppression but no stimulant effect [1]. Diethylpropion (Tenuate, Tepanil), phenmetrazine (Preludin) and phenteramine (Ionamin) are among the earlier, less successful, attempts in this direction (Fig. 6-1). In the special case of fenfluramine, it was found that adding the trifluoromethyl group to the phenyl ring removed the stimulant effects of the structure in animal testing. The $NH_2$ compound proved toxic, but the present $CF_3 - NH - C_2H_5$ compound was safe, sedative and anorectic [2].

The drug has now been on the market in the United States for two years and, together with mazindol (Sanorex) [3,4], a somewhat more stimulant antiobesity agent, constitutes the "new look" in pharmacological war on fat.

None of our anorectic agents are highly effective in the treatment of obesity in man. Differences between active drug and placebo in this area tend to run about a pound or so greater weight loss per week on the active drug. The effect may continue for as long as three months. Nevertheless, a recent, but pre-fenfluramine survey by Lasagna [5] showed that one-third of the doctors polled did not use appetite suppressants at all, while the others used them with varying degrees of optimism and enthusiasm and varying degrees of concern about either side effects or abuse potential.

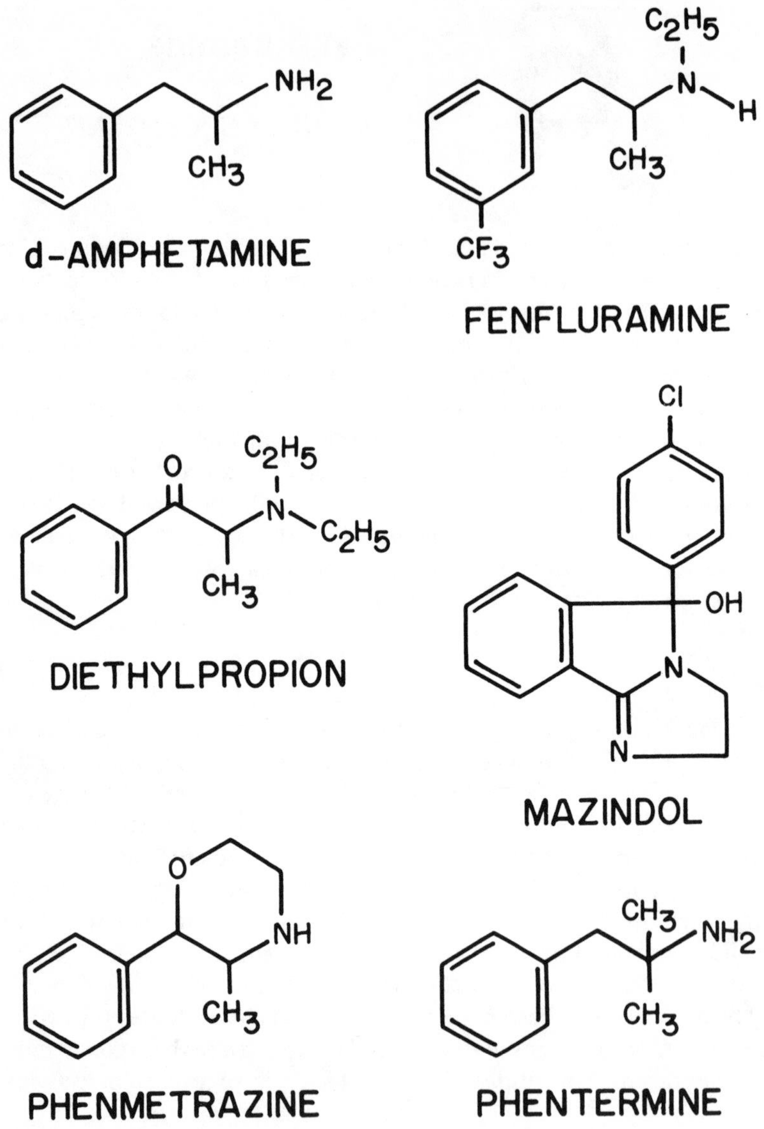

**Figure 6-1.** Chemical Structures of d-Amphetamine and Related Anorectic Drugs

**Mechanism of Action**

Amphetamine and other stimulant anorexics are presumed to act principally by releasing dopamine at brain synapses and, perhaps, by direct stimulation of these synapses; some amphetamine actions may be noradrenergic rather than dopaminergic. In any event, alpha-methyltyrosine, which blocks synthesis of both dopamine and noradrenalin, also blocks amphetamine's effect on appetite [6]. Fenfluramine has an effect on dopaminergic systems that is opposite to the effect of amphetamine. Fenfluramine is a blocker of dopamine receptors, while amphetamine stimulates the same receptors [7]. Fenfluramine is, in fact, as potent as chlorpromazine in blocking the stereotyped behaviors elicited in rats by amphetamine or other dopaminergic drugs.

On the other hand, fenfluramine's effects on appetite appear to be mediated through the serotonin systems of the brain. Destroying the serotoninergic neurons in the midbrain raphe of animals lowers brain serotonin and eliminates the anorectic effect of fenfluramine. Fenfluramine lowers both serotonin and its main metabolite, 5-hydroxyindolacetic acid, and fenfluramine's action on appetite is blocked by a serotonin-receptor blocker called methergolin [6] and by other serotonin antagonists. Thus, although the exact mechanism by which fenfluramine activates serotonergic systems is unclear, the drug's potency in this brain system is evident [7].

At the neurophysiological level, there is evidence that amphetamine's effects on appetite are mediated through a "hunger" center in the lateral hypothalamus. Bilateral lesions in that area reduce amphetamine's effect on hunger in the rat, while such lesions enhance fenfluramine's antiappetite effect [8]. Fenfluramine may act instead (or in addition) through a "satiation" center in the ventro-medial area of the hypothalamus; fenfluramine increases electrical activity in that area [9].

The latter effect is positively correlated with fenfluramine's ability to increase glucose uptake by muscle tissue. Fenfluramine has, in fact, a hypoglycemic effect—it flattens glucose tolerance test curves appreciably even in diabetics, which may make it a drug of choice in the treatment of obese diabetics [9].

The drug also has a mild hypotensive effect in man, producing statistically significant drops in blood pressure on the order of 10 mm systolic and 5 mm diastolic in nonhypertensive patients and more impressive decreases in hypertensive patients.

Fenfluramine appears to mix well with other antihypertensive drugs and to be safe in patients with cardiovascular disease [9].

## Pharmacokinetics

After a single large oral dose (60 mg), peak blood level occurs at about three hours. Norfenfluramine, the drug's major metabolite, appears within two hours after the drug is taken and, by four hours, achieves plasma levels about as high as those of the intact drug. On regimens of 20 mg t.i.d., plateau steady-state blood levels are reached after three to four days, at which time comparable levels of norfenfluramine are also present and stable. The plasma half-life of the drug is about 20 hours (the drug level in the plasma will drop 50% in 20 hours if no more drug is given). Probably a level of 100 ng/ml of plasma is effective in reducing appetite in man; levels over 120 ng/ml are associated with excessive sedation, dizziness, dry mouth, and nausea. Fenfluramine levels in plasma correlate better with appetite suppression in man than do norfenfluramine levels.

The drug passes the placental barrier in animals and must be assumed to do so in man. Urinary pH influences the renal excretion of fenfluramine, which resembles amphetamine in having its excretion speeded when urinary pH is acid. The above information is derived from the excellent review of the drug's pharmacology by Pinder et al. [9].

**Psychological Effects**

In animals, fenfluramine tends to decrease motor activity; however, it has a stimulant effect [9] in animals pretreated with a monoamine oxidase (MAO) inhibitor. In Fink's early human study of fenfluramine's effect on the human electroencephalogram, he picked up both clear subjective sedation and a barbiturate-like pattern of EEG changes (increased beta activity, increased alpha amplitude, and decreased delta activity) [10].

Along with other stimulant appetite suppressants, fenfluramine suppresses REM sleep but only fenfluramine also increases slow-wave sleep. At higher dosages (40 to 80 mg at bedtime) it interferes with sleep [11,12], and even low chronic dosages (40 to 120 mg/day) cause an increase in number of awakenings during the night [12].

In clinical trials of fenfluramine in obese patients, sedation occurs as a side effect in a minority of patients (usually 10% to 15%). Its effects on mood and subjective state in single doses in studies oriented toward the drug's potential for abuse liability are very unclear. In one study, by Gotestam et al. [4] of Swedish prisoners with a history of heavy stimulant abuse, 80 mg (a large dose) of fenfluramine was compared with 50 mg of amphetamine, 2 mg of mazindole, and placebo. Mazindole was found to resemble amphetamine and fenfluramine to be indistinguishable from placebo. However, Gagnon et al. compared single doses of 20, 40, and 60 mg of fenfluramine with placebo and 5 mg of amphetamine in "young nurses." The two higher fenfluramine doses and amphetamine all produced more stimulation and euphoria (not defined) than placebo [14]. Fatigue was least in the 60 mg fenfluramine subjects. To confuse matters further, Griffith et al., evaluating fenfluramine at single doses of 60, 120, and 240 mg (a huge dose) in volunteer ex-opiate-addict prisoners, found the drug to be a weak hallucinogen, even causing visual and olfactory hallucinations, cyclic mood alterations, distorted time sense, and fleeting psychotic ideation, in three of eight subjects at the highest dose. The drug did not appear amphetamine-like in their hands [15]. Pinder et al., in their review [9], summarize a South African paper by Levin that was not available to me. Levin is quoted as reporting that 25% of a group of over 400 drug abusers had abused fenfluramine and judged it to resemble a mixture of cannabis and amphetamine when taken in large doses (up to 400 mg). Only two patients preferred fenfluramine to other drugs. In most users, its tendency to cause nausea and diarrhea made it a drug taken only when preferred drugs were not available [9].

**Use in Obesity**

In general, the literature of fenfluramine in the treatment of obesity, as reviewed by both Pinder et al. [9] and Burland [2], supports the efficacy of the drug on the basis of published placebo-controlled studies. In comparisons with other older anti appetite drugs, fenfluramine causes at least comparable degrees of weight loss; the only drug modality reported to be superior to fenfluramine is a long-acting diethylpropion preparation [16]. The intermittent use of long-acting preparations (of both diethylpropion [17] and phentermine [18]) may have a value in the treatment of obesity by effecting weight loss while avoiding the development of tolerance and psychological dependence. If so, although fenfluramine given continuously was shown to be as effective as the intermittent therapies in two of the three reported studies, fenfluramine cannot readily be given intermittently. If fenfluramine administration is stopped abruptly after four weeks at 20 mg t.i.d., mild to moderate mood depression is likely to occur [19].

There is one report in the literature of four cases of clinically manifest depression necessitating psychiatric treatment occurring after abrupt cessation of fenfluramine therapy. In three of these cases, replacement of the fenfluramine relieved the depression. Once the patient was stabilized, fenfluramine could then be gradually withdrawn and depression did not occur [20]. Two double-blind fenfluramine-placebo studies [19,21] found depression to occur in degrees detectable on self-reported forms, peaking on the third to fifth day after abrupt fenfluramine discontinuation. Only one of the 16 patients studied by Oswald et al. [21] showed depression severe enough—"cried all weekend" ten days after drug withdrawal—to be clinically obvious, although a few other subjects noticed themselves to be unaccountably depressed for a few days. This study led Oswald to postulate that fenfluramine might be a drug "of dependence but not of abuse."

It is hard to assess the real risks of depression associated with the use of fenfluramine in the treatment of obesity generally. Gradual tapering of dosage over a two-week period may well avoid depressive downswings entirely.

## Use in Psychiatric Patients

Fenfluramine has been studied in nonpsychotic obese patients and was found to be modestly effective in reducing both weight and psychiatric symptoms in one study, though the drug appeared more useful in anxious than in depressed patients [22]. In contrast, a straightforward trial of fenfluramine against placebo in lower social class, somatically focused outpatients with chronic anxiety, carried out by Rickels' group [23] found fenfluramine to be less effective than placebo. Since Hughes [24] found fenfluramine to be about equal to diazepam in anxious, tense psychiatric outpatients, the exact status of fenfluramine in psychiatric outpatients, with anxiety or depression remains uncertain. An article not available to me on the use of fenfluramine in neuroleptic-induced obesity apparently exists [25] in the Scandinavian literature. Fenfluramine's dopamine-blocking activity suggests that it might be more compatible with antipsychotic drugs than are anorectics, which resemble amphetamine closely.

On the other hand, three cases of activation or precipitation of acute psychosis have been reported in patients with a history of psychosis or emotional lability who were receiving fenfluramine. Fenfluramine will also occasionally elicit facial dyskinesias or bruxism [9], suggesting that the drug's amphetamine-like effects may sometimes be more prominent than its sedative actions.

Fenfluramine has been tried in the treatment of mania by two groups. Pearce [26] treated four manic patients with dosages as high as 180 mg/day and observed a "definite response" in 48 hours. Three patients relapsed when the drug was stopped. Two of these were switched to placebo and were unaware that the drug had been discontinued. Although Pearce used the drug because it was serotonergic and caused depression, his logic seems dubious since the drug is also a dopamine blocker and could act like chlorpromazine, and it mainly causes depression *after* its use has been stopped for three days. Goodwin et al. [27] have failed to replicate Pearce's findings in a second small series of manic patients.

To complete the heterogeneous nature of this review of an ambidextrous anorectic drug, fenfluramine has been reported, not unreasonably, to have been used to substitute for d-amphetamine in six patients heavily dependent on stimulants, using dosages of about 120 mg/day of fenfluramine in the beginning [28]. Initial hypertension and peculiar skin sensations occurred in all patients; diarrhea was a more persistent side effect. The patients were withdrawn gradually from fenfluramine after being maintained on it for six months. Fenfluramine has also been claimed to decrease alcohol intake in rats and has been tried, tentatively, after detoxification in alcoholics [9].

## Discussion

Reviewing the current literature on fenfluramine leaves one intrigued but unsatisfied and mildly apprehensive. The drug is clearly a useful, nonstimulating appetite-reducing agent without too many side effects if one begins with 20 mg t.i.d. and does not expect its full effect on appetite to occur immediately. Increasing the dosage to 40 mg t.i.d. may be useful later. When stopping the drug the dosage should be slowly tapered.

When used in this manner, psychiatric complications should be minimal, and some anxious patients may feel both less hungry and less anxious.

Since the drug acts on appetite quite differently than does amphetamine, one would guess that some patients will lose weight better on one drug than on the other.

When fenfluramine is used in patients with serious psychiatric illnesses or on other psychoactive drugs, the patients should be carefully observed. One McLean Hospital patient with a major pathological preoccupation with food became relatively asymptomatic two weeks after fenfluramine was added to her ongoing amitriptyline regimen. The next two comparable patients showed no clear response to fenfluramine. The drug should be combined with MAO inhibitors only with great caution, since it causes excitement when given to animals pretreated with these drugs.

The appearance of rebound depression following the use of fenfluramine makes one wonder about the role of serotonin in depression. If amitriptyline is really most effective in serotonin-poor depressions, fenfluramine, as a serotonergic drug, might ultimately be found to be of use in such depressions, either alone or in combination with amitriptyline.

Fenfluramine seems to contain the properties of a sedative, a stimulant, and an hallucinogen all in the same drug. The hallucinogenic effects only appear at rather high dosages. Sedative effects are more common at lower dosages (i.e. 20 to 40 mg t.i.d.) but amphetamine-like effects seem to occur occasionally. The single six-patient study hinting that fenfluramine may be the "methadone" of the amphetamine-like drug class [28] is intriguing in this regard.

Despite Oswald and associates' idea that drugs like fenfluramine can produce "dependence but not abuse," this appears to be a misnomer [21].

Fenfluramine produces some type of tolerance and physical dependence, which appears to be so unlike psychological dependence that patients do not even associate their depression with their recently discontinued drug therapy.

In any event, fenfluramine is an interesting addition to our pharmacological armamentarium. It deserves cautious clinical use in some psychiatric patients with serious weight problems. Its specific benefits and risks when given along with antipsychotics, antidepressants, and lithium—all of which often cause undesirable weight gain—deserve systematic study.

## Commentary

This somewhat-sedative, serotonergic appetite suppressant is still not widely used either in obesity or psychiatry despite the passage of three years since this article was originally written. However, it is an interesting medication and deserves further study.

Soon after writing this paper I was consulted on the treatment of a chronically depressed young woman who had, in addition, most of the symptoms of anorexia nervosa—constant preoccupation with eating, fear of eating, fear of obesity, overactivity, episodic gorging and vomiting with secondary guilt—except emaciation. She was gorging too frequently to be thin. She had been treated previously with d-amphetamine with minimal improvement. After two months on 200 mg/day of amitriptyline, she was still depressed and still had all the above symptoms. When reluctantly started on fenfluramine (Pondimim) she markedly improved in four days, losing both her depression and her life-long preoccupation with eating and not eating. She stayed well for at least several months and was then lost to follow-up. A second, very thin, patient with anorexia nervosa had no response. However, I and my associates have added fenfluramine to the prior tricyclic therapy of about 20 patients whose depressions were not responding to the tricyclic therapy alone. It is our impression that the fenfluramine was helpful in improving mood in about one-third of the patients. Two remarkably treatment-resistant patients who had failed for several years on a range of other drugs are being maintained on desipramine-fenfluramine combinations with marked improvement for a year or more. Other cases have been followed on fenfluramine plus other tricyclics for shorter periods with good initial response. One patient with rapid cycling bipolar manic-depressive illness is better controlled on fenfluramine plus lithium than on lithium alone. Several plump schizophrenic patients have been placed on fenfluramine, in addition to their antipsychotics, without aggravation of their psychosis but without dramatic effect on their weight. To date, no patient has developed euphoria of the stimulant type on fenfluramine.

The drug is clearly sedative. I have usually prescribed it at bedtime in dosages increasing from 20 mg/day to 60 mg/day over a one-week period and stabilized the patient at that dosage for a week or two, sometimes then increasing the dosage gradually to 120 mg/day maximum. The major side effects have been sedation and ataxia, the latter sometimes occurring in the absence of sedation.

The drug clearly deserves systematic study. Our informal experience suggests that fenfluramine is sometimes useful in depression but it certainly does not prove that this is so. Even if it helps when added to a tricyclic, fenfluramine might help by increasing the plasma level of the tricyclic, something we have not systematically checked. Since fenfluramine shares with carbamazepine (Tegretal) [29] and L-tryptophan [30] some ability to improve both mania and depression, it deserves some consideration as an alternative to lithium carbonate in bipolar patients whose cyclic illnesses are not responsive to that more conventional drug.

**References**

1. Samuel PD, Burland WL: Drug treatment of obesity, pp 419-428. *In* Bray G (ed). Obesity in Perspective. DHEW publication (NIH):75-708, GPO, Washington, DC, 1975.

2. Burland WL: A review of experience with fenfluramine, pp 229-440. *In* Bray G (ed). Obesity in Perspective. DHEW publication (NIH): 75-708, GPO, Washington, DC 1975.

3. Smith DE: A new anorexiant: clinical evaluation. Rocky Mountain Med J 71:41-44, 1974.

4. Gotestam GK, Gunne LM: Subjective effects of two anorexigenic agents, fenfluramine and AN 448 in amphetamine-dependent subjects. Brit J Addict 67:39-44, 1972.

5. Lasagna L: Attitudes toward appetite suppressants: a survey of US physicans. JAMA 225:44-48, 1973.

6. Jespersen S, Scheel-Kruger J: Evidence for a difference in mechanisms of action between fenfluramine and amphetamine-induced anorexia. J Pharm Pharmac 25:49-54, 1973.

7. Garattini S, Buczko W, Jori A, et al: The mechanism of action of fenfluramine. Postgrad Med J 51 (supp 1):27-38, 1975.

8. Blundell J, Leshem M: Central action of anorexic agents: effects of amphetamine and fenfluramine in rats with lateral hypothalamic lesions. Europ J Pharmacol 28:81-88, 1974.

9. Pinder R, Brogden R, Sawyer P, et al: Fenfluramine: a review of its pharmacological properties and therapeutic efficacy in obesity. Drugs 10:241-323, 1975.

10. Fink M, Shapiro D, Itil T: EEG profiles of fenfluramine, amobarbital and d-amphetamine in normal volunteers. Psychopharmacologia 22:369-376, 1971.

11. Gagnon MA, Bordeleau JW, Tetreault L: Fenfluramine: study of its central action through its effects on sleep. Internat J Clin Pharmocol, Ther, Toxicol 1:74, 1969a.

12. Gagnon MA, Tetreault L, Bordeleau JM: Psychometric studies on sleep for the evaluation of central effects of drugs. The effects of fenfluramine on sleep. Activ Nerv Sup 21:202, 1969b.

13. Lewis SA, Oswald I, Dunleavy DL: Chronic fenfluramine administration—some cerebral effects. Brit Med J 3:67-70, 1971.

14. Gagnon MA, Gauthier R, Tetreault L: Subjective vs objective measurement of appetite and feeding: evidence for central stimulation in man by fenfluramine. Clin Pharm Therapeut 15:205-206, 1974.

15. Griffith JD, Witt JG, Jasinski DR: A comparison of fenfluramine and d-amphetamine in man. Clin Pharm Therapeut 18:563-570, 1975.

16. Rooyen JR, van der Merwe M: Comparison of diethylpropion (Tenuate Dospan) and fenfluramine. Med Proc 17:420, 1971.

17. Silverstone JT: Intermittent treatment with anorectic drugs. Practioners 213:245, 1974.

18. Munro JF, MacCuish AC, Wilson EM, et al: Comparison of continuous and intermittent anorectic therapy in obesity. Brit Med J 1:352, 1968.

19. Steel JM, Munro JF, Duncan LJP: A comparative trial of different regimens of fenfluramine and phentermine in obesity. Practioner 211:232, 1973.

20. Harding T: Depression following fenfluramine withdrawal. Brit J Psychiat 121:338-339, 1972.

21. Oswald I, Lewis SA, Dunleavy DL, et al: Drugs of dependence though not of abuse: fenfluramine and imipramine. Brit Med J 3:70-73, 1971.

22. Gaind R: Fenfluramine in the treatment of obese psychiatric outpatients. Brit J Psychiat 115:963-964, 1969.

23. Raich WA, Rickels K, Raab E: A double-blind evaluation of fenfluramine in anxious somatizing neurotic medical clinic patients. Curr Ther Res 8(1):31-33, 1966.

24. Hughes BD: Double-blind trial in anxiety and tension in patients referred to psychiatric outpatient department. So Afr Med J 45 (suppl):37, 1971.

25. Jensen P, Kirk L: Fenfluramine-treatment of neuroleptic-induced obesity. Nord Psykiatr Tidsskr 26:367, 1972.

26. Pearce JB: Fenfluramine in mania. Lancet 1:427, 1973.

27. Goodwin F, et al: Fenfluramine in mania. Paper presented at July 8-12, 1976, meeting of the Collegium Internat Neuropsychopharm, Quebec City, Canada, 1976.

28. Jones HS: Fenfluramine used as a substitute for methylamphetamines and dexamphetamines in the treatment of dependence on these drugs. So Afr Med J (suppl):31-32, 1971.

29. Ayd F: Carbamazepine: a potential alternative for lithium therapy for affective disorders. Int Drug Ther Newsletter 14:29-32, 1979.

30. Cole J, Hartmann E, Brigham P: L-tryptophan: clinical studies. McLean Hosp J, 1980. In press.

# 7

## Drugs and Senile Dementia

*Jonathan O. Cole, M.D.* and
*Roland J. Branconnier, M.A.*

The draft version of *DSM-III* [1] defines senile dementia as a dementia with insidious onset after age 65 and a uniformly progressive deteriorating course in a patient for whom all other specific causes for dementia have been ruled out. Dementia, to be diagnosed, requires a decrement in intellectual functioning after brain maturation (age 15) of sufficient severity to interfere with social or occupational functioning or both. The changes must involve memory impairment plus (a) impairment in abstract thinking, (b) impairment in judgment, or (c) personality change or impairment in impulse control. Drugs have long been sought which might ameliorate or even reverse the organic and social disabilities of these often tragic and helpless patients. A number of drugs are now marketed in the United States for use in this condition, and a much larger number are in clinical use in Europe. The purpose of this paper is to review these drugs and to comment on their relative place in clinical psychopharmacology.

### Clinical Syndrome Problems

The first issue concerns diagnosis. The most dramatic results in the treatment of apparent senile dementia are achieved by diagnosing and treating some other condition that is masquerading as senile dementia. A variety of noncerebral organic illnesses—heart failure, infection, uremia, hypothyroidism, vitamin deficiency—can present with memory difficulty and confusion. Toxicities from a variety of medical drugs and, commonly, alcohol can also affect brain function. Treating the medical problem or withdrawing the offending drug can often clear the patient's sensorium and return him to his pre-illness status. Normal pressure hydrocephalus, usually manifested by rather rapidly progressive dementia with ataxia and incontinence, can be treated neurosurgically [2]. Dementia secondary to a small cerebral infarct will often clear spontaneously; multiple infarct dementia (*DSM-III*'s version of psychosis with cerebral arteriosclerosis) often has an episodic, irregular course in contrast to the slowly progressive course of senile dementia.

An equally important problem is the pseudodementia often seen with depressive episodes in the elderly. This will respond nicely to antidepressant drugs or, in more severe cases, electroconvulsive therapy. There is evidence that American psychiatrists, in contrast to their British counterparts, tend to underdiagnose depression when confronted with newly hospitalized elderly patients [3].

A separate type of problem is posed by elderly patients living in the community in retirement who have the subjective impression that their memory is failing a little. These people probably have a normal decrease in memory which may not be progressive but which may be aggravated by the stresses of low income, lack of meaningful work, decreasing social contacts, etc. Some memory problems seen in the institutionalized elderly may have a similar, relatively nonorganic etiology. Lack of hope, meaningful activity, and social contacts can lead to withdrawal and apathy with a secondary weakening or loss of old capacities and interests.

Since some studies of drugs intended to be effective in senile dementia include patients with "normal" or situationally aggravated cognitive deficits, the data are difficult to interpret.

In studies involving heterogeneous institutional populations of elderly people with memory and behavioral deficits, most of them may, in fact, have senile dementia. However, one must watch for both the apathetic nonorganic patient and the elderly chronic schizophrenic often placed in such facilities these days.

Dementia secondary to cerebral arteriosclerosis deserves special mention since many of our current "geriatric" drugs are vasodilators. This condition is less common than senile dementia, has a different course, and could, at least in theory, respond differently to drug therapy.

**Cerebral Vasodilators**

The major drugs in this group currently available in the United States are papaverine (Pavabid), dihydrogenated ergot alkaloids (Hydergine), cyclandelate (Cyclospasmol) and isoxsuprine (Vasodilan). In Europe, other similar drugs such as naftidrofuryl (Praxilene), nicergoline (Sermion), and butalamine (Surheme) are also in common use. Recently, a generic form of Hydergine, deapril-ST, was approved for use in this country.

These drugs pose a conceptual problem. If they really work by dilating brain arteries or arterioles, should this effect be helpful? If blood flow is reduced by arteriosclerosis, it is difficult to envision how a drug can affect a sclerosed artery; in fact, by dilating the normal arteries a vasodilator might shunt blood *away* from brain areas with reduced blood supply. Current evidence suggests that brain-blood flow is reduced in senile dementia, but this reduction is secondary to the decrease in active brain tissue, not a cause of the cell loss. Elaborate studies of changes in regional blood flow are being carried out in Sweden; these may both help explain the nature of the deficits seen in various senile organic states and could be used to assess the actual local effects of vasodilating drugs [4]. There is also the possibility, unproven, that vasodilators may dilate capillaries or increase the deformability of red blood cells and thus improve the tissue blood supply in this manner [5,6].

Despite the weakness of the general concept of vasodilators as an important pharmacological basis for the treatment of senile dementia, it remains a useful paradigm for screening drugs at the animal level. Several drugs originally proposed as treatments for senile dementia were initially identified as cerebral vasodilators but are now claimed to have other pharmacodynamic properties, such as improving brain metabolism. Until recently, a good animal model of senile dementia had not been available.

Recent evidence obtained by Obris [7] would suggest that reduced cerebral blood flow is the result and not the cause of cerebral atrophy. Moreover, it has been independently demonstrated by Corsellis [8] and by Roth et al. [9] that there exists a strong positive correlation between the density and the location of neurofibrillary degeneration (NFD) with the severity of neuropsychological impairment observed in senile dementia. At present, it appears that this form of neuropathology may be primarily responsible for the cortical dysfunction in both Alzheimer disease and senile dementia. Indeed, Tomlinson [10] has suggested that 83% of all cases of senile organic brain syndrome may have NFD as their primary neuropathology.

Klatzo et al. [11] observed that subarachnoid injections of aluminum salts in animals produced NFD. This led Crapper et al. [12] to investigate the possibility of this element playing an etiological role in the pathogenesis of the NFD that had been observed in Alzheimer disease by Terry [13].

The atomic absorption study conducted by Crapper et al. [12] on autopsied human NFD and $AL^{+3}$-induced feline NFD showed that both lesions contained a high concentration of aluminum, on the order of 9 to 12 mg/gm. This is in contrast to normal brain tissue that has an average concentration of only 0.23 to 2.70 mg/gm. Indeed, they showed that intracisternal injections of $AlCl_3$, which produce tissue concentrations of $Al^{+3}$ in excess of 12 mg/gm of brain, will cause a profound NFD as well as a slow development of behavioral deficits in both short-term memory and associated learning in their cats.

It is enticing to speculate on the usefulness of aluminum-induced NFD as an animal model for senile dementia. Indeed, the evidence would suggest that such a model might be utilized in the preclinical assessment of agents of putative value in geriatric psychopharmacology. However, in the absence of experimental data on this model of senile dementia, the vasodilator approach may be with us for some time to come.

*Papaverine*

This ancient nonanalgesic and nonaddicting opium alkaloid has been used in senile conditions for decades. The most widely used preparation is Pavabid, a primitive spansule in which layers of drug alternate with layers of shellac in slow-release micropellets. The usual dosage of two 150 mg tablets b.i.d. is remarkably free of side effects. The three available placebo controlled studies show a mild advantage for the drug over placebo, especially in the areas of ameliorating conceptual disorganization, mannerisms, and uncooperativeness [14-16]. The most recent study conducted at Boston State Hospital's Geriatric Psychopharmacology Unit in symptomatic community-resident volunteers showed a little more mood improvement on Pavabid than on placebo [17]. This study, plus two earlier ones [18,19], suggest that Pavabid does in fact alter EEG frequencies in the direction of "normality"; however, this effect has little value if unaccompanied by real clinical improvement.

The fact that papaverine turns out to be a dopamine-blocking agent [17,20] as are the antipsychotic drugs, coupled with the data from the more positive of the studies noted above, makes one wonder if the drug is not serving as a mild neuroleptic in elderly patients.


*Dihydrogenated Ergot Alkaloids*

A preparation containing three dihydrogenated ergot alkaloids in equal amounts is marketed as Hydergine. This drug appears to improve glucose metabolism and oxygen utilization in brain tissue, in addition to increasing blood flow. Seven controlled studies have shown Hydergine to be superior to placebo and two have shown it to be better than papaverine, although the latter drug was used at only 300 mg/day (possibly below minimal effective dose). The problem with these studies is not the lack of difference from placebo but that the areas of superiority vary unsystematically from study to study. The effects are sometimes seen on mood, self-care, somatic symptoms, attitude, appetite, emotional instability, anxiety, and so on. If all studies showed effects on all these target symptoms, the drug might indeed seem wondrous, but the results are spotty. Notably, the areas of clear drug-placebo difference do not include memory and cognition. Further, drug-placebo differences occur very gradually over the three-month period usually employed in these studies. The dosages used were usually either 1.5 mg b.i.d. in US studies, and 1.5 mg t.i.d. in European studies [21].

The drug has no clear side effects. However, it is usually given as a sublingual lozenge, and the cooperation necessary to handle this type of medication may be lacking in demented patients. There appears to be, as yet, no evidence that conventional oral administration would be better or worse than sublingual.

The data on the other presumed vasodilators (cyclandelate, isoxsuprine) are less extensive. For cyclandelate, one controlled study showed improvement in long-term memory and reasoning [22]; our controlled study of isoxsuprine in geriatric symptomatic volunteers was essentially negative [23].

Our attempt to confirm a previous controlled study of naftidrofuryl, which was clearly positive [24], was only partially successful [25]. This left us wondering whether relatively normal elderly subjects with subjective complaints of poor memory and documented deficits in some areas of neuropsychological functioning are sensitive to the effects of these vasodilator drugs.

Anticoagulants have also been claimed to improve brain oxygenation by decreasing blood sludging [26]. The evidence is mainly anecdotal and the potential hazards of this approach lead one to avoid it for the present.

*Hyperbaric Oxygen*

The seductive notion that more oxygen could be pumped into a failing brain by subjecting patients to hyperbaric pressure chambers led to positive findings in an initial controlled study [27]. Other investigators, notably Gerhon's group, have failed to replicate the initial results on several occasions [28,29].

**Stimulants**

Patients with senile dementia, or related conditions, often are withdrawn, apathetic, and inert, as well as having memory and cognitive deficits. For this reason, stimulants of various sorts have been tried for decades in an attempt to energize failing brains. One notable failure in this area has been Alertonic, an alcohol-containing elixir that also includes several vitamins and 2.5 mg of pipradol, an amphetamine-like stimulant. It tasted rather like good sherry and filled a psychic ecological niche—every tired old person needs a tasty, mild tonic. Unfortunately, an extensive program of controlled studies developed by Blackwell failed to demonstrate any clear efficacy for this seductive preparation [30]. However, the idea persists that there should be a good stimulant out there somewhere which will help restore mental activity or at least increase useful activity in the elderly.

*Pentylenetetrazol*

The ancient and honorable drug in this area is pentylenetetrazol (Metrazol), which has been studied in senile conditions since 1953. It reflects dramatically the state of all other geriatric drugs. There are a number of very positive uncontrolled studies reporting that chronically institutionalized impaired patients blossom under the drug and at least 14 controlled studies that are much less impressive. Only two show Metrazol to be clearly superior to placebo [31,32]; five show some modest advantage for Metrazol over placebo [16,33-36]; and seven are pretty clearly negative [37-43]. In the studies that show improvement, it is usually on clinical global ratings or on, for example, total assets on the NOSIE ward behavior scale. It is not shown on psychological test performance. Dosages vary from 100 mg t.i.d. to 300 mg t.i.d. with no clear relationship appearing between dose used and likelihood of clinical improvement. It is interesting to note, however, that one very positive study used 100 mg given six times a day [32]. If the drug is very short-acting, this type of regimen should be superior. Side effects are often more common on Metrazol than on placebo and include nausea and gastric distress, dizzyness, faintness, syncope, and jitteriness. Although Metrazol has been used prior to the advent of electroconvulsive therapy and in much higher intravenous doses to induce grand mal seizures, only three seizures were observed in the 14 studies reviewed. One occurred on placebo; the other two were noted in a study using a regimen of 200 mg q.i.d. [43].

We have recently been involved in a study comparing Metrazol (600-800 mg/day for 12 weeks) with placebo in elderly community volunteers with mild memory complaints. A preliminary analysis shows, as noted above, a modest superiority for Metrazol over placebo on our battery of neuropsychological tests when these data are pooled to form an "impairment index" score. Further, the type and quantity of side effects on Metrazol did not differ significantly from placebo [44].

On balance, in the absence of really effective drugs, pentylenetetrazol may be worth trying occasionally in elderly patients with memory deficit and behavioral problems. There are animal data showing that the drug improves the retention of learned material, at least in mice [45]. The drug seems safe in dosages under 800 mg/day [44]. Frequent small doses might have an advantage. A trial of at least six weeks, if the drug is well tolerated, may be necessary to see if improvement is occurring.

*Amphetamine-like Drugs*

Methylphenidate (Ritalin) has been studied a little in elderly patients, as has magnesium pemoline (Cylert) [46,47]. The latter drug created a burst of interest 15 years ago when it was believed, incorrectly, that it increased brain nucleic acid [48]. It is now marketed for use in hyperkinetic children but may be worth trying as a mild stimulant in elderly patients. Deanol (Deaner) is another marketed antidepressant stimulant which may well act by cholinergic activation in the brain [49]; the other drugs noted above act through adrenergic mechanisms. Gershon's group finds elderly volunteers to be underreactive to methylphenidate [50]. Unfortunately, when they finally show a response to a fairly high dosage (e.g., 40 mg/day) they develop side effects.

We think it may be appropriate to try stimulant drugs cautiously in elderly patients who are underactive and not grossly demented. Since methylphenidate and deanol may have different mechanisms of action, both should be investigated carefully.

The larger question is whether the behavior for which one might prescribe a stimulant is really a form of depression, in which case treatment with a tricyclic antidepressant might be more rational. The patient's cardiac status might be an issue in the decision. Patients with partial heart block should be given tricyclics only with caution and regular electrocardiographic monitoring. Low doses of adrenergic stimulants, though they may cause some rise in pulse rate and blood pressure, probably have less effect on cardiac conditions.

There is a sleeper in our current pharmacopeia. If Robinson is right, and elderly individuals have elevated levels of the enzyme monoamine oxidase (MAO) in their brains [51], the use of an MAO inhibitor such as phenelzine (the one best studied at present) may be rational. The fear of hypertensive crises leading to strokes tends to dampen our enthusiasm for this approach, but we wish somebody else would do the necessary studies to determine efficacy and safety in elderly patients with depression or related symptoms.

**New Approaches**

Four new approaches are worth mentioning at this time:

1. There is some evidence that the enzyme choline acetyletransferase is reduced in the aged [52]. Feeding patients a lot of choline, the precursor of acetylcholine, an approach that appears to be useful in tardive dyskinesia, may not work because of the reduced level of synthetic enzyme. Physostigimine, which acts by reversibly inhibiting acetylcholine esterase, needs study in senile dementia. However, even if it improves cognitive function, it will not do as a treatment because of its short duration of action and the probable need to give it parenterally. A long-acting oral cholinergic drug would need to be developed. It would probably need to be combined with

an anticholinergic drug like methscopolamine that would block peripheral cholinergic side effects while remaining politely outside the blood-brain barrier to allow our imaginary drug to act freely on brain cholinergic centers.

2. The growing interest in polypeptide neurohormones has led to the discovery that a fraction of the large polypeptide adrenocorticotropic hormone (ACTH), namely ACTH 4—10 (the fourth through the tenth amino acids in ACTH) has a marked effect on rat behavior, improving memory and increasing drive [53]. We have studied this drug in elderly volunteers and find a marked improvement in self-reports of mood on the POMS, an adjective check list, and some hint that it may help subjects retrieve previously learned material from their memory store [54]. Unfortunately, the drug can only be given parenterally and has a half-life in the body of about 90 seconds! Organon, the company that developed ACTH 4—10, is working on longer lasting oral analogues. We have recently completed a study on the first of these; at the dose used the results were not impressive [55].

3. Piracetam (Nootropil) is an odd drug created by cyclizing gamma-aminobutyric acid (GABA), a straight-chain compound. The resulting drug does not appear to act like GABA but does protect animals against the behavioral impairments caused by hypoxia and also vertigo [56,57]. Controlled European studies have been positive and make the drug worthy of further study in this country [58,59].

4. A radical treatment approach might be suggested based upon the evidence that chronic accumulation of aluminum in the brain could lead to NFD [60]. If, indeed, aluminum-induced NFD is the primary neuropathology of Alzheimer disease, as well as senile dementia, then pharmacologic intervention with a chelator might be indicated. Most chelating agents exhibit approximately the same order of preference for metals [61]. Since the binding constants for lead and aluminum with calcium disodium edetate are similar, it can be hypothesized that aluminum-induced NFD might be reversed by this agent. While no clinical trials have been conducted, there is a report in the literature of a case of "dialysis dementia" (an aluminum-induced encephalopathy) that failed to respond to treatment with BAL (dimercaprol) [62]. At present, there are not enough data to justify clinical trials; however, animal studies should be conducted to assess the value of this approach.

## Conclusions

The best existing treatment for senile dementia is, unfortunately, the positive diagnosis of some other more-treatment-responsive condition that masquerades as senile dementia. If true senile dementia is clearly present, the best available drug therapies are Hydergine and pentylenetetrazol, with Hydergine having better evidence for efficacy. Neither drug has clinically dramatic effects; both have slow and subtle effects over periods of several weeks.

The most interesting newer drugs include polypeptides with clear memory-improving effects in animals and piracetam, a drug marketed in Europe but not yet available in the United States.

## Commentary

This paper was written to summarize the status of drug therapies for senile dementia as we saw them in 1977. Since that time, I have had the opportunity to review, in more detail, the original studies on Hydergine, the most widely used drug in this area, and I have incorporated new data on cholinergic deficits and cholinergic drugs in Alzheimer disease in a separate paper included in this volume. The area has also been reviewed by Doctors Barry Riesberg and Samuel Gershon [63].

A more detailed examination of the literature on Hydergine reveals that the drug has several possible mechanisms of action [64]. It may improve brain-blood flow. It may improve neuronal "equilibrium." It has alpha-adrenergic blocking properties. It is a mild and atypical dopamine agonist (i.e., it is probably a weak stimulant). At the clinical level, in dosages up to 4.5 mg/day compared to placebo or to papaverine in 16 controlled studies mainly in nursing home patients but two in outpatients, Hydergine is superior to placebo or papaverine on one-sixth to one-half of the clinical symptoms assessed. The pattern of changes varies widely from study to study with such diverse areas as dizziness, self-care, subjective confusion, anxiety, and depression responding sometimes in some studies. Overall, one can make a better case for the drug improving mood than for the drug improving memory dysfunction. Whatever it does, it does it slowly and insidiously with differences from placebo being greater at three months than at one month, but even at three months, the improvement is modest. The drug is now available as an oral, swallowable, tablet as well as a sublingual lozenge.

The company (Sandoz) is conducting a multiunit collaborative study comparing 6 mg/day of the oral tablet with placebo and is attempting to assess Hydergine's effects on memory and cognition. This work may lead to clearer data on the real assets and limitations of Hydergine.

There is also interesting preliminary work on the ability of vasopressin or related polypeptides to improve memory in both senile dementia [65,66] and even in depression [67]. Since these agents are given by nasal spray, their mechanism of action is unclear. It is far too early to tell whether this approach will prove useful clinically.

It is still true, unfortunately, that the best "treatment" for senile dementia is the diagnosis of some other treatable medical or psychiatric condition.

## References

1. Diagnostic and Statistical Manual III (Draft), Task Force on Nomenclature and Statistics. American Psychiatric Association, Washington, D.C., 1977.
2. Katzman R: Normal pressure hydrocephalus. *In* Wells CE (Ed): Dementia. Philadelphia, FA Davis, 1977, Chap 4.
3. Gurland BJ: The comparative frequency of depression in various adult age groups. J Gerontol 31:283-286, 1976.
4. Hagberg B, Ingvar DH: Cognitive reduction in presenile dementia related to regional abnormalities of the cerebral blood flow. Br J Psychiat 128:209-222, 1976.
5. Meier-Ruge W, Enz A, Gygax P, et al: Experimental pathology in basic research of the aging brain. *In* Gershon S, Raskin A (Eds): Aging. New York, Raven Press, 1975, pp 55-126.
6. Hess H, Franke I, Jauch M: Improvement in the fluidity of blood with medication. Fortschr Med 91:743-748, 1973.
7. Obrist WD: Cerebral physiology of the aged. Influence of circulatory disorders. *In* Gaitz CM (Ed): Aging and the Brain. New York, Plenum, 1972, pp 117-133.
8. Corsellis JAN: Mental Illness and the Aging Brain. London, Oxford Univ Press, 1962.
9. Roth M, Tomlinson BE, Blessed G: Correlation between scores for dementia and counts of senile plaques in cerebral gray matter of elderly subjects. Nature (London) 209: 109-110, 1966.
10. Tomlinson BE: Morphological brain changes in non-demented old people. *In* van Praag HM, Kalverboer AF (Eds): Aging of the Central Nervous System. Haarlam, The Netherlands, De Erven and Bohn, 1970, pp 38-57.
11. Klatzo I, Wisniewski H, Streicher E: Experimental production of neurofibrillary degeneration. I. Light microscopic observations. J Neuropath Exp Neurol 24: 187-199, 1965.
12. Crapper DR, Krishman SS, Dalton AJ: Brain aluminum distribution in Alzheimer's disease and experimental neurofibrillary degeneration. Science 180:511-513, 1973.
13. Terry RD: The find structure of neurofibrillary tangles in Alzheimer's disease. J Neuropath Exp Neurol 22:629-642, 1963.
14. Ritter RH, Nail HR, Tatum P, et al: The effect of papaverine on patients with cerebral arteriosclerosis. Clin Med 78:18-22, 1971.

15. Stern FH: Management of chronic brain syndrome secondary to cerebral arteriosclerosis, with special reference to papaverine hydrochloride. J Am Geriat Soc 18:507-512, 1970.

16. Lu L, Stotsky BA, Cole JO: A controlled study of drugs in long-term geriatric psychiatric patients. Arch Gen Psychiat 25:284-288, 1971.

17. Branconnier RJ, Cole JO: Effects of chronic papaverine administration on mild senile organic brain syndrome. J Am Geriat Soc 25:458-462, 1977.

18. McQuillan LM, Lopec CA, Vibal JR; Evaluation of EEG and clinical changes associated with Pavabid therapy in chronic brain syndrome. Curr Ther Res 16:49-58, 1974.

19. Cole JO, Branconnier RJ, Martin GF: Electroencephalographic and behavioral changes associated with papaverine administration in healthy geriatric subjects. J Am Geriat Soc 23:295-300, 1975.

20. Gardos G, Cole JO, Sniffin C: An evaluation of papaverine in tardive dyskinesia. J Clin Pharm 16:304-310, 1976.

21. Shader RI, Goldsmith GN: Dihydrogenated ergot alkaloids and papaverine: A status report on their effects in senile mental deterioration. In Klein D, Gittleman-Klein R (Eds): Progress in Psychiatric Drug Treatment. New York, Brunner-Mazel, 1976, pp 540-554.

22. Smith WL, Lowery JB, Davis JA: The effects of cyclandelate on psychological test performance in patients with cerebral vascular insufficiency. Curr Ther Res 10:613-617, 1968.

23. Branconnier RJ, Cole JO: Unpublished data.

24. Judge TG, Urquhart A: Naftidrofuryl—A double-blind cross-over study in the elderly. Curr Med Res Opinion 1:166-172, 1972.

25. Braconnier RJ, Cole JO: The impairment index as a symptom-independent parameter of drug efficacy in geriatric psychopharmacology. J Gerontol (In press).

26. Walsh AC, Walsh BH: Senile and presenile dementia: Further observations on the benefits of Dicumarol-psychotherapy regimen. J Am Geriat Soc 20:127-131, 1972.

27. Jacobs EA, Winter PM, Alvis HJ, et al: Hyperoxygenation effect on cognitive function in the aged. N Eng J Med 281:753-757, 1969.

28. Raskin A, Gershon S, Crook TH, et al: Tables for the effects of hyper- and normobaric oxygen on cognitive impairment in the elderly. Presented at the Annual Meeting of The American College of Neuropsychopharmacology, San Juan, Puerto Rico, December 11, 1975.

29. Goldfarb AI, Hochstadt NJ, Jacobson JH, et al: Hyperbaric oxygen treatment of organic mental syndrome in aged persons. J Gerontol 27:212-217, 1972.

30. Blackwell B: Personal communication.

31. Lapinsohn LI: Metrazol or glutamic acid in treating certain mental disorders. Penn Med J 58:42-44, 1955.

32. Linden ME, Courtney D, Howland AO: Interdisciplinary research in the use of oral pentylenetetrazol (Metrazol) in the emotional disorders of the aged. Studies in gerontologic human relations. V. J AM Geriat Soc 4:380-399, 1956.

33. Leckman J, Anath JV, Ban TA, et al: Pentylenetetrazol in the treatment of geriatric patients with disturbed memory function. J Clin Pharmacol 11:301-303, 1971.

34. Stotsky BA, Cole JO, Lu L, et al: A controlled study of the efficacy of pentylenetetrazol (Metrazol) with hard-core hospitalized psychogeriatric patients. Am J Psychiat 129:47-51, 1972.

35. Mead S, Mueller EE, Mason EP, et al: A study of the effects of oral administration of Metrazol (R) in old individuals. J Gerontol 8:472-476, 1953.

36. Swenson WM, Grimes BP: Oral use of Metrazol in senile patients. Geriatrics 8:99-101, 1953.

37. Swenson WM, Anderson DE, Grimes BP: A re-evaluation of the oral use of Metrazol in senile patients. J Gerontol 12:401-403, 1957.

38. Sheard MH, Coyne E, Hammons P: A trial of oral pentamethylenetetrazol in senile patients. Quart Rev Psychiat Neurol 20:34-37, 1959.

39. Gericke OL, Lobb LG: Effect of Metrazol on the memory of the aged. Psychiat Studies Projects 2:2-7, 1964.

40. Ananth JV, Deutsch M, Ban TA: Senilex in the treatment of geriatric patients. Curr Ther Res 13:316-321, 1971.

41. Williams JR, Csalany L, Misevic G: Drug therapy with or without group discussion: Effects of various regimens on the behavior of geriatric patients in a mental hospital. J Am Geriat Soc 15:34-40, 1967.

42. Barrabee P, Wingate JH, Phillips BD, et al: Effects of L-Glutavite compared with Metrazol and vitamins on aged female psychotic patients. Postgrad Med 19:485-491, 1956.

43. Robinson DB: Evaluation of certain drugs in geriatric patients. Arch Gen Psychiat 1:41-46, 1959.

44. Branconnier RJ, Cole JO: Unpublished data.

45. Krivanek J, McGaugh JL: Effects of pentylenetetrazol on memory storage in mice. Psychopharmacologia 12:303-321, 1968.

46. Raskind M, Eisdorfer C: Psychopharmacology of the aged. *In* Simpson LL (Ed): Drug Treatment of Mental Disorders. New York, Raven Press, 1976, pp 237-266.

47. Connors CK (Ed): Clinical Use of Stimulant Drugs in Children. The Hague, Excerpta Medica, 1974.

48. Plotnikoff N: Learning and memory enhancement by pemoline and magnesium hydroxide. Recent Adv Biol Psychiat 10:102-120, 1968.

49. Re O: 2-Dimethylaminoethanol (Deanol): A brief review of its clinical efficacy and postulated mechanism of action. Curr Ther Res 16:1238-1242, 1974.

50. Crook T, Ferris G, Sathananthan G, et al: The effect of methylphenidate on test performance in the cognitively impaired elderly. Psychopharmacologia 52:251-255, 1977.

51. Robinson DS: Changes in monoamine oxidase and monoamines with human development and aging. Fed Proc 34:103-107, 1975.

52. Signorelli A: Influence of physostigmine upon consolidation of memory in mice. J Compar Physiol Psychol 90:658-664, 1976.

53. Flood JF, Jarvik ME: Effects of ACTH peptide fragments on memory formation. The neuropeptides. Pharmacol Biochem Behav 5:41-51, 1976.

54. Branconnier RJ, Cole JO, Gardos G: ACTH 4—10 in the amelioration of symptomatology associated with mild senile organic brain syndrome. Paper presented at the Annual New Clinical Drug Evaluation Unit Program, Key Biscayne, Florida, May 19-21, 1977.

55. Branconnier RJ, Cole JO: Unpublished data.

56. Piracetam, basic scientific and clinical data. UCB-Pharmaceutical Division, Brussels, Belgium, 1974, pp 40-41.

57. Giurgea CE, Moyersoons F, Evraerd ACA: GABA related hypothesis on the mechanism of action of the antimotion sickness drugs. Arch Intern Pharmacodyn Therap 166:238-251, 1967.

58. Stegink AJ: The clinical use of Piracetam, a new nootropic drug. The treatment of symptoms of senile involution. Arzneim-Forsch (Drug Res) 22:975-977, 1972.

59. Mindus P, Cronholm B, Levander S, et al: Effects of piracetam on anxiety and mental performance in middle-aged healthy volunteers. Paper presented at VII European Congress of Clinical Gerontology, September 1974.

60. Crapper DR, Krishnan SS, Quittkat S: Aluminum, neurofibrillary degeneration and Alzheimer's disease. Brain 99:67-80, 1976.

61. Albert A: Selective Toxicity, the Physico-Chemical Basis of Therapy. London, Chapman & Hall, 1973, p 350.

62. Mahurkar SD, Dhar SK, Salta R, et al: Dialysis dementia. Lancet 1:1412-1415, 1973.

63. Riesberg B, Gershon, S. _____ In Cole JO, Barrett J (Eds): Psychology and aging. Raven Press. In press.

64. Cole JO: Drug therapy of senile organic brain syndromes. Psychiatric J of the Univ of Ottawa. In press.

65. Oliveros JC, Jandali MK, Timsit-Berthier M, et al: Vasopressin in amnesia. Lancet 1(8054):42, 1978.

66. Legros JJ, Gilot P, Seron X, et al: Influence of vasopressin on learning and memory. Lancet 1(8054):41-42, 1978.

67. Gold P, Weingartner H, Ballenger J, Goodwin K, Post R: Effects of 1-desamo-8-d-arginine vasopressin on behavior and cognition in primary affective disorder. Lancet ii:992-994, 1979.

# 8

# Lecithin and Choline in Alzheimer Disease

*Jonathan O. Cole, M.D.*

Alzheimer disease in the elderly appears to be essentially identical with senile dementia [1]. It is characterized neuropathologically by the presence of excessive numbers of senile plaques and neurofibrillary tangles. Their concentration in the cerebral cortex correlates well with the degree of dementia present prior to death [2]. Younger patients (ages 45 to 65) with a similar progressive dementia show the same pathological findings and are usually diagnosed as having presenile dementia. The two conditions seem to share a common basis but differ chiefly in age of onset. They are both usually called Alzheimer disease. The younger patients may show a more rapid and extensive deterioration. Senile dementia is much more common than vascular (multi-infarct) dementia in those elderly patients who suffer from a clear and progressive organic brain dysfunction without other diagnosable causes [3].

Although the diagnosis of Alzheimer disease is usually made by exclusion, as the current diagnostic criteria in *DSM-III* clearly state [4], the clinical diagnosis is often confirmed at autopsy and occasionally by brain biopsy during life. To date, the clear neuropathological changes have not been therapeutically relevant; existing standard and research drug therapies have been related to either putatative changes in brain blood flow, metabolism, or to nonspecific stimulant effects. One suspects that the generally weak effects shown by the currently available marketed drugs (e.g. Hydergine, papaverine, pentylenetetrazol, methylphenidate) or newer investigational drugs are as likely to be attributed to their mild antidepressant or antianxiety actions as to any specific effect on the neuropathology of senile dementia [5,6]. Certainly, vasodilation seems an unlikely way to affect brain function in this condition. Until recently, the only quasirational approach to Alzheimer disease would have to be based on preliminary data suggesting that aluminum ion caused a similar neuropathology in experimental animals and that human neurofibrillary tangles were rich in aluminum. The use of chelating agents to leach aluminum out of the brain might be rational but, to my knowledge, has never been tried. Fortunately, or unfortunately, more recent studies of aluminum levels in the brains of patients with Alzheimer disease have been negative [7].

In the last four years, however, there has been a breakthrough in our understanding of the biochemistry of Alzheimer disease, which is even more clearly conducive to the development of rational therapies. Seven studies have all found marked reductions in choline acetyltransferase (CAT) levels in the cortex of patients with Alzheimer disease; this enzyme catalyzes the conversion of choline to acetylcholine in the neuron.

Bowen et al., in a most detailed and rigorous study, identified a 50% decrease in CAT levels in the parietal cortex of senile dementia patients compared with aged normal controls [8]. Davies and Maloney confirmed this and found a concomitant fall in the activity of the acetylcholine-destroying enzyme, acetylcholinesterase [9], which suggests, but by no means proves, the loss of cholinergic neurons, while Perry et al. discerned a normal level of muscarinic acetylcholine receptors, suggesting that the postsynaptic cholinoceptive cells are intact [10].

Spillane et al. found a two-thirds reduction of cortical CAT activity both in autopsy material and in brain biopsy material. Tissue from a single biopsy was used to study choline uptake into the cells and this also was markedly reduced [11]. Bowen et al. also studied both necropsy and biopsy materials and identified a 65% reduction of CAT activity in autopsy tissue and a 54% reduction in biopsy specimens [12]. The White et al. report is an earlier study by the same group with similar findings in a smaller group of necropsy samples [13]. Reisine et al. reported a comparable two-thirds reduction in a small sample of patients with Alzheimer disease compared with control subjects [14]. A variety of other brain enzyme levels have been measured in several of these studies without any other abnormality of comparable magnitude being observed [8,12-14]. Four of the studies assessed the levels of cholinergic (muscarinic) receptors in Alzheimer disease and control patients and determined these to be normal in amount [10,12-14]. Since all of these studies used age-matched controls, the CAT reduction appears to be relatively disease-specific, although some studies saw similar reductions in demented elderly subjects with some admixture of vascular brain disease. Three studies disagree somewhat as to the restriction of CAT reduction to the cortex, two finding slightly reduced [9,10] and the other markedly reduced [14] levels of CAT in the caudate nucleus. The hippocampus was reported in two studies to show low CAT levels in senile dementia [9,14].

Since there is no direct method for identifying individual cholinergic neurons as yet, it is impossible to say whether lowered CAT levels are caused by the death of cholinergic neurons, by reduced levels of enzyme in remaining cells, or by both. Although neuronal loss has been assumed to occur in Alzheimer disease to a greater extent than in normal aging, this presumption has not been fully validated [15] and may, in fact, be incorrect [3,16].

The changes in CAT found in Alzheimer disease are at least as impressive as the changes in gamma-aminobutyric acid enzymes found in Huntington chorea. Some patients with the latter condition also show a loss of both CAT *and* muscarine receptors [17].

The observations that acetylcholine synthesis and, presumably, cholinergic neuronal activity are reduced in senile dementia fit well with Drachman's evidence that the specific neuropsychological deficits in these patients closely resemble those produced by the anticholinergic drug, scopolamine, in normal younger subjects [18]. Other controlled studies of the effects of scopolamine in normal volunteers have shown impairment in the registration and recall of new information [19,20].

**How to Increase CNS Cholinergic Activity**

Most marketed cholinergic drugs, such as bethanechol or neostigmine, do not pass the blood-brain barrier and, therefore, are of no potential value in Alzheimer disease. Physostigmine, a short-acting drug, usually given parenterally, *does* enter the brain and is used to reverse anticholinergic delirium [21]. It acts by blocking acetylcholinesterase (ACE), the enzyme that deactivates acetylcholine by converting it to choline. Although it might be useful in senile dementia, it would only be helpful if enough acetylcholine is being synthesized by CAT in the neuron to make blocking its destruction useful. Further, physostigmine causes peripheral cholinergic effects such as bradycardia, vomiting, salivation, diarrhea, and abdominal cramps. When given to patients, a peripheral anticholinergic drug must also be given to block these unpleasant and, in the elderly, potentially serious side effects [22]. In the past, methylscopolamine has been used as the peripheral blocker but is no longer commercially available. Propantheline (Probanthine) and glycopyrrholate (Robinul) are possible alternative peripheral anticholinergic drugs. Another possible central-acting cholinergic drug is arecoline, a chemical found in the betel nut and possibly its active principle [20]. This appears to be a direct cholinergic agonist and might be effective even when neuronal acetylcholine is absent.

The other, indirect precursor, approach to increasing brain acetylcholine has been studied most extensively by Growdon, Wurtman, and their associates. They have shown that both choline [23] and lecithin [24,25] given orally to experimental animals can cause a doubling of brain acetylcholine levels. They have indirect evidence that this rise is accompanied by increased cholinergic activity as inferred from secondary increases in tyrosine hydroxylase in the caudate nucleus, an effect that could be blocked by atropine, an anticholinergic drug. Similar changes are observed in the adrenal medulla [26].

The major source of dietary choline is lecithin (phosphatidylcholine) in foods such as eggs, meat, wheat germ, butter or margarine. In phosphatidylcholine, the phosphacholine is bound to glycerol and two fatty acids. It is absorbed into the intestinal wall from the gut as lysolecithin, one of lecithin's two fatty-acid molecules being split off in the intestine. In the gut wall, two molecules of lysolecithin become one molecule of phosphatidylcholine with two fatty acids and one molecule of glycerol phosphorylcholine with none. The phosphorylcholine goes into the plasma and is re-excreted into the gut in the bile bound to bile salts. The phosphatidylcholine goes into the lymph and causes a slow, gradual rise in plasma phosphatidylcholine levels after a single large dose of oral lecithin. After oral choline, plasma choline levels rise rapidly [27]. In either situation, either phosphatidylcholine or free choline can pass the blood-brain barrier and become available to cholinergic neurons. Other sources of choline for the brain can come from the liver, which can synthesize choline from other organic compounds and from acetylcholine released from the nerve synapses in the brain and hydrolyzed to choline by ACE. The brain itself does not synthesize choline.

The situation is complicated by the fact that neurons have two ways of taking in choline [28]. There is a high-affinity system at the synapses, which are near saturation at ordinary plasma choline levels, and a low-affinity system in the cell bodies, which is not saturated at normal choline levels. When either choline or lecithin are fed in large amounts, the low-affinity system pulls more choline into the cells where it is synthesized into acetylcholine by the enzyme CAT. This process also requires acetylcoenzyme A (acetyl-CoA) derived from glucose via pyruvate, a system that needs both thiamine and adequate plasma glucose levels.

Of the two methods of raising brain acetylcholine levels, choline has the advantage of specificity and rapidity. Its disadvantages include choline's bitter taste and metabolism in the intestine to trimethylamine, a substance that causes subjects to emit a foul dead-fish odor. It may also be more likely to cause abdominal distress, nausea, and diarrhea than is lecithin, though both substances can do this. There is also the possibility that choline itself may have direct effects on brain cholinergic receptors [29,30]. Lecithin, on the other hand, does not cause foul body odor but is a more complex substance.

Lecithin of the type sold in health food stores contains only about 20% to 25% phosphatidylcholine mixed with a variable array of other fatty substances. If 50 to 100 gm/day is an effective dose of this type of lecithin for doubling plasma choline levels (mostly as phosphatidylcholine), then the eight calories per gram of the mixed substance can be a large calorie load [27]. Even if "pure" phosphatidylcholine were readily available, which is not the case, the specific fatty acids incorporated in the larger molecule are variable. Thus, lecithin *could* have effects due to the presence of essential fatty acids or other unknown constituents.

### Clinical Applications

Increasing brain acetylcholine is of theoretical interest in a number of psychiatric and neurological conditions, including tardive dyskinesia, Huntington chorea, and mania, as well as senile or presenile dementia. In the first three conditions, the abnormal state is believed to be due to dopaminergic overactivity (absolute or relative) in the brain; raising brain acetylcholine might improve the condition by correcting the balance between cholinergic and dopaminergic systems in the brain [31]. In Huntington disease there is also evidence that some, but not all, patients show a decrease in CAT in the basal ganglia [17]. Although large numbers of patients have not been treated with either choline or lecithin for any of the above conditions, a double-blind study has shown 10 gm/day of choline to be more effective than placebo in reducing dyskinetic movements in chronic psychotic inpatients [32]. A few cases of tardive dyskinesia, Huntington chorea, and mania have also been reported to improve on choline [33]. More recently, Growdon's group has used lecithin (about 20% phosphatidylcholine) in a few cases of tardive dyskinesia with good results at dosages up to 100 gm/day for about three months [34]. Lecithin appears to be free of choline's tendency to make patients smell like dead fish and may have fewer gastrointestinal cholinergic side effects as well.

Since both lecithin and choline have been shown to raise brain acetylcholine levels in experimental animals, it seems reasonable to assume that lecithin is the more acceptable agent for use in man. It should be noted that the Palo Alto group (K. Davis) feels strongly that choline, as the only available pure substance, deserves priority in studies because results obtained could be more clearly interpretable [35].

To date, we are aware of only three studies of choline in senile dementia and two of lecithin—one unpublished—in presenile dementia.

Smith et al., in London, did a crossover study (two weeks of choline bitartrate at 9 gm/day, one week washout, two weeks placebo) in 10 patients with senile dementia (mean age: 77) [36]. Three patients seemed less confused after two weeks on choline, while three others showed increased urinary incontinence. Gastrointestinal discomfort occurred in some patients. No statistically significant changes were seen in a battery of cognitive and memory tests, perhaps because of the short duration of study treatment.

In Edinburgh, Boyd et al. treated seven elderly patients with choline (5 gm/day for two weeks, then 10 gm/day for two weeks) [37]. Again, clinical observers believed the patients became less irritable and more aware of their surroundings, but the cognitive and behavioral measures used did not detect any clear changes. The higher dosage caused nausea and diarrhea. Two patients were improved on testing, particularly in the first 24 hours of the trial.

Signoret et al. treated eight patients with Alzheimer disease (ages 59 to 78) with choline citrate (9 gm/day for 21 days) [38]. The presentation of the results defies understanding, but, apparently, a few "younger" patients with shorter duration of illness showed some improvement on memory tests as did some relatives of patients who seem also to have been given choline.

Etienne et al. treated seven outpatients with Alzheimer disease of less than three years' duration with lecithin (Centrolex F 3.7 gm choline/100 gm lecithin) in dosages beginning with 25 gm/day, increasing by 25 gm/day every week for four weeks [39]. Plasma choline levels were increased from about 11 nmol/ml to 36 nmol/ml. Three patients showed some improvement on paired associate learning; two of these showed improved visual retention. No changes occurred on immediate or remote memory or constructional ability. Some digestive side effects were noted but no foul odor, depression, or cholinergic toxicity. The average tolerated lecithin dose was about 75 gm/day.

At a recent meeting, Christie reported on the use of lecithin (20% to 30% phosphatidylcholine) at 100 gm/day in 11 patients with presenile dementia (average age 60, average duration of illness 3.8 years) [40]. Patients received choline up to 5 gm/day for five days before going on lecithin. The least-impaired and the seven most-impaired patients showed no change, but the three intermediate patients improved on orientation, speech, and dyspraxia. One patient became more irritable on choline, and, in general, choline slightly worsened ward behavior, while lecithin slightly improved ward behavior. One patient has now been maintained on lecithin for a year with no further deterioration.

In general, the available studies suffer from small sample size and short duration of treatment. They show suggestive changes. Some patients with senile or presenile dementia may respond to choline or lecithin with mild degrees of improvement, which may be more apparent in general social functioning than on discrete memory tasks, although both may improve. Lecithin seems reasonably well tolerated, although high doses may cause anorexia and gastrointestinal discomfort. The foul odor caused by choline does not seem to occur. Depression, which has been reported to occur occasionally with choline use in tardive dyskinesia, has not been reported in senile dementia patients on lecithin or choline to date.

There is also some evidence that cholinergic drugs may improve memory generally. There is one study of a patient with a memory defect caused by herpes simplex encephalitis who was given several doses of physostigmine in a double-blind trial [41]. An "impressive" gain on a selective reminding memory test was observed on 0.8 mg of physostigmine given subcutaneously but not after higher or lower doses. The authors felt the data suggested a drug effect on both memory storage and retrieval. The patient seemed calmer and more goal-directed during testing on the proper physostigmine dose.

Smith and Swash studied repeated single doses of 1 mg physostigmine given subcutaneously to a 42-year-old man with early presenile dementia [42]. Compared with placebo, the physostigmine did not improve positive verbal memory but did significantly decrease inappropriate responses on the tests. The patient's brain, on cortical biopsy, showed only 23% of the amount of CAT found in normal brains.

Davis et al. studied the effects of a one-hour intravenous infusion of 1 mg physostigmine on memory in normal volunteers, using a double-blind crossover design with a saline placebo control [22]. Physostigmine had no effect on short-term memory and only a suggestive effect on retrieval of words learned before drug administration. However, both learning and retrieval were improved by physostigmine on a word list learned after half the drug had been given.

Sitaram et al. studied the effects of arecoline (4 mg) and scopolamine (0.5 mg) on the number of times needed to learn 10 words from a familiar category (e.g. vegetables) [19]. Arecoline (with possible peripheral side effects blocked by methscopolamine 0.3 mg) improved learning and memory, and scopolamine impaired them relative to placebo. Arecoline, at 6 mg intramuscularly, reversed the effects of scopolamine on learning and memory. A single 10 gm oral dose of choline chloride was also compared with placebo in normal subjects on the number of times needed to learn lists of 10 uncategorized words. Choline improved performance significantly. Subjects who performed initially less well on these learning tasks, in either study, showed significantly larger drug effects with all three drugs tested. Davis et al. report a similar trend in their physostigmine study [35].

## Conclusion

Thus, there are suggestions in the available literature that cholinergic drugs at a proper dose may improve retention and recall in both normal and organically impaired subjects on tasks where there is room for improvement. It may be possible to improve psychological functioning in the elderly with cholinergic agents, even if the basic defect in senile dementia is not a loss of cholinergic function in the central nervous system. If the elderly in general, and senile dementias in particular, have a major loss in presynaptic cholinergic neurons or in the enzyme necessary to synthesize acetylcholine, then drugs like choline and lecithin—which require, presumably, conversion into acetylcholine intracellularly—as well as drugs like physostigmine—which block the destuction of synthesized acetylcholine at the synapse—should be more effective in patients showing lesser degrees of cholinergic cell or enzyme loss. If, in more severe degrees of dementia, cholinergic neurons are lost but postsynaptic receptors are intact, direct cholinergic agonists, such as arecoline, might be more effective. There is also a suggestion that dose may be a crucial issue; too low a dose should be ineffective, while too high a dose might both cause cholinergic side effects and interfere with learning or memory.

One word of caution is necessary. Cholinergic synapses abound in the brain, and probably are involved in a variety of functions. Karczmar's review [30] suggests that increasing cholinergic activity in the brain could equally well elicit aggression, tremor, eating behavior, temperature alterations, or sexual activity, as well as improved memory. Nevertheless, the data to date are promising enough to warrant further clinical studies in senile dementia, a serious disease currently lacking any useful or rational therapies.

## Commentary

This paper grew out of our excellent conference on the subject held in December, 1978. Material from the conference is now available in book form [43].

Since the paper was written, work has continued at several centers on cholinergic drugs and Alzheimer disease. From discussions with investigators at meetings, my impression is that choline alone has not proven useful at one center, while preliminary work with lecithin at another center may be more promising. Intravenous physostigmine at a proper dose, probably somewhere between 0.25 and 0.50 mg improves memory performance for an hour or two in most Alzheimer patients, higher as well as lower doses being ineffective. To my knowledge no direct cholinergic agonists (which should not depend on the brain's ability to synthesize acetylcholine) have been studied in senile dementia to date. It is still too early to tell whether the interesting research reports summarized in my paper will or will not lead to any useful therapy for Alzheimer disease.

## References

1. Constantinidis J.: Is Alzheimer's disease a major form of senile dementia? Clinical, anatomical, and genetic data. *In* Katzman R, Terry R, Bick K (Eds): Alzheimer's Disease: Senile Dementia and Related Disorders. Vol 7. New York, Raven, 1978, pp 15-25.

2. Blessed G, Tomlinson B, Roth M: The association between quantitative measures of dementia and of senile change in the cerebral grey matter of elderly subjects. Br J Psychiat 114:797-811, 1968.

3. Terry R: Aging senile dementia and Alzheimer's disease. *In* Katzman R, Terry R, Bick K (Eds): Alzheimer's Disease: Senile Dementia and Related Disorders. Vol 7. New York, Raven, 1978, pp 11-14.

4. Diagnostic and Statistical Manual III (Draft), Task Force on Nomenclature and Statistics. Washington, D.C., American Psychiatric Association, 1977.

5. Cole JO, Branconnier R: Drugs and senile dementia. McLean Hosp J 2:210-221, 1977.

6. Cole JO: Drug therapy of senile-organic brain syndromes. Psychiat J Univ Ottawa (in press).

7. Crapper D, Karlik S, DeBoni U: Aluminums and other metals in senile (Alzheimer) dementia. *In* Katzman R, Terry R, Bick K (Eds.): Alzheimer's Disease: Senile Dementia and Related Disorders. Vol 7. New York, Raven, 1978, pp 471-491.

8. Bowen DM, Smith CB, White P, et al: Neurotransmitter-related enzymes and indices of hypoxia in senile dementia and other abiotrophies. Brain 99:459-496, 1976.

9. Davies P, Maloney AJF: Selective loss of central cholinergic neurons in Alzheimer's desease. Lancet 2:1403, 1976.

10. Perry KK, Perry RH, Blessed G, et al: Necropsy evidence of central cholinergic deficits in senile dementia. Lancet 1:189, 1977.

11. Spillane JA, White P, Goodhardt MJ, et al: Selective vulnerability of neurones in organic dementia. Nature 7:558-559, 1977.

12. Bowen DM, Spillane JA, Curzon G, et al: Accelerated aging or selective neuronal loss as an important cause of dementia? Lancet 1:11-14, 1979.

13. White P, Hiley CR, Goodhardt MJ, et al: Neocortical cholinergic neurons in elderly people. Lancet 1:668-671, 1977.

14. Reisine TD, Yamamura HI, Bird ED, et al: Pre- and post-synaptic neurochemical alterations in Alzheimer's disease. Brain Res 159:477-481, 1977.

15. Tomlinson B: Morphological changes and dementia in old age. *In* Smith L., Kinsbourne M. (Eds): Aging and Dementia. New York, Spectrum, 1977, pp 25-56.

16. Terry R: Discussion. *In* Katzman R, Terry R, Bick K (Eds): Alzheimer's Disease: Senile Dementia and Related Disorders. Vol 7. New York, Raven, 1978, pp 396-399.

17. Bird ED: The brain in Huntington's chorea. Psychol Med 8:357-360, 1978.

18. Drachman D: Central cholinergic system and memory. *In* Lipton M., DiMascio A, Killan K (Eds): Psychopharmacology: A Generation of Progress. New York, Raven, 1978, pp 651-662.

19. Safer D, Allen R: The central effects of scopolamine in man. Biol Psychiat 3:347-355, 1971.

20. Sitaram N, Weingartner H, Gillin JC: Human serial learning: Enhancement with arecoline and choline and impairment with scopolamine. Science 201:274-276, 1977.

21. Granacher R, Baldessarini R: Physostigmine. Arch Gen Psychiat 32:375-380, 1975.

22. Davis K, Mohs R, Tinklenberg J, et al: Physostigmine: Improvement of long-term memory processes in normal humans. Science 201:272-274, 1978.

23. Cohen EL, Wurtman RJ: Brain acetylcholine: Control by dietary choline. Science 191:561-562, 1976.

24. Hirsch MJ, Wurtman RJ: Lecithin consumption elevates acetylcholine concentrations in rat brain and adrenal gland. Science 202:223-225, 1978.

25. Wurtman RJ, Hirsch MJ, Growdon JH: Lecithin consumption raises serum-free-choline levels. Lancet 1:68-69, 1977.

26. Ulus IH, Hirsch, MJ, Wurtman RJ: Trans-synaptic induction of adrenomedullary tyrosine hydroxylase activity by choline: Evidence that choline administration increases cholinergic transmission. Proc Nat Acad Sci 74:788-790, 1977.

27. Wurtman RJ: Sources of choline and lecithin in the diet. *In* Growdon J, Wurtman RJ, Barbeau A (Eds): Uses of Choline and Lecithin in Neurological and Psychiatric Disorders. New York, Raven, 1979 (in press).

28. Jenden D: An overview of choline and acetylcholine metabolism in relation to the therapeutic uses of choline. *In* Growdon J, Wurtman RJ, Barbeau A, (Eds): Uses of Choline and Lecithin in Neurological and Psychiatric Disorders. New York, Raven, 1979 (in press).

29. Karczmar A: Overview: Cholinergic drugs and behavior—What effects may be expected from a "cholinergic diet?" *In* Growdon J, Wurtman RJ, Barbeau A (Eds): Uses of Choline and Lecithin in Neurological and Psychiatric Disorders. New York, Raven, 1979 (in press).

30. Karczmar A, Dun N.: Cholinergic synapses: Physiological, pharmacological and behavioral correlates. *In* Lipton M, DiMascio A, Killam K (Eds): Psychopharmacology: A Generation of Progress. New York, Raven, 1978, pp 293-305.

31. Jenden D: The neurochemical basis of acetylcholine precursor loading as a therapeutic strategy. *In* Davis K, Berger P (Eds): Brain Acetylcholine and Neuropsychiatric Disease. New York, Plenum, 1978.

32. Growdon J, Hirsch M, Wurtman RJ, et al: Oral choline administration to patients with tardive dyskinesia. New Eng J Med 297:524-527, 1977.

33. Tamminga C: Choline and lecithin in affective illness. *In* Growdon J, Wurtman RJ, Barbeau A (Eds): Uses of Choline and Lecithin in Neurological and Psychiatric Disorders. New York, Raven, 1979 (in press).

34. Growdon J, Gelenberg A, Doller J, et al: Lecithin can suppress tardive dyskinesia. New Eng J Med 298:1029-1030, 1978.

35. Davis K: Clinical and preclinical experience with choline chloride in Huntington's disease and tardive dyskinesia. Paper presented at the Symposium on the Uses of Choline and Lecithin in Neurologic and Psychiatric Diseases, Tucson, Arizona, December 4-6, 1978.

36. Smith C, Swash M, Exton-Smith A, et al: Choline therapy in Alzheimer's disease. Lancet 2:318, 1978.

37. Boyd W, Graham-White J, Blackwood G, et al: Clinical effects of choline in Alzheimer senile dementia. Lancet 2:711, 1977.

38. Signoret J, Whiteley A, Lhermitte F: Influence of choline on amnesia in early Alzheimer's disease. Lancet 2:837, 1978.

39. Etienne P, Gauthier S, Dastoor D, et al: Lecithin in Alzheimer's disease. Lancet 2:1206, 1978.

40. Christie J: Effects of choline and lecithin administration to patients with Alzheimer's disease. Paper presented at Symposium on the Uses of Choline and Lecithin in Neurologic and Psychiatric Diseases, Tucson, Arizona, December 4-6, 1978.

41. Peters B, Levin H: Memory enhancement after physostigmine treatment in the amnestic syndrome. Arch Neurol 34:215-219, 1977.

42. Smith C, Swash M: Physostigmine in Alzheimer's disease. Lancet 1:42, 1979.

43. Barbeau A, Growdon J, Wurtman R (Eds): Choline and Lecithin in Brain Disorders. New York, Raven, 1979.

# L-Tryptophan: Clinical Studies

*Jonathan O. Cole, M.D.*
*Ernest Hartmann, M.D.*
*Peter Brigham, M.D.*

L-Tryptophan (TP), an essential amino acid that has been the subject of clinical psychiatric research for almost 20 years, has been reported to be useful in depression, mania, schizophrenia, obsessive-compulsive disorders, and insomnia, generally when used in amounts in excess of the usual human dietary intake (about 1 gm/day).

Since TP is readily available both as a dietary supplement in health food stores and as a prescription drug, it can be used as a psychopharmacological therapy or as a self-medication, even though it has not been approved by the Food and Drug Administration (FDA) for use in any psychiatric condition. It is not available as a drug in the United States, although some drugstores carry it as a dietary supplement. It is, however, available in England for use in depression. The purpose of this paper is to review the available evidence on the utility of TP as a psychoactive drug, either alone or in combination with other agents.

It should be noted that the legal status of physicians in the United States using available medications for indications not approved by the FDA is equivocal. Physicians are generally given the prerogative to use whatever treatments seem clinically indicated to help their patients, and the FDA does not usually interfere in this aspect of the practice of medicine. On the other hand, if a physician uses a drug for a nonapproved indication he may be in a weak position if a malpractice suit ensues. If a drug such as TP will be used frequently or systematically in the treatment of a particular type of psychiatric patient, the physicians would be well advised to file a formal research protocol with the FDA and obtain an Investigational New Drug number. This is a relatively simple procedure which brings with it FDA sanction for the use of drugs such as TP under the specific conditions proposed.

L-Tryptophan is readily absorbed in the intestine. It is carried in the plasma in both free and bound forms. Ordinarily, 10% to 20% is in free form, the rest is bound to serum albumin at sites shared competitively with free fatty acids and certain drugs, such as salicylates, benzodiazepines, chlorpromazine, and diphenylhydantoin. L-Tryptophan crosses the blood-brain barrier into the central nervous system readily, but the transport is

119

shared with other large neutral amino acids (mainly leucine, isoleucine, phenylalanine, tyrosine, and valine). The effect of this is that TP given alone elevates both plasma TP and brain serotonin. However, an equal amount of TP given with large amounts of other large neutral amino acids does not increase brain serotonin because the other amino acids are shunted into the brain preferentially. The transport mechanism that carries TP across the blood-brain barrier handles all six amino acids, and they compete with each other for transports. Thus, the relative amounts of TP, compared with the levels of the other amino acids, have more effect on brain levels of TP than does the proportion of free (or total) TP in the plasma. Because carbohydrate feedings cause insulin release, which in turn lowers plasma-free fatty acids and frees more albumin sites to bind TP, carbohydrate feedings increase total plasma tryptophan and, as a result, brain tryptophan; protein feedings that contain only modest amounts of TP and large amounts of the other neutral amino acids in fact decrease brain tryptophan.

All this is of more than academic interest because TP is the main precursor of an important brain amine, 5-hydroxytryptamine (serotonin), and TP administration leads to rapid increases of brain serotonin.

In the brain, TP is converted by the enzyme tryptophan hydroxylase to 5-hydroxtryptophan (5-HTP); 5-HTP is then converted to serotonin by the enzyme-aromatic amino acid decarboxylase. Although it might appear that administering 5-HTP, the more immediate precursor, would be a more efficient way to increase brain serotonin, the presence of aromatic amino acid decarboxylase is widespread in nonserotonergic neurons, making it likely that the serotonin produced after 5-HTP administration may activate a much wider range of synapses and have more complicated effects. TP has the advantage that tryptophan hydroxylase occurs only in serotonergic neurons, making the serotonin increase elicited by TP administration more "physiological" and more likely to specifically rectify the serotonin deficiency believed to be present in some depressions and other conditions.

TP is chiefly metabolized by the liver enzyme tryptophan pyrrolase. This enzyme is induced by TP administration and also by cortisol. Tryptophan pyrrolase activity is reduced both by allopurinol, a drug used to treat gout, and by nicotinic acid or nicotinamide (vitamin $B_3$). The enzymes that convert TP to serotonin require pyridoxine (vitamin $B_6$) and ascorbic acid (vitamin C) to form coenzymes. These facts have served to complicate clinical studies of TP use, since pyridoxine and ascorbic acid are often added to facilitate serotonin synthesis or other substances (e.g. nicotinic acid, allopurinol, or decarboxylase inhibitors) are added to decrease peripheral destruction of the tryptophan. The magnitude and importance of these effects are a bit unclear. For more extensive reviews of the whole matter, the recent detailed review by Young and Sourkes is recommended [1], as is a recent book, *Nutrition and the Brain*, which contains excellent chapters on neurotransmitter precursors in the diet by Growdon [2], on vitamin therapy and the brain by Lipton [3], and on nutrients and cofactors required for brain monoamine synthesis by Sourkes [4].

## L-Tryptophan in Normal Subjects

There have been four published studies of the effects of single doses of TP in waking normal subjects. In the earliest of these, Smith and Prockop [5], using increasing doses from about 2 to 6 gm of TP, adjusted for the subjects' weight, on separate days observed drowsiness to appear within the first hour after drug administration. Five of the seven subjects napped after the 6 gm dose. Five also reported euphoria when roused, and three became hyperactive and uninhibited in conversation, laughing or being socially obnoxious. All subjects had trouble concentrating. Nystagmus developed in all subjects at the higher dosages. Oswald et al. [6] also observed slight euphoria, a mild feeling of drunkenness, and some drowsiness coming on about 20 minutes after a single dose of 5 gm TP and also noted some tendency for the subjects' conversation to become "lewd." On the other hand, Greenwood et al. in two studies [7,8], one using an infusion of 100 mg TP/kg and one using 5 gm TP orally, found only drowsiness and increased slow-wave activity on the EEG. Subjects were subjectively slowed down, drowsy, and clumsy. Nausea was a major side effect in the oral study that used tablets but not in earlier studies that used powdered material mixed with applesauce or juices [5,6].

Oates and Sjoerdsma [9] gave TP in doses ranging from 20 to 50 mg/kg to hypertensive subjects pretreated with a monoamine oxidase inhibitor (Catron) for at least four days. Both patients receiving 30 mg/kg and one of the two receiving 50 mg/kg reported either "jovial irresponsibility" or alcohol-like intoxication accompanied by pleasant euphoria. Three patients, two on 20 mg/kg and one on 50 mg/kg, became drowsy without euphoria.

It is difficult to explain the differences between the Smith and Oswald studies and the second oral Greenwood study; doses and rates of administration were similar. Perhaps differences in setting were responsible. Although setting is not well described in any of the papers, the Smith study appears to have occurred in a ward atmosphere with a variety of people (and social stimuli) around, whereas the second Greenwood study was high on complex measures and may have been conducted in a laboratory setting with isolated testing rooms and less social stimulation.

## L-Tryptophan and Sleep

There has been a great deal of interest in the effects of TP on sleep. We shall review first a group of studies investigating effects related to sleepiness or fatigue: whether TP produces subjective fatigue or sleepiness in humans. Then we shall review sleep laboratory studies that investigate effects of TP on measures of laboratory-recorded sleep.

### Subjective Sleepiness

As we have seen above, Smith and Prockop [5] and others reported sleepiness as a prominent side effect of large daytime doses of TP. Oswald et al. [6] reported sleepiness as a prominent side effect after TP is taken at bedtime. Similarly, Hartmann [10, 11] reported that when TP (5 to 10 gm) was given 30 minutes before bedtime, some subjects started to fall asleep before they were even put to bed in the sleep laboratory. Griffiths et al. [12] reported clear sleepiness before subjects were put to bed in their study using large doses (7.5 gm and 12 gm) of TP, and Wyatt et al. [13] similarly reported sleepiness in their study using 7.5 gm tryptophan in normal subjects and insomniacs.

Subjective sleepiness was investigated more methodically by Hartmann et al. [14]. They administered 4 gm TP, 4 gm L-leucine, and 4 gm of a placebo powder to each of 12 subjects at 9 p.m. Each subject underwent each treatment condition. Results were measured on the Stanford Sleepiness Scale, filled out every 15 minutes after ingestion by the waking subjects, for a period of two hours. L-Tryptophan, but not L-leucine, significantly increased subjective sleepiness at each time point, starting 45 minutes after administration.

Hartmann et al. [15] performed a further study with a more complicated design in which 2 gm TP, 2 gm L-leucine, or placebo powder was combined with either a high-protein or a high-carbohydrate "meal" given at 6 p.m. Each of 12 subjects underwent each of six treatment conditions. The carbohydrate diet produced somewhat more subjective sleepiness than the mixed high-protein diet, as was predicted according to data of Fernstrom and Wurtman [2]; this was significant at only one time point. L-Tryptophan increased subjective sleepiness, although the results were not as dramatic as when it was administered without food. L-Leucine had no effect.

Hartmann et al. [16] performed a dose-response study along the same lines. Each of six subjects underwent each of five treatment conditions, all at lunchtime (1 p.m.). A "meal" containing approximately 600 calories was made from casein hydrolysate, which contains all other natural amino acids but only a negligible amount of TP. One condition was vehicle alone; the other conditions were vehicle plus ¼ gm of TP, vehicle plus ½ gm TP, vehicle plus 1 gm TP, and vehicle plus 4 gm TP. Free and albumin-bound serum TP levels were measured, and it could be demonstrated that both increased in a dose-dependent manner. Subjective sleepiness was clearly increased by casein hydrolysate plus 4 gm TP, again starting 45 minutes after administration. L-Tryptophan (1 gm) produced a trend in the same direction.

*Nighttime Sleep Studies*

A large group of studies of nighttime sleep have been done. In most cases, the methodology involved all-night polygraphic recordings, but we shall also review a few studies involving regular nighttime observations of sleeping subjects by nurses or other observers, and studies of nighttime sleep in which the outcome measures were subjective reports by the subjects or patients.

Sleep-laboratory studies generally involve all-night polygraphic recordings, including the EEG, a submental electromyogram (EMG), and sometimes respiration and EKG as well. A number of variables of theoretical interest can be derived from a single sleep-laboratory study and attempting to present all the results would be quite complicated. Early studies of TP were concerned with changes in the sleep cycle, especially possible changes of distribution of S (synchronized or non-REM) and D (desynchronized, dreaming, or REM) sleep. We shall mention these only briefly, since tryptophan has little clear-cut effect on these measures. The chief emphasis will be on variables that can be relevant in terms of the possible clinical use of tryptophan: changes in sleep latency (time to fall asleep), waking time, or sleep time.

Early studies by Oswald et al. [6] and Hartmann et al. [10, 11] reported subjective sleepiness before sleep onset. In both studies, the chief emphasis was on distribution of sleep states rather than sleep latency or waking time. Oswald did not report results on sleep latency but did report a significant reduction in D-latency (time to the first D-period) after TP in normal people and even more prominently in a group of narcoleptic subjects. Hartmann, summarizing his results, reported a significant reduction in sleep latency, with a slight nonsignificant increase in sleep time and in D-time.

Hartmann et al. [17] investigated doses of 2 to 5 gm TP 20 minutes prior to bedtime, compared with placebo, in a group of 24 hospitalized, chronic psychiatric patients complaining of insomnia. Each patient was studied for eight nights—four nights of placebo, one night on each of four different doses of TP in a balanced design. This was not a sleep laboratory study: sleep was rated behaviorally by a trained observer examining patients every 15 minutes during the night. The two higher doses of TP (4 gm and 5 gm) produced a significant decrease in waking time and an increase in sleep; the lower dose (2 gm and 3 gm) produced nonsignificant trends in the same direction. Sleep latency was not accurately estimated since checks were performed only every 15 minutes.

In a similar study, Makipour et al. [18] studied the effects of 5 gm of TP in a group of 29 male chronic alcoholic patients experiencing insomnia two to three weeks after withdrawal from alcohol. As in the above study, sleep was estimated by observers with no sleep-laboratory recordings. In this study, TP decreased sleep latency (which was unusually long in these subjects) significantly as well as significantly increasing total sleep time.

A dose-response study to estimate effects of seven different doses of TP was performed by Hartmann et al. [19]. Ten adult males who reported sleep latencies of over 15 minutes at home (a mean of 30 minutes) slept in the laboratory for a complete all-night polygraphic recording on 12 separate occasions—usually one night per week for 12 weeks. The first two nights were considered adaptation nights and were not used in data analysis. In the subsequent 10 laboratory nights (10 weeks), each subject took a placebo on three occasions and TP on seven occasions in a random design. The seven nights on TP included one night on each of seven doses: 1 gm, 2 gm, 3 gm, 4 gm, 5 gm, 10 gm, and 15 gm. Sleep latency was significantly reduced by TP at all doses: sleep latency showed a mean value of 24 minutes across the 30 nights on placebo and a mean of 12 minutes on the nights on 1 gm TP (the lowest dose). There was no difference between the various doses of TP: mean values of sleep latency ranged from 11 to 16 minutes. Thus, no dose-response curve was established, but all doses of TP, including the 1 gm dose, reduced sleep latency.

Aside from the effects on sleep latency, other effects on sleep were not dramatic. Total waking time was reduced with some of the doses of TP, including the 1 gm dose; however, if only waking after sleep onset was considered, the results were not significant. Sleep time was not significantly affected nor was D-time or time of any of the stages of sleep affected by doses up to 5 gm TP. The very high doses (10 gm and 15 gm) produced a significant, though not numerically large, decrease in D-time and an increase in slow-wave sleep (stages 3 and 4).

In a more recent study, Hartmann and Spinweber extended the dose-response study downward, using a similar design to study the effect of doses of ¼ gm, ½ gm, and 1 gm of TP compared with placebo [20]. One gram produced a significant decrease in sleep latency; there was only a slight non-significant trend at the lower doses. Considering these two dose-response studies together, it appears that, at least in relatively normal subjects with long sleep latencies, a dose of 1 gm TP is sufficient to reduce sleep latency.

Wyatt et al. [13] reported a carefully performed and somewhat complicated three-part study. First, five normal females underwent a 22-night design in which, after two adaptation nights, subjects received 7.5 gm TP on 10 consecutive nights and placebo on 10 consecutive nights in a balanced design. There was a significant increase in total sleep time after TP and an increase in slow-wave sleep (stages 3 and 4). D-time decreased significantly.

Although the authors report that changes in sleep latency were not significant, data are not presented.

In the second portion of the study, TP was administered to seven patients with severe insomnia, including two seriously depressed patients. Each had four or five adaptation nights followed by, in some cases, 15 consecutive days of study and in other 30 consecutive days of study. The 15 (or 30) days consisted of five (or 10) consecutive days on placebo, followed by the same number of days of 7.5 gm TP given 30 minutes before bedtime, and a final 5- (or 10-) day placebo period. In this study, total sleep was significantly increased, and the amount of intermittent waking time significantly decreased. Sleep latency decreased from the first continuous placebo period to the TP period; however, sleep latency did not reincrease in several of the subjects when they returned to placebo for the second long stretch of recordings. There was also a significant decrease in "early morning wakefulness," and in "intermittent wakefulness" during the night.

In a third portion of this study, two patients with carcinoid tumor were given TP on a number of nights with or without PCPA (an inhibitor of tryptophan hydroxylase). Different doses of TP were used in an increasing dosage design. the finding here was that the sedative effect of TP was quite pronounced, even in the patients taking PCPA; therefore, the authors suggest that a mechanism not involving tryptophan hydroxylation may be involved in the sedative effect of TP.

Griffiths et al. [12] administered single bedtime doses of 7.5 gm and 12 gm of TP in a group of normal males. A reduction in sleep latency was found after both doses. Thse authors also describe some changes not found in other studies—a significant and sizable increase in REM sleep is reported after the 12 gm dose.

Davis et al. [21] reported on the effects of 1 gm and 2 gm doses of TP in a single administration (20 minutes prior to bedtime), using a group of 24 long-sleep-latency males and females. When the entire group, which included many subjects who actually had very short sleep latencies, was considered, the results regarding sleep latency were of borderline significance: sleep latency to stage 2 was significantly reduced while the closely related and the more usual measure used in most studies above—sleep latency to the first stage 1 leading to stage 2—just missed significance. When only subjects who actually met the originally defined criteria of sleep latency of 20 minutes or more under baseline conditions were considered, 1 gm and 2 gm doses of TP both proved to reduce sleep latency significantly relative to placebo. D-sleep and the other stages of sleep were not altered in this study.

Hartmann and Elion [22] performed one study in which the first night in the laboratory—usually discarded as an adaptation night—was used as the experimental night. In this study, 42 normal males and females were divided into three groups, matched on the basis of age, sex, and reported home sleep latency. Each slept in the laboratory for one night of polygraphically recorded sleep. Twenty minutes prior to bedtime, one group received placebo, one group received 1 gm TP, one group received 3 gm TP. Results demonstrated a significantly reduced sleep latency in both TP groups compared with the placebo group. There was no difference between the two doses of TP. No significant effects aside from sleep latency were found.

Nicholson and Stone [23] reported a dose-response study investigating the effects of single doses of 2 gm, 4 gm, and 6 gm of TP on sleep in six normal males. This group reported negative results—no significant changes in sleep stages or states and no significant reduction in sleep latency. The subjects used in this study were not long-latency subjects; the average sleep latency, both on placebo and on tryptophan was approximately 12 minutes. The authors also investigated effects of TP (1 gm, 3 gm, and 4 gm) on daytime sleep in the same six subjects and found no clear-cut effects.

Spinweber et al. [24] likewise studied the effects of TP on polygraphically recorded sleep in the daytime to differentiate possible time-of-day effects. In a group of 20 young males, 4 gm TP or placebo was administered in a balanced design at either 9 a.m. or 1 p.m. During the first hour after administration, waking EEGs and several psychological tests were administered. Subjects were placed in bed for polygraphic recordings 60 minutes after administration of TP. Under these conditions, 4 gm TP produced a significant reduction in sleep latency compared to placebo at both times of administration. There was no significant difference between the two times of administration. The remainder of sleep was left unaltered.

Overall there is some disagreement as to the exact effect of TP on D-sleep, S-sleep, and the distribution of the various stages. There appears to be a tendency across studies for total sleep to be increased and for the "deep" portions of S-sleep (stages 3 and 4) to increase. However, there is enough disagreement so that none of these effects can be considered firmly established.

The effect in reducing sleep latency (the sleep-inducing effect) appears to be relatively clear. The articles reviewed above do include one negative study [23] and, as mentioned, an additional study [21] was negative or equivocal when all *normal subjects* were considered. It is of interest that these two negative results can be seen to involve subjects with normal (approximately 10 minutes) sleep latencies, whereas a majority of the positive studies involved either normal subjects with long latencies or mild insomniacs. There are two reasons why this might be important. First, there is the "basement effect." Since sleep latencies of less than four or five minutes are almost unknown in the sleep laboratory (except in narcoleptics) it would be almost impossible to demonstrate a reduction in sleep latency in someone whose latency is only a few minutes longer than this minimum. In addition, a review of the time curves for the daytime effects on sleepiness, mood, EEG, etc., shows that the effects of TP only begin to be manifested within 30 to 45 minutes and are of significance only at 45 minutes or longer. Therefore, when TP is administered 20 minutes before bedtime to a person whose sleep latency is 10 or 15 minutes on placebo, the effect would have to take place within 30 to 35 minutes after drug administration in order to produce any reduction in latency. In the studies reviewed, when time from administration to sleep onset has been 45 minutes or longer, positive effects have been demonstrated.

Most of the studies so far have been small-scale laboratory studies and often have involved normal subjects, or longer latency subjects, rather than persons who could be called true insomniacs. From a clinical point of view, a large-scale study involving insomniacs is obviously needed. One such study is in progress in Hartmann's laboratory, comparing TP with placebo, secobarbital, and flurazepam.

**Depression**

One intriguing study of TP in depression was conducted by Chouinard [25]: a random double-blind comparison of TP and nicotinamide (NA), imipramine (IMI), and their combination, on a sample of 25 depressed patients. Criteria were: ages 18 to 60 and a diagnosis of primary affective disorder by Feighner criteria [26]. Patients with complicating diagnoses (e.g., physical illness, schizophrenia, alcoholism, etc.) were excluded. In addition, patients were classified as having unipolar illness (UPI) or bipolar illness (BPI) according to the Research Diagnostic Criteria (RDC) [27].

The sample was divided randomly into three groups, TP/NA (8), IMI (8), and TP/NA plus IMI (9). There were 21 females and four males of which 15 were UPIs and 10 BPIs; the three experimental groups were not significantly different in sex, age, diagnosis (UPI/BPI) or previous hospitalizations. The TP/NA group received 2 gm TP and 0.5 gm NA the first week, 4 gm TP and 1.0 gm NA the second week, and 6 gm TP and 1.5 gm NA the third and fourth weeks. The IMI group received 75 mg IMI the first week, 150 mg the second, and 225 mg the third and fourth weeks. The TP/NA plus IMI group received both medications according to the same schedules; the experiment was double-blind, with appropriate placebos (TP placebo for IMI patients and vice versa). Assessment was done each week with a modified Hamilton Depression Rating Scale (HAM), performed by a psychiatrist, and a Beck self-rating scale completed by the patient. Plasma was drawn for determination of total and free TP and total kynurenine, the major TP metabolite.

There were no significant differences between the three groups in response on total HAM score or on total Beck score. There were significant (Dunnett test, two-tailed) differences in various HAM subscales: at day 14, TP/NA was found superior to IMI for general somatic symptoms and depersonalization/derealization and inferior to IMI for gastrointestinal somatic symptoms, and TP/NA plus IMI was found inferior to IMI for late insomnia and insight. At day 28, TP/NA was no longer superior to IMI for any item but was inferior to IMI for late insomnia, gastrointestinal somatic symptoms, and weight loss. L-Tryptophan and nicotinamide plus IMI was no different from IMI. There was an overall trend in mean total HAM scores toward worsening of TP/NA patients over the last two weeks compared with day 14, largely ascribable to the above subscales. There was significant heterogeneity of covariance at day 28 for psychic anxiety, with individual regression slopes suggesting that TP/NA was inferior to IMI for patients with high baseline levels of psychic anxiety. Chouinard suggests that this might explain the higher rate of use of p.r.n. diazepam observed in the TP/NA group (diazepam p.r.n. was the only other drug used during the study).

Because 36% of the patients showed little or no response, the sample was divided, post hoc, into marked-, moderate-, or nonresponders, on the basis of their improvement in the HAM scores. There was little difference between the treatment groups in the distribution of response for UPI patients; however, there tended to be more nonresponders among BPI patients than UPI patients in the TP/NA group (p = 0.07) and IMI group (p = 0.11). Of the three BPI patients in the TP/NA group, none showed a response (as compared with two marked responders and two moderate responders out of five UPI patients given TP/NA). The only BPI patients showing marked response were two of the four given TP/NA plus IMI.

Plasma total and free-TP levels significantly increased over the course of the trial for those patients taking TP/NA. The TP/NA group was found to have a positive correlation (between-subject coefficients) between rise in free TP and improvement in HAM and Beck scores, while for the TP plus IMI group the correlation was a negative one. If within-subject correlations between weekly free-TP level and weekly Beck total score are considered, the UPI patients showed uniformly negative correlation coefficients (p = 0.001) (meaning, in this case, better clinical response with higher TP levels).

The three bipolar patients, however, could not be adequately judged by this measure as they all were dropouts due to failure to respond. L-Tryptophan-nicotinamide-imipramine patients, whether UPI or BPI, showed no within-patient correlations between plasma TP and response. Overall, initial TP levels were positively correlated with final TP levels—i.e., those patients with high TP at the outset showed greatest increase in plasma TP. Plasma levels in the TP/NA group reached a plateau after two weeks but continued to rise for the duration of the trial for the TP/NA plus IMI group.

Chouinard concludes: (1) TP/NA showed antidepressant effects comparable to IMI for the first two weeks; (2) TP/NA tended to lose some of its effects during the last two weeks; (3) since rise in total and free TP was correlated with clinical response, that response was possibly a drug effect; (4) a therapeutic response to TP/NA alone was seen only in UPI patients, not in BPI patients; and (5) some depressed patients metabolize TP slowly and thus have higher pretreatment-plasma TP and higher rises in plasma level with exogenous TP administration (and better clinical response).

Chouinard then gives a quick review of relevant literature and suggests that there is a therapeutic window for TP, that UPI patients respond to doses of 6 gm/day or less of TP or 4 gm/day or less of TP/NA; that BPI patients may respond to doses greater than 6 gm/day of TP or 4 gm/day of TP/NA; and that if tricyclics are combined with TP, the dose of TP should be halved for UPI patients. He also suggests that TP should be given in divided doses to minimize plasma-level fluctuations. The plateauing of response for weeks 3 and 4 in the TP/NA patients is explained by the rise in dose for that period, thus exceeding the therapeutic window.

We shall limit discussion of this and other individual studies in favor of an extended discussion of the entire body of research later in this chapter. Let it suffice for the moment to list several points of interest for later discussion: (1) the trial was four weeks in length; (2) average total HAM scores at 28 days remained greater than 20 (relatively high) for all three treatment groups; (3) there are alternative explanations for the leveling off of TP effects after the first two weeks. Nevertheless, Chouinard's conclusions about UPI/BPI dose-response differences are worth keeping in mind while reviewing other studies.

Chouinard's pilot study for this investigation is worth summarizing [28]. One BPI and ten UPI depressed patients (by Feighner and RDC criteria) were given TP/NA in the same doses and schedule as described above. Assessment was with HAM, Clinical Global Improvement (CGI), and Beck rating scales. At 14 days, average total HAM scores had dropped significantly (p < .01) but was still above 20, where it remained for the second two weeks. Beck and CGI dropped significantly (p < .01 each). On the basis of HAM scores, there were three marked-, four moderate-, and four non-responders. The single BPI patient was a nonresponder. The same relationships as reported in the later study were found here between free-plasma TP initially and at day 28 (a positive correlation) and between rise in plasma TP and decrease in Beck and HAM scores; the latter, however, was of borderline significance. Within-subject correlations were found between rise in plasma TP and improvement as measured by Beck total score for the

UPI patients, and a reverse correlation was observed for the single BPI patient (who did not respond clinically). This open study is limited by the small sample size and the lack of controls; it is, however, entirely consistent with the later controlled double-blind study. It is flawed by the high post-treatment HAM scores, even for "marked responders." Usually pretreatment scores over 18 are considered high enough to warrant including patients in antidepressant drug trials.

Of the other uncontrolled studies on TP in depression in the literature, Broadhurst's is of interest because of his subject sample [29]. His paper primarily reports the outcome of a controlled study of TP versus IMI, but he briefly describes an additional uncontrolled trial of TP in 36 treatment resistant "chronic or frequently relapsing depressive" patients, all of whom had been previously treated with tricyclic antidepressants, monoamine oxidase (MAO) inhibitors, and electroconvulsive therapy (ECT) at various times. Using a modified HAM, he reports that 22 out of 36 patients were markedly improved (75% improvement in HAM scores) after 28 days of TP; he does not state the doses used. Twenty-one out of the 22 showed improvement "progressive beyond 75%" and 12 of the 21 had transient mood swings when TP was discontinued. The mood swings reversed when TP was restarted. Of the 14 out of 36 who showed "no early response," six improved "more slowly." Eight patients had no response. This study also is unusual in that 20 patients (including 17 out of 22 early responders) were followed for one year or longer.

Shopsin tried TP in eight male "endogenous depressives" with gout who were already on allopurinol (which should decrease peripheral TP destruction) [30]. Five showed marked improvement in HAM depression scores (from 34 to 41) on doses of 4 gm to 6 gm TP and 100 to 200 mg of allopurinol per day. He makes the UPI-BPI distinction in reporting his data, and the five responders were four UPI patients treated with 4 to 6 gm TP/day and one BPI patient treated with 6 gm TP/day. The three partial or nonresponders were two UPI patients treated with 6 gm TP/day and one BPI patient on 6 gm TP/day. Dunner and Goodwin looked at clinical response and cerebrospinal fluid (CSF) 5-hydroxyindoleacetic acid (5-HIAA) levels of five depressed patients on TP—three BPI and two UPI patients [31]. They reported no significant improvement on a scale devised by Bunney and Hamburg for measuring depression. The dose used was 9 gm/day; the study period was only two weeks.

Moller et al. ran an interesting, initial, uncontrolled study that was biochemically oriented [32]. Eleven UPI patients and eight BPI patients (all depressed except one BPI patient who was manic) were included (17 female and one male) and modified HAM and amino acid levels were done in an attempt to correlate biochemical findings with clinical response. Some of their patients received racemic tryptophan (150 to 200 mg/kg), most took TP (100 to 160 mg/kg) and some got both at different times. Assuming an average body weight of 60 kg, this dose was equivalent to 4.5 to 6 gm or 6 to 9.6 gm of TP, respectively. No adjunctive drugs were given. Five of 19 patients "remitted" within one week, with 90% reduction in HAM scores. Seven of the other 17 were treated further with TP for two to three weeks or longer "without significant improvement." The five responders were four female BPI patients (including the manic patient) and one female UPI patient. The manic patient remained on the lithium she had been taking for two and a half years. Four of these five subjects were found to have a low age-corrected ratio of plasma TP to competing amino acids (valine, isoleucine, and leucine). The nonresponders all had the same amino acid pattern as a group of controls. Problems with this study include a lack of controls and, for the ten "failures," a study time of only one week.

A very recent report by Moller extends his earlier findings and involves a new series of 32 endogenously depressed patients [33]. His evidence is clear on the following issues: (1) depressed patients do not differ from controls on total or free plasma TP; (2) depressed patients do not differ from controls on plasma or urine levels of kynurenine, the major peripheral TP metabolite (and by inference in rate of TP metabolism); (3) they do not differ in the range of observed ratios of TP to other competing amino acids. However, in the new study, with the ratio of plasma TP levels to the sum of levels of valine, leucine, isoleucine, tyrosine, and phenylalanine, depressed patients with low ratios (the bottom 15% or 30 % of normal range, corrected for age) show much higher improvement rates on TP than do patients with higher ratios. Eight of 10 patients in the lowest 15% of normal values improved on 100 mg/kg/day of TP; 3 of the 8 patients falling in the 15% to 30% range improved; only one of 14 patients with ratios in the upper 70% of normal ratios improved. Bipolar patients were overrepresented in the lowest ratio subgroup. Most patients who improved did so in the first week. A few patients are being maintained for prolonged periods on TP since they are unresponsive to other antidepressants.

It seems clear from the above data that Moller's TP responsive depressives have normal plasma TP levels and may differ from other depressives in having elevated plasma levels of the other amino acids. The reason for this difference is unclear. It should be noted that Moller's first study took plasma samples one hour after breakfast, while the second study used fasting samples. The ratios were more abnormal in the first study, suggesting that some depressed patients may metabolize amino acids abnormally after absorption from the intestine.

The evaluation of the antidepressant activity of TP, however, must rest on controlled studies. Investigators have compared TP to placebo [34-38], to tricyclic antidepressants [25,29,39,40-44], and to ECT [45-47]. In addition, TP has been studied as an adjunct to tricyclic antidepressants, MAD inhibitors and ECT.

In the earliest of the TP-placebo studies, Bunney et al. used a National

Institute of Mental Health (NIMH) double-blind crossover design [34]. Eight depressed patients, diagnosed as "manic depressive or psychotic depressive," were given 8 gm/day TP (average dose) for 16 days (average duration). Using the depression rating scale devised by their own group, they found no difference from placebo overall, with only one patient showing decrease in depression scores on TP and rise on placebo. Defects of this study include uncertain or unreported inclusion criteria and, hence, possibly a heterogeneous sample, small sample size, and short trial durations. Mendels et al. studied 15 depressed BPI and UPI men [35]. Using the Bunney, the Beck, and HAM rating scales, they found no difference between the effects of TP and those of L-dopa or placebo. L-Tryptophan was begun at 3 gm/day and was increased to "a maximum of 15 gm per day," with an average maximum of 14 gm and a daily average of 7.5 gm (range 5.9 to 9.9 gm).

Duration was 42 days. One patient improved slightly on TP, whether UPI or BPI is not reported. All patients were subsequently discharged on standard antidepressants, ruling out a treatment-resistant sample. Inclusion criteria appear to be adequate, and this study has no obvious fault in design. Of note is the high dose of TP used. Dunner and Fieve studied TP alone, and with L-dopa, double-blind, using intraindividual control periods on placebo [36]. With doses of 8.4 to 9 gm/day, six patients received TP for 10 to 17 days following a placebo period; one patient received TP for 16 days followed by L-dopa for four days and then placebo; and five received TP for 14 to 18 days, then TP and L-dopa for 6 to 13 days, and then placebo. Patients were diagnosed as having primary affective disorder by Feighner criteria and were further described as UPI and BPI. Of the six who received only TP, four (all UPI) had no response as measured by "a global rating scale for mood" and "a structured interview for assessment of symptoms of mania and depression." One BPI patient had "equivocal" response, i.e., improvement on TP without relapse on placebo, and one UPI patient had "good" response, i.e., TP improvement with placebo relapse. The one UPI patient who received TP and L-dopa consecutively was unimproved and all five of the TP/TP plus L-dopa patients (three UPI and two BPI) had no response to TP alone; only one of these had a "fair" response to TP and L-dopa. This study can be criticized for a short trial duration and unreported rating criteria.

Murphy et al. studied 24 depressed and 10 manic patients, double-blind in a nonrandom alternating TP-placebo schedule [37]. Criteria were "affective symptoms severe enough to require hospitalization." Sixteen of the 24 depressed patients were diagnosed UPI and eight were called BPI on the basis of history. Average dose of TP was 9.6 gm/day and average duration was 20 days. Using the Bunney and Hamburg rating scale, one of the 16 UPI patients "improved partially" without relapse on placebo, and five of the eight BPI patients "improved partially," of whom three had a relapse on placebo. One of the 15 UPI nonresponders got worse on TP, and one of the BPI got hypomanic. Flaws in this study are the vaguely stated inclusion criteria and the complete absence of raw-score data and undefined "improvement" criteria.

The 1976 paper by Farkas et al. has some of the same faults [38]. Sixteen patients, depressed according to Feighner criteria, were studied in another double-blind alternating TP-placebo design, using doses of 6 to 9 gm/day of TP (average 8.36 gm/day). HAM and nurses' global rating scales were used to evaluate clinical status. Of 10 UPI patients, one was a "responder" and nine were "nonresponders." Of two BPI I patients, one was a "nonresponder," and one was an "equivocal responder," with no relapse on placebo. Of four BPI II patients, two were "nonresponders" and two were "responders;" one was improved enough for discharge and the other responded better to phenelzine than TP after the trial period. No data or "response" criteria are given in the report.

Investigations comparing TP with tricyclic antidepressants while theoretically perhaps less vigorous in testing TP efficacy, have the advantage of stirring up fewer ethical reservations now that depression is considered a relatively treatable illness. The most recent of these, Chouinard's study [25], has been discussed. The earliest of these was reported in 1970 by Broadhurst [29]. He compared 6 gm/day TP with 150 mg/day IMI in 24 patients in an open trial for 28 days. Patients were diagnosed as having "acute primary depressive illness" (criteria unstated) and Beck self-rating scores were employed to follow their clinical course. He found no difference between the two groups, and 65% of all patients, evenly distributed, showed "substantial improvement"—defined as discharge without readmission for six months. The report is flawed by the vague inclusion criteria, the absence of raw data or explicit statistics, and the exclusive reliance on a self-rating scale.

Coppen et al. compared TP with IMI, with and without liothyronine in a double-blind nonrandom study of 33 patients diagnosed with "primary depression" by Kline criteria [39]. Thirty were "unipolar" with 16 out of 30 having had "at least one previous depressive attack." Three were bipolar. Average ages of the four treatment groups ranged from 54 to 60. L-Tryptophan dose was 9 gm/day in divided doses; IMI dose was 150 mg/day. Using a modified HAM and Beck self-rating scales, no significant difference was found between TP and IMI. Triiodothyronine did not affect TP efficacy. Only one of the BPI patients was treated with TP, and she received triiodothyronine as well for two of the four weeks; she showed no response at all and recovered slowly with ECT after the study period. The UPI/BPI distinction here may be blurred by the absence of previous affective illness in 14 of the patients, although given the age of the sample, the unwitting inclusion of some (potentially) BPI patients in the UPI group is unlikely.

Kline and Shah conducted an open study of TP versus IMI with 34 depressed patients (17 male/17 female). For six weeks 3 to 6 gm/day TP was compared with 150 to 225 mg/day IMI using a three-point global rating scale measuring overall severity of depression [40]. They found no difference between TP and IMI, but the study is seriously flawed by vague inclusion criteria and the crude rating scale.

Gayford et al., in 1973, compared 10 patients on 6 gm/day of TP with three patients on 175 mg/day of amitriptyline (AMI) [41]. Subjects were described as having "endogenous depressive illness." The trial was open; study duration was 14 days; and the patients were rated either "informally" or with a HAM scale. All AMI patients and only one TP patient "recovered." The one TP responder had a higher pretreatment plasma total TP and his plasma TP rose more than the nonresponders. Inclusion criteria, study duration, ratings, and "recovery" criteria are all inadequate, or at least inadequately reported.

Jensen et al., in 1975, studied 42 inpatients diagnosed with "endogenous depression," either BPI or UPI, with diurnal variation and a total score of 5 for HAM items one, two, and eight. TP (6 gm/day) was compared with IMI (150 mg/day) for 21 days, in a random double-blind design [42]. TP and IMI groups both improved significantly as measured by HAM scores; IMI was judged to have "more rapid" effect than TP. Unipolar and bipolar differences, if any, are unreported. One possible criticism, perhaps related to a study duration of only three weeks, is the relatively elevated final HAM scores of both groups (16.5 for TP and 13.4 for IMI). In addition, no statistical comparison *between* the two groups was done.

Herrington et al. ran one of the few studies with any long-term follow-up [43]. They compared 20 Medical Research Council (MRC) diagnosed depressives on TP with 20 on AMI; however, they excluded those with "mild depressive reactions, marked social problems, and those whose depression was of such severity that ECT was the treatment of choice." As a consequence, on the Carney neurotic/endogenous depression scale, only 3 out of 20 TP patients and 8 out of 20 AMI patients scored greater than 6 out of 12 points and were thus judged "likely to be endogenous." L-Tryptophan doses were 6 gm/day for the first two weeks and 8 gm/day for the remaining two weeks; AMI doses were 75 mg/day for one week and 150 mg/day for three weeks. Assessment was with a modified HAM, MRC, Beck, and Taylor scores, and a global rating scale, and the design was random and double-blind. The authors found no significant difference between the two groups except for a tendency for the improvement of the TP patients to fade between the third and fourth weeks. Outcome was not correlated with baseline depression scores except for a significant negative correlation between initial anxiety and improvement on TP. At the conclusion of four weeks, only one patient continued on TP and the others were either well

(8 out of 20 on TP and 11 out of 20 on AMI) or treated with further tricyclics or ECT. There was a trend toward a lower relapse rate in the TP patients over the six-month follow-up but this did not reach the 0.05 level of significance.

Rao and Broadhurst conducted a four-week random double-blind trial of nine patients on TP and seven on IMI [44]. Inclusion was on the basis of modified MRC criteria, doses were 6 gm/day of TP and 150 mg/day of IMI, and assessment was with HAM scores. They also found no significant difference between the two groups, and the strength of the finding is heightened by the low HAM scores at the end of the fourth week (less than five for each group).

Three British groups compared TP with ECT. For methodological reasons, an open design was used in each case. Carroll et al. used matched pairs of patients with "severe primary depressive illness" judged suitable for ECT on the basis of extent of symptomatology [45]. L-Tryptophan at 7 gm/day was compared with bilateral ECT three times a week for 21 days, using HAM scores. They concluded that ECT was superior to TP. Of TP patients, one out of 12 was symptom-free and 11 out of 12 required posttrial ECT; of ECT patients, 3 out of 12 were symptom-free and 4 out of 12 required further ECT. The chief criticism of this study is the brevity of the study period. The severity of depression in their sample is noteworthy.

Herrington et al., in 1974, used HAM, RMC, Beck, Taylor and global severity scales to compare 21 patients on ECT with 22 patients on TP [46]. Patients were randomly given ECT twice a week (for a total of six to eight treatments) or 6 gm/day TP for two weeks followed by 8 gm/day for two more weeks. At day 14, there was no significant difference between the two groups (e.g., HAM scores dropped from around 27 to around 14 in both groups). Ratings for TP patients leveled off for the following two weeks, while ECT patients continued to improve, all 21 requiring no further treatment; 14 out of 22 TP patients, however, subsequently needed and responded to ECT or AMI. Relapse rates were similar in the two groups in a six-month follow-up. The authors concluded that the two-week improvement in the TP group could be due to nonspecific factors.

MacSweeney reported a trial of TP versus ECT in 25 "severe unipolar" depressives, with no prior history of mania or hypomania or family history of mania in first-degree relatives [47]. He used 3 gm/day TP with 1 gm/day NA and compared it with unilateral ECT for four weeks. The only rating scale used was the Beck self-rating scale. No significant difference was found between the two treatments at 28 days, and TP/NA were found more effective after 21 days. The study can be criticized for its use of only one rating scale, a self-reporting inventory.

L-Tryptophan has been investigated in combination with each of the three major treatments for depression: tricyclic antidepressants, MAO inhibitors, and ECT. Two studies of ECT ± TP found TP to be no more effective than placebo when used in conjunction with ECT [48,49]. Five studies compared tricyclic antidepressants with tricyclic antidepressants plus TP, one using either IMI or AMI [50], one using clomipramine (CMI) or desipramine (DMI) [52], and two using CMI [53,54]. The Pare study found no difference between the presence or absence of 7.5 gm/day TP in combination with either IMI or AMI [50]. Lopez-Ibor et al. found 3 gm/day TP without significant effect in combination with AMI, although there was a trend toward faster improvement on the combination [51]. Shaw et al. found TP in unreported doses an ineffective supplement to CMI or DMI [52]. Roos declared TP (at about 3 gm/day) a useful supplement to CMI in elevating mood [53], and Walinder et al. found TP (at about 3 gm/day) likewise useful in combination with CMI in improving depression/anxiety scores [54]. Although all of these studies were double-blind, all have one or more serious flaws including vaguely defined inclusion criteria ("various forms of depression"), unstated doses, short or unspecified study times, and inadequately presented data or statistics.

There have been four controlled or semicontrolled studies showing that TP is more effective than placebo in improving depression when added to an MAO inhibitor. Coppen et al. [55] added 14 gm of racemic tryptophan (7 gm/day TP plus pyridoxine and B vitamins) during only the second week of a four-week course of treatment with tranylcypromine (30 to 50 gm/day, adjusted for patients' weight) in 25 older, apparently endogenous, patients with "severe depressive illness." Both TP and placebo groups improved, but TP patients showed significantly superior outcome (a 75% drop in HAM scores compared with a 50% drop in the placebo group). This difference was highly significant at all ratings in the third and fourth weeks of the study. Slightly increased hypotension occurred when TP was added; patients noted drowsiness and feeling "slightly drunk" on the first day.

Glassman and Platman also treated 20 older (average age: 59) endogenously depressed patients with phenelzine 60 mg/day for three weeks [56]. Half the patients received 12 to 18 gm racemic tryptophan (6 to 9 gm TP) adjusted by patients' weight. Again, the tryptophan group showed a greater decrease in HAM scores (70% on drug; 40% on placebo), significant at about the 5% level.

Ayuso-Gutierrez and Lopez-Ibor compared 6 gm of racemic tryptophan with placebo in apparently severely endogenously depressed inpatients who were receiving daily intravenous nialamide infusions of 500 mg/day for 20 days [57]. The tryptophan group contained more anxious patients and fewer retarded patients than did the placebo group. Ten of 14 tryptophan patients achieved "complete remission" versus 5 of 15 placebo patients. Differences in HAM scores were statistically significant after both 8 and 20 days. L-Tryptophan patients had more side effects, chiefly nausea, dizziness, and throbbing headache.

Pare treated 14 patients who had improved on various MAO inhibitors whose symptoms had returned when the dose was tapered [50]. Without raising the inhibitor dose, he added 7.5 mg/day or more TP. Six of 14 such patients showed a "striking" improvement within two or three days of adding the TP, which gradually faded within a week after placebo was substituted. Five of the 14 patients developed marked nausea and drowsiness when TP was added, necessitating stopping the TP. Two patients developed muscular twitching and hyperreflexia, also necessitating stopping the drug. Adding TP to 10 similar patients, who were developing more depression when tricyclic antidepressant dosage was lowered, was clinically helpful in only one patient.

Only the Coppen and Glassman reports deal with well-studied MAO inhibitors. In both cases, effective doses, likely to cause clear improvement alone, were used [58].

## Mania

Four trials of TP in mania have been conducted. Murphy et al. gave TP in a double-blind study, with a nonrandom alternating TP-placebo schedule, to 10 manic or hypomanic patients [59]. Using Bunney and Hamburg's mania rating scale and doses of 9.6 ± 0.4 gm/day for an average of 20 days, they noted improvement in seven patients and no improvement in three. Three of the seven responders relapsed with placebo. Better response was noted with hypomanic patients: three of four patients had only partial improvement. Interestingly, depression ratings, which were elevated during the manic period, also improved in eight of the 10 patients, including all but one of the responders. One nonresponder, in fact, became more delusional and disorganized on TP. While generally positive, these results are open to question because of the small sample, the lack of raw scores reported, and the unstated criteria for "improvement."

A study by Prange et al. compared TP and chlorpromazine (CPZ) in a double-blind crossover experiment [60]. Ten manic patients, all of whom had previous affective episodes and had never received lithium, were randomly assigned to either TP for 14 days followed by 14 days on CPZ or to CPZ for 14 days followed by TP for 21 days. Doses were adjusted by weight; a 67 kg person received 400 mg CPZ or 6 gm/day TP in divided dosages. The CPZ dose was kept a bit less than optimal; this choice reflected the authors' prior experience with TP in open trials in which it had shown clear effects but seemed less potent than high-dose antipsychotic medication. All patients received pyridoxine 50 mg/day through the study. L-Tryptophan patients tended to improve by the fourth day; CPZ patients improved more slowly in general during the first two weeks; three of five TP patients improved, one became depressed, and one was unchanged. CPZ patients' response was more erratic. On most measures TP was superior to CPZ, but the differences did not reach statistical significance. After crossover, matters were, on the average, more confusing with both groups staying somewhat improved but with unexplained shifts in pathology in individual patients, thus confounding matters. Side effects were significantly more common on CPZ, particularly dry mouth, blurred vision, palpitations, and urinary difficulty.

Moller et al. also describe one manic patient who recovered within a week on about 7 gm/day TP [32].

On the basis of the above three studies, it seems likely that TP at doses of 6 gm/day or higher can cause improvement in some hypomanic and perhaps even manic patients, but the evidence is only suggestive, not definitive.

**Schizophrenia**

The evidence for a therapeutic utility of TP in schizophrenia is far weaker than in affective disorders. Two early studies added TP to iproniazid, the original MAO inhibitor, and elicited increased activity and affect in withdrawn chronic schizophrenics with some element of mood elevation in the NIMH study patients [62] but with mainly an increase in anxiety and agitation in the Chicago patients [63]. In the NIMH study, methionine was also added separately to the iproniazid and caused more obvious psychotic disorganization than did TP. In neither study did the TP cause clear clinical improvement but rather it caused a change in psychotic state.

More recently, Bowers gave six schizophrenics 2 to 4 gm/day TP, along with 100 mg/day pyridoxine for periods of 8 to 12 days. He noted some decrease in anxiety and tension, but even the most improved schizophrenic patient responded less well than she ultimately did on a phenothiazine. Gillin et al., having found some modest improvement in schizophrenics on 5HTP in a previous study, gave doses of 9 to 20 gm/day TP plus 100 mg/day pyridoxine for 11 to 28 days to eight chronic schizophrenics [65]. The patients had been off all antipsychotic drugs for a month before beginning the study and received placebo double-blind for an additional two weeks before starting on TP. No clear tryptophan-related changes occurred, although one patient was a little better on TP and two a little worse.

Chouinard et al. added benzerazide (to inhibit liver tryptophan pyrrolase and decrease TP destruction) to 2 to 6 gm/day TP in 16 schizophrenics, mainly chronic or process, and compared them with 16 comparable patients receiving 300 to 900 mg/day CPZ, in a double-blind controlled study [66]. Five of the TP patients and none of the CPZ patients had to be withdrawn from the six-week study. More TP than CPZ patients required p.r.n. CPZ during the study. On most measures from the nursing and interview scales, the CPZ group was superior to the TP group if the end-of-study scores on the four TP treatment failures were included. If these patients were excluded from the analysis, no significant treatment differences on clinical measures remained, although the trends still favored CPZ. Nausea and vomiting occurred in 4 of the 15 TP patients, while dry mouth and dizziness or syncope were more common in CPZ patients. Tardive dyskinesia scores increased on TP and decreased on CPZ; the differences between the two treatments in this area are significant. Although the authors interpret their data as suggesting that TP has some antipsychotic effect of slow, gradual onset (hence the early dropouts), it is hard to be convinced by a study of the sort reported in the absence of a placebo group. Plasma tryptophan levels were elevated by TP plus benzerazide only for the first three weeks of this six-week study.

Overall, these studies fail to elicit any real enthusiasm for the utility of TP, with or without an MAO inhibitor, in chronic schizophrenia.

**Obsessive-Compulsive Disorders**

Only Yaryura-Tobias and associates have studied TP in obsessive-compulsive disorders. In their most recent paper, they note moderately good results with TP plus niacinamide and pyridoxine in seven such patients and claim to have treated 294 patients with obsessive-compulsive symptoms with chlorimipramine with good results [67]. When TP plus vitamins were added to chlorimipramine, the dose of the serotonergic tricyclic antidepressant could be cut in half. No clear outcome data are reported.

**Neurological Conditions**

Growdon reviews the efficacy of both 5-HTP and TP in posthypoxic intention myoclonus occurring in patients who have survived transient brain anoxia [2]. This beneficial effect was observed in nine open studies in small numbers of patients at doses of from 300 to over 1,000 mg/day 5-HTP, with or without added carbidopa, an amino acid decarboxylase inhibitor. Tryptophan has also been used in a few patients and seems a bit less effective.

L-Tryptophan, added to L-dopa, was reported by Coppen et al. to reduce depression in parkinsonian patients [68]. This effect was only significant in a pre-to-post test score analysis in the combined drug group, there being no significant difference between TP-L-dopa patients and placebo-L-dopa patients overall in outcome. Sourkes [4] suggests that

L-dopa therapy could reduce brain TP levels by competing with TP for absorption from the intestine. Prange et al. [61] have reported that TP alone had no effect on parkinsonian patients; however, when pyridoxine was added, the patients developed severe rigidity. In this study, pyridoxine alone was *not* given to parkinsonian patients. Sourkes suggests that pyridoxine alone can worsen parkinsonism by facilitating the metabolism of L-dopa and reports that the vitamin does, in fact, clinically interfere with the efficacy of L-dopa therapy in parkinsonism [4].

Hyyppa et al. describe a modest amelioration of depression and of neurological symptoms due to TP administration in patients with multiple sclerosis [69]. The effect was most obvious early in the 30-day treatment period. No concurrent placebo control group was used, making the results of dubious value.

## L-Dopa-Induced Side Effects

In parkinsonian patients treated with large doses (3 to 10 gm/day) of L-dopa, psychiatric or behavioral side effects are quite common—they are reported as occurring in up to 30% of cases in some series. These effects include agitation, nightmares, occasional depression, and psychotic episodes usually of a paranoid, delusional type. These side effects are among the most common reasons for reducing or stopping L-dopa therapy in patients who are otherwise benefiting from it. Birkmayer and Newmayer [70] as well as Miller and Nieburg [71] reported that TP can reverse these side effects of L-dopa, without otherwise interfering with treatment. Dosage used was generally between 1 to 3 gm/day TP. These authors claim that most of the patients could be maintained on their optimal L-dopa therapy with the addition of TP. They state that they have helped several hundred patients in this way, but the papers do not provide detailed information.

## L-Tryptophan Side Effects

Given the large number of published clinical trials of TP in depression and the moderate number in other psychiatric and neurological conditions, it is remarkable that most studies do not mention side effects at all. Two hypotheses are tenable to explain this. One is that the substance is almost free of side effects in the doses used. The other is that discussion of biochemical data and rationales take up so much space that side-effect data are simply not included.

Many clinical papers on TP are letters to *Lancet*, brief clinical reports, or include TP as one of several drugs studied. Three studies suggest that TP does not improve sleep in depressed patients [35,39,59]. A few state there were no troublesome side effects [43] or that the TP group showed fewer side effects than the group receiving the comparison treatment [42, 53,54]. Coppen et al. found more side effects on TP than on IMI, but note that one very hypochondriacal patient was in the TP group [39]. Chouinard et al., in their initial open TP study, found tremor, nausea, vomiting, and dry mouth in more than half their patients [28]. However, in their subsequent double-blind study, TP caused less of these effects and compared favorably to IMI, being less likely to cause hypotensive symptoms [25]. In their study comparing TP to CPZ in chronic schizophrenics, the TP group showed a significant worsening of dyskinesia, probably due to the absence of dopamine-blocking drug effects [66]. When TP is added to MAO inhibitors, drowsiness [55] or, in large doses, myoclonus [56] can occur.

On the basis of the literature and very limited personal experience using TP in treatment-resistant depressed patients, sedation, nausea, and tremors have all been seen and may constitute the commoner side effects.

The literature also includes rare cases of sexual excitation both in normal subjects [6] and, after prolonged therapy, in depressed patients [72-74]. On the other hand, Broadhurst and Rao deny having seen any sexual effects in a series of over 500 patients treated with TP [75].


**Discussion**

The use of TP as a treatment for depression has seductive aspects. If it really were effective, it would indirectly support the hypothesis that some depressions are improved when brain serotonin is raised. Also TP is a "natural substance," which implies, but by no means proves, that it should be safer and obscurely better than the synthetic "unnatural" drugs usually used to treat depressions.

Grossly, the evidence that TP is an effective antidepressant is weak; even uncontrolled open studies with the exception of those by Broadhurst [29] and Shopsin [30] are relatively or completely negative. Placebo-controlled trials are even less promising. If one pools all available data from the open and placebo-controlled studies, ignoring dosage, adjuvant drugs, and failure to relapse when an improved TP patient is shifted to placebo, a gross improvement rate of 48 of 136 patients (35%) is obtained, which resembles the rate often reported for placebo in double-blind trials of tricyclic antidepressants.

On the other hand, seven studies have compared TP to a tricyclic antidepressant, usually IMI and usually at rather low fixed doses of 150 mg/day. The six larger studies, all unfortunately without a placebo group

group, found TP to be as effective as the tricyclic. To further confuse matters, one study found TP equivalent to ECT in efficacy, although two others found TP clearly inferior. Adding TP to ECT confers no additional benefit, while adding TP to tricyclics has been without benefit in most studies. Two studies, both using clomipramine, report adding TP was valuable; why the most serotonergic tricyclic antidepressant drug should be most aided by the addition of a serotonin precursor is unclear.

It is reasonably certain that TP potentiates the antidepressant effect of MAO inhibitors. However, these drugs are quite effective without TP added. If one were to try adding TP to MAO inhibitor nonresponders, Pare's approach [50] of starting with over 7gm/day seems unwise, since several patients developed severe side effects; beginning with 500 mg. b.i.d. seems more appropriate.

Beyond this there are some intriguing but unsubstantiated hints available in the literature. Perhaps BPI depressions respond best to high TP doses [25,32,37,38] of over 6 gm/day, as Chouinard suggests. Perhaps there is a therapeutic window for TP in UPI depressions, such that dosages over 4 to 6 gm/day are no longer effective. Two studies, Chouinard's [25] and Herrington's [43] certainly showed a failure to sustain improvement on TP after the first two weeks, at which time the TP dose was raised; this certainly does not prove that the dose increase was responsible. All one can really say about the dose issue is that the studies that found TP equal to a tricyclic or ECT in efficacy tended to use doses of 6 gm/day or less while the more negative placebo-controlled studies used higher doses. Mendels' clearly negative placebo-controlled study went up to 15 gm/day, for example [35].

Another hint in the literature is that patients with high pretreatment anxiety levels are unlikely to do well on TP [25,43]. At the biochemical level there is a suggestion, which seems counterintuitive, that patients with high pretreatment plasma TP levels are most likely to respond to oral TP [25,41]. This is particularly odd if there is a therapeutic window for TP. Moller's two groups of patients with low ratios of plasma TP to plasma levels of other competing amino acids who responded uniquely to TP therapy [32,33] make one feel that this clue should be pursued further in future TP trials in depression.

It is hard to infer anything clear from the use of added pyridoxine, ascorbic acid, or niacin to make TP work better, but studies that have used such adjuvants do not seem to achieve better results than those using TP alone. It is also worth noting that giving TP to depressed patients does not improve their sleep; in fact, TP seems inferior to tricyclic antidepressants in this regard. Perhaps TP, which is a reasonable hypnotic agent, works differently in depression or perhaps the dosage schedules (usually breakfast and supper) used in depression are inappropriately chosen. TP may be most effective in inducing sleep if given 45 minutes before sleep is expected and may be much less effective in promoting prolonged sleep.

If a maximum increase in plasma TP is desired, basic studies suggest that the medication should not be given with protein meals but given alone or with carbohydrates. In Moller's two studies, he gave TP with meals in the first study and alone in the second and got good results in a subset of patients in each. In the second study, patients appear to have been preselected to have a higher proportion with low tryptophan ratios; in any event, he obtained a higher improvement rate in the second (20 of 42) than in the first (5 of 19).

All in all, TP remains interesting, enigmatic and worthy of further study. If it becomes possible to predict which depressed patients will respond to TP or if it proves to really be as effective as the more side-effect-prone antipsychotics in mania and if it is a safer and "better" treatment for insomnia than benzodiazepines, clinical psychopharmacological practice will benefit, as will patients. As with many new drug therapies, the combination of clinical and basic studies may advance our rapidly growing knowledge of the interrelationships between brain metabolism, neurotransmitters, behavior, and clinical psychopathology.

## Summary

More than 70 studies of the effects of TP in a variety of clinical conditions are reviewed. The available evidence is incomplete and sometimes contradictory, but the following tentative conclusions seem reasonable:

1. L-Tryptophan may have antidepressant effects in some depressed patients. Negative placebo-controlled studies are balanced out by studies showing TP to be as effective as tricyclic antidepressants. Issues such as dose, pretreatment plasma TP levels, and ratios with competing amino acids, and bipolar versus unipolar depressive diagnosis all seem potentially important. There is some question as to whether initial antidepressant response to TP may or may not fade on continued therapy. Side effects (nausea, drowsiness, tremors) seem relatively uncommon.

2. L-Tryptophan seems to increase the antidepressant effect of MAO inhibitors.

3. On the basis of two controlled studies, TP may have some efficacy in hypomania.

4. L-Tryptophan speeds sleep onset in individuals with some trouble falling asleep. Doses from 1 to 7 gm have about the same effect.

5. In normal subjects, TP increases sleepiness and may occasionally produce a euphoric inebriated state.

6. L-Tryptophan may counteract psychopathology induced by L-dopa in parkinsonian patients.

7. L-Tryptophan may work by increasing brain serotonin. Maximum elevations in plasma TP should occur if TP is given between meals or with nonprotein meals.

8. The value of adding various vitamins (C, B$_3$, B$_6$) to TP is unclear.

9. L-Tryptophan is not approved as a drug in the United States but is available as a dietary supplement in pharmacies and health-food stores.

L-Tryptophan therefore remains an interesting substance that may yet turn out to be valuable in some medical and psychiatric conditions. It is of special interest and relevance in the treatment of affective disorders.

### References

1. Young S, Sourkes T: Tryptophan in the central nervous system: regulation and significance. Adv Neurochem 2:133-191, 1977.

2. Growdon JH: Neurotransmitter precursors in the diet: Their use in the treatment of brain diseases. *In* Wurtman R, Wurtman J (Eds): Nutrition and the Brain, Vol. 3. New York, Raven, 1979, pp 117-181.

3. Lipton MA: Vitamins, megavitamin therapy, and the nervous system. *In* Wurtman R, Wurtman J (Eds): Nutrition and the Brain, Vol. 3. New York, Raven, 1979, pp 183-264.

4. Sourkes T: Nutrients and cofactors required for monoamine synthesis in nervous tissue. *In* Wurtman R, Wurtman J (Eds): Nutrition and the Brain, Vol. 3. New York, Raven, 1979, pp 265-299.

5. Smith B, Prockop D: Central nervous system effects of ingestion of L-tryptophan by normal subjects. New Eng J Med 267:1338-1341, 1962.

6. Oswald I, Ashcroft G, Berger R, et al: Some experiments in the chemistry of normal sleep. Brit J Psychiat 112:391-399, 1966.

7. Greenwood M, Friedel J, Bond A, et al: The acute effects of intravenous infusion of L-tryptophan in normal subjects. Clin Pharmacol 2:165-172, 1975.

8. Greenwood M, Lader M, Kantameneni B, et al: The acute effect of oral (-)-tryptophan in human subjects. Brit J Clin Pharmacol 2:165-172, 1975.

9. Oates J, Sjoerdsma A: Neurological effects of tryptophan in patients receiving a monoamine oxidase inhibitor. Neurology 10:1076-1078, 1960.

10. Hartmann E: Some studies on the biochemistry of dreaming sleep. Proceedings of the IV World Congress of Psychiatry, Madrid, Spain, September 1966. Exerpta Med Internat Cong Series No 150, 1966, pp 3100-3102.

11. Hartmann E: The effect of tryptophan on the sleep dream cycle in man. Psychosom Sci 8:479-480, 1967.

12. Griffiths WJ, Lester BK, Coulter JD, et al: Tryptophan and sleep in young adults. Psychophysiol 9:345-356, 1972 (abstract).

13. Wyatt RJ, Engelman K, Kupfer DJ, et al: Effects of L-tryptophan (a natural sedative) on human sleep. Lancet 1:842-845, 1970.

14. Hartmann E, Spinweber C, Ware C: L-tryptophan, L-leucine, and placebo: Effects on subjective sleepiness. Sleep Res 5:57, 1976.

15. Hartmann E, Spinweber C, Fernstrom J: Diet, amino acids, and sleep. Sleep Res 6:61, 1977.

16. Hartmann E, Oldfield M, Carpenter J: Tryptophan, dietary intake: Effect on subjective sleepiness. Sleep Res (in press).

17. Hartmann E, Chung R, Chien C: L-tryptophan and sleep. Psychopharmacologia 19:114-127, 1971.

18. Makipour H, Iber FL, Hartmann E: Effects of L-tryptophan on sleep in hospitalized insomniac patients. Report to the Assn Psychophysiological Study of Sleep, Lake Minnewaske, New York, 1972. Abs: Sleep Res 1:65, 1972. Los Angeles, Brain Information Service, UCLA.

19. Hartmann E, Cravens J, List S: Hypnotic effects of L-tryptophan. Arch Gen Psychiat 31:394-397, 1974.

20. Hartmann E, Spinweber C: Sleep induced by L-tryptophan: Effects of dosages within the normal dietary intake. J Nerv Ment Dis 167:497-499, 1979.

21. Davis D, Tyler J, Hartmann E: Effects on human sleep of L-tryptophan, one and two grams. Sleep Res 4:72, 1975.

22. Hartmann E, Elion R.: The insomnia of "Sleeping in a strange place." Psychopharmacologia 53:131-133, 1977.

23. Nicholson AN, Stone BM: L-tryptophan and sleep in healthy man. EEG Clin Neurophysiol 47:539-545, 1979.

24. Spinweber C et al: (unpublished manuscript).

25. Chouinard G, Young S, Annable L, et al: Tryptophan-nicotinamide, imipramine and their combination in depression. A controlled study. Acta Psychiat Scand 59:394-414, 1979.

26. Feighner J, Robins E, Guze S, et al: Diagnosis criteria for use in psychiatric research. Arch Gen Psychiat 26:57-62, 1972.

27. Spitzer R, Endicott J, Robins E: Research diagnostic criteria. Ed 3. Biometrics Research, New York, State Psychiatric Institute, 1977.

28. Chouinard G, Young S, Annable L, et al: Tryptophan-nicotinamide combination in the treatment of newly admitted depressed patients. Comm Psychopharm 2:311-318, 1978.

29. Broadhurst A: L-tryptophan v.s. ECT. Lancet 1:1392-1393, 1970.

30. Shopsin B: Enhancement of the antidepressant response to L-tryptophan by a liver pyrrolase inhibitor. Neuropsychobiol 4:188-192, 1978.

31. Dunner DL, Goodwin FK: Effects of L-tryptophan on brain serotonin metabolism in depressed patients. Arch Gen Psychiat 26:364-366, 1972.

32. Moller SE, Kirk L, Fremming KH: Plasma amino acids as an index for subgroups in manic depressive psychosis: Correlation to effect of tryptophan. Psychopharmacologia 49:205-213, 1976.

33. Moller SE: Tryptophan availability in endogenously depressed patients. (Paper presented at meeting of the American College of Neuropsychopharmacology, San Juan, Puerto Rico, December 14, 1979).

34. Bunney WE Jr, Brodie HK, Murphy DL, et al: Studies of alpha-methyl-para-tyrosine, L-dopa and L-tryptophan in depression and mania. Am J Psychiat 127:872-881, 1971.

35. Mendels J, Stinnett JL, Burns D, et al: Amine precursors and depression. Arch Gen Psychiat 32:22-30, 1975.

36. Dunner DL, Fieve RR: Affective disorder: Studies with amine precursors. Am J Psychiat 132:180-183, 1975.

37. Murphy DL, Baker M, Goodwin FK, et al: L-tryptophan in affective disorders: Indoleamine changes and differential clinical effects. Psychopharmacologia 34:11-20, 1974.

38. Farkas T, Dunner DL, Fieve RR: L-tryptophan in depression. Biol Psychiat 11:295-302, 1976.

39. Coppen A, Whybrow PC, Noguera R, et al: The comparative antidepressant value of L-tryptophan and imipramine with and without attempted potentiation by liothyronine. Arch Gen Psychiat 26:234-241, 1972.

40. Kline NS, Shah BK: Comparable therapeutic efficacy of tryptophan and imipramine: Average therapeutic ratings versus "true equivalence." An important difference. Curr Ther Res 15:484-487, 1973.

41. Gayford J, Parker A, Phillips E, et al: Whole blood 5-hydroxy-tryptamine during treatment of endogenous depressive illness. Brit J Psychiat 112:597-598, 1973.

42. Jensen K. Freuensgaard K, Ahlfors U, et al: Tryptophan-imipramine in depression. Lancet 2:920, 1975.

43. Herrington R, Bruck A, Johnstone E, et al: Comparative trial of L-tryptophan and amitriptyline in depressive illness. Psychol Med 6:673-678, 1976.

44. Rao B, Broadhurst A: Tryptophan and depression. Brit Med J 1:460, 1976.

45. Carroll B, Mowbray R, Davis B: Sequential comparison of L-tryptophan with ECT in severe depression. Lancet 1:967-969, 1970.

46. Herrington R, Bruce A, Johnstone E: Comparative trial of L-tryptophan and ECT in severe depressive illness. Lancet 2:731-734, 1974.

47. MacSweeney D: Treatment of unipolar depression. Lancet 2:510-511, 1975.

48. Kirkegaard C, Moller SE, Bjorum N: Addition of L-tryptophan to electroconvulsive treatment in endogenous depression. A double-blind study. Acta Psychiat Scand 58:457-462, 1978.

49. D'Elia G, Lehmann J, Raotma H: Evaluation of the combination of tryptophan and ECT in the treatment of depression: I. clinical analysis. Acta Psychiat Scand 56:303-318, 1977.

50. Pare CMB: Potentiation of monoamine-oxidase inhibitors by tryptophan. Lancet 2:527-528, 1973.

51. Lopez-Ibor A, Ayso Gutierrez JL, Iglesias JLM: Tryptophan and amitriptyline in the treatment of depression: A double-blind study. Int Pharmacopsychiat 8:145-151, 1973.

52. Shaw DM, Johnson LJ, MacSweeney DA: Tricyclic antidepressants and tryptophan in unipolar affective disorder. Lancet 2:1245, 1972.

53. Roos BE: Tryptophan, 5-hydroxytryptophan and tricyclic antidepressants and tryptophan in unipolar affective disorder. Lancet 2:1245, 1972.

54. Walinder J, Skott A, Carlsson A, et al: Potentiation of the antidepressant action of clomipramine by tryptophan. Lancet 1:79-81, 1963.

55. Coppen A, Shaw D, Farrell J: Potentiation of the antidepressive effect of a monoamine oxidase inhibitor by tryptophan. Lancet 1:79-81, 1963.

56. Glass A, Platman S: Potentiation of a monoamine oxidase inhibitor by tryptophan. J Psychiat Res 7:83-88, 1969.

57. Ayuso Gutierrez J, Lopez-Ibor AJ: Tryptophan and an MAOI (nialamide) in treatment of depression. Internat Pharmacopsychiat 6:92-97, 1971.

58. Quitkin F, Rifkin A, Klein D: Monoamine oxidase inhibitors. Arch Gen Psychiat 36:749-764, 1979.

59. Murphy D, Baker M, Goodwin F, et al: L-tryptophan in affective disorders: Indolamine changes and differential clinical effects. Psychopharmacologia 34:11-20, 1974.

60. Prange A, Wilson I, Lynn C, et al: L-tryptophan in mania. Arch Gen Psychiat 30:56-62, 1974.

61. Prange A, Sisk J, Wilson I, et al: Balance, permission, and discrimination among amines: A theoretical consideration of the actions of L-tryptophan in disorders of movements and affect. In Barchas J, Usdin E (Eds): Serotonin and Behavior. New York, Academic, 1973.

62. Pollin W, Cardon P, Kety S: Effects of amino acid feedings in schizophrenic patients treated with iproniazid. Science 133:104-095, 1961.

63. Lauer J, Inskip W, Bernsohn J, et al: Obersvations on schizophrenic patients after iproniazid and tryptophan. AMA Arch Neurol Psychiat 80:122-130, 1958.

64. Bowers MB: Cerebrospinal fluid 5-hydroxyindoles and behavior after L-tryptophan and pyridoxine administration to psychiatric patients. Neuropharmacol 9:599-604, 1970.

65. Gillin J, Kaplan J, Wyatt R: Clinical effects of tryptophan in chronic schizophrenic patients. Bio Psychiat 11:635-639, 1976.

66. Chouinard G, Annable L. Young S, et al: A controlled study of tryptophanbenzerazide in schizophrenia. Comm Psychopharmacol 2:21-31, 1978.

67. Yaryura-Tobias J, Neziroglu F, Ghagavan H: Obsessive-compulsive disorders: A serotonergic hypothesis. *In* Saletu B, Berner P, Hollister L (Eds): Neuropsychopharmacology: Proceedings of the 11th Congress of the CINP. Oxford, England, Pergamon, 1979, pp 117-125.

68. Coppen A, Metcalfe M, Carroll J, et al: Levodopa and L-tryptophan therapy in parkinsonism. Lancet 1:654-658, 1972.

69. Birkmayer W, Neumayer E: Die behandlung der dopa psychosen mit L-tryptophan. Nervenaerzt 43:76-78, 1972.

70. Hyyppa M, Jolma T, Riekkinen J, et al: Effects of L-tryptophan treatment on central indoleamine metabolism and short lasting neurologic disturbances in multiple sclerosis. J Neural Transmiss 2:297-304, 1975.

71. Miller EM, Nieburg HA: L-tryptophan in the treatment of levodopa-induced psychiatric disorders. Dis Nerv Sys 35:20-23, 1974.

72. Egan G, Hammad G: Sexual disinhibition with L-tryptophan. Brit Med J 2:701, 1976.

73. Hullin R, Jerram T: Sexual disinhibition with L-tryptophan. Brit Med J 2:1010, 1976.

74. Morgan R: Tryptophan overdosage. Brit J Psychiat 131:548, 1977.

75. Broadhurst A, Rao B: L-tryptophan and sexual behavior. Brit Med J 1:51-52, 1977.

# Part II
# Drug Side Effects

# 10 Tardive Dyskinesia

*Jonathan O. Cole, M.D.*
*George Gardos, M.D.*

Tardive dyskinesia has been described by a recent American College of Neuropsychopharmacology and Federal Drug Administration task force as "The syndrome . . . characterized by rhythmical involuntary movements of the tongue, face, mouth, or jaw (e.g., protrusion of tongue, puffing of cheeks, puckering of mouth, chewing movements). Sometimes these may be accompanied by involuntary [choreoathetoid] movements of extremities [1]." There is reasonable evidence, based essentially on guilt by association, that patients who have received antipsychotic drugs are liable to develop persistent abnormal movements of the sort just described.

The presumption that all patients getting any antipsychotic drug at any dose are at some risk of developing abnormal movements that may not go away when the drug is stopped is properly worrisome to all psychiatrists using these drugs. It raises a number of practical and logical questions, most of which are difficult to answer. This communication will attempt to provide answers that reflect current research evidence, such as it is, as well as the authors' clinical experiences and beliefs.

**Q. Do all patients who develop abnormal movements on antipsychotic drugs have tardive dyskinesia?**

A. No. Abnormal movements occurring in the first few days or weeks on antipsychotic medication are predominantly extrapyramidal symptoms and respond to antiparkinsonian medication. Certain parkinsonian symptoms, such as tremor, can occur even in patients who have been on drugs for years. Some patients show coexisting parkinsonianism and tardive dyskinesia. Bona fide neurological disorders producing abnormal movements may also occur in patients on antipsychotics. Huntington chorea somewhat resembles tardive dyskinesia, but the movements are more severe, and the condition, unlike tardive dyskinesia, progresses relentlessly toward total disability. In elderly patients, a condition known as "senile chorea" may be seen that resembles tardive dyskinesia but more closely resembles Huntington chorea, being a severe, progressive dyskinesia. Dyskinetic chewing, mouthing, and tongue movements are seen in the elderly, associated with edentia, chronic institutionalization, and dementia. This syndrome is called "orofacial dyskinesia" and is hard to differentiate from tardive dyskinesia; the coexistence of choreoathetoid movements of the extremities makes the diagnosis of tardive dyskinesia probable. Gilles de la Tourette syndrome may be differentiated by its coprolalia, vocal utterances, and early onset.

In addition to the conditions just mentioned, there are numerous disorders of the extrapyramidal or pyramidal motor systems, brain stem, or cerebellum, which may produce abnormal movements and may even mimic tardive dyskinesia.

Schizophrenic patients, especially hospitalized ones, had been observed to show striking movement abnormalities long before phenothiazines came into use. These movements tend to go under the title "schizophrenic mannerisms" and include a great variety of automatic, semipurposeful, and ritualistic movements. Although the distinction between mannerisms and dyskinetic movements is sometimes easy to make, we think that there are some cases where one is hard put to decide which condition is being encountered. Kraepelin described dyskinetic movements and American-trained psychiatrists visiting psychiatric hospitals in Egypt and Turkey, where antipsychotic drugs are rarely available for financial reasons, have observed and even filmed patients with typical tardive-dyskinesia-like movements who have never received an antipsychotic drug. The senior author has seen one patient who developed chewing movements and tongue protrusion immediately after a prefrontal lobotomy in 1956; she had had brief prior exposure to perphenazine. The movements were mild but are still present today. Rocking movements, commonly seen in institutionalized retarded patients in the predrug era, are often part of a larger picture of buccolingual and choreiform movements. An excellent review of this general area has been published by Marsden, Tarsy and Baldessarini [2].

Despite these alternative explanations for abnormal movements, it seems likely that the high and apparently increasing prevalence of dyskinetic movements observed on chronic wards in public mental hospitals—almost 50% at Boston State Hospital [3]—is attributable in large part to tardive dyskinesia secondary to antipsychotic drug exposure.

Of the 14 patients hospitalized at McLean Hospital for more than 10 years, three show clear tardive dyskinesia with buccolingual and extremity movements and four others show mild symptoms suggestive of the condition. One of these has shown tongue protrusion in the past but currently shows only mild lip movements.

**Q. What kinds of movements make up tardive dyskinesia?**

A. Patients who have abnormal movements after exposure to antipsychotic drugs and presumably have tardive dyskinesia, no other diagnosis being likely, can show a wide range and variety of movements.

The typical movements are in the tongue, jaws, and mouth. The tongue will rarely show only tremor but more commonly will roll, writhe, and wander around the mouth and lips. Sometimes the tongue will protrude from the mouth repetitively. Semirhythmic chewing movements usually occur, but other patients have yawning or side-to-side jaw movements. The lips may smack, purse, pout, or suck. Rapid eye blinking or tonic eyebrow arching also occurs, as do facial tics, grimaces and tooth grinding.

Breathing disturbances—respiratory grunting or alterations in speech rhythm—can occur. Head nodding and body rocking can be present as can more dystonic twisting movements of the neck and torso. Thrusting pelvic movements (called axial hyperkinesia) sometimes occur.

Fine choreiform finger movements and grosser finger counting and hand clenching movements are relatively common. Wrist movements are often also present. More violent hemiballistic or writhing athetoid movements of the whole arm are rarer but can occur.

Similar movements occur in the toes and ankles. In addition, patients may swing their legs or stamp or tap their feet repetitively in a way indistinguishable from the akathisia seen in patients in their first weeks on an antipsychotic drug. On standing, patients may rock from foot to foot sideways, do pelvic thrusting movements or stamp their feet. Finger movements may be exaggerated when patients walk.

Movements vary with patient's arousal level, being least when the patient is drowsy or asleep. Stress will usually increase dyskinesia. Patients can almost always inhibit a movement if they need to—even marked dyskinesia rarely interferes with eating or drinking. However, asking a patient to concentrate on one tonic complex posture (e.g., standing with eyes closed and arms extended) or on a complex action (e.g., touching thumbs to each finger in turn rapidly) will often bring out or exaggerate dyskinesia in other muscle groups not involved in the task.

The exact types and severities of movements vary widely from patient to patient. Probably mild choreiform finger movements and tongue writhing are the earliest and most common manifestations of the disorder.


**Q. When a patient on antipsychotic drugs develops chewing, tongue movements, or choreoathetoid movements of the extremities or some combination of these, what does this mean? What should the psychiatrist do then?**

A. The psychiatrist should be aware that the patient may have developed "tardive" (e.g., late appearing, long-lasting, semipermanent) dyskinesia. However, other, less serious, dyskinesias may present in a similar way.

Occasionally, a patient with chronic schizophrenia, under the influence of either acute agitation or antiparkinsonian drugs, or both, will develop typical dyskinetic movements, which will disappear when the antiparkinsonian medication is stopped or the patient's clinical status improves. One such patient on trifluoperazine plus benztropine showed these symptoms which faded when benztropine was stopped. When trifluoperazine was also stopped for three weeks, no dyskinetic movements emerged, though the patient became progressively more active, bizarre, and sleepless.

Some patients, after a few months or years of antipsychotic drug therapy, develop dyskinetic movements. The movements often appear while the patient is still on the drug. They may temporarily worsen when the antipsychotic drug is stopped but will then slowly improve, disappearing after weeks or months. Such dyskinesias are obviously not permanent and may be called "treatment-emergent" dyskinesias. The senior author has now seen three neurotic and three younger schizophrenic patients in whom this syndrome has emerged and has then waned over a period of six weeks to one year, eventually disappearing entirely. In the cases of two schizophrenic patients, the psychosis worsened as the movements faded and both had to be started on antipsychotic medication again. One is asymptomatic after 18 months on clozapine and the second has moderate dyskinesia and moderate paranoid schizophrenia on trifluoperazine; he has refused clozapine treatment. The third patient's movements had disappeared after a year of low-dose thioridazine, but she remained quite psychotic.

The psychiatrist, faced with dyskinesia in an ambulatory, socially adjusted schizophrenic with a history of overt, severe psychosis doing well on maintenance antipsychotics therapy, is in an uncomfortable position. Stopping the antipsychotic medication has to be seriously considered but may lead rapidly to relapse and rehospitalization. A clinical decision has to be made that takes into account the patient's history of drug response and relapse. In a patient who clearly relapses rapidly when taken off drugs, continued drug therapy at the lowest possible dose seems the best therapy of the total problem. Since antiparkinsonian drugs sometimes (but not always) aggravate or even induce dyskinetic movements, stopping such drugs would also be indicated.

If the patient has been well adjusted for a prolonged period or if the patient's response to antipsychotic drugs is less obviously good, a watchful trial off drugs is indicated in the hope that the movements will gradually fade away. Obviously, the undesirability of the dyskinesia must be weighed against the hazards of psychotic relapse.

In patients without schizophrenic illness, the antipsychotic drug should be stopped, and alternative treatments tried instead. Having now seen nine nonpsychotic patients in the past two years with clear tardive dyskinesia, we feel very strongly that these drugs should be strenuously avoided in the treatment of depression, anxiety states, borderline states, or personality disorders unless other drug classes have failed to help the patient and antipsychotic drugs really benefit the patient's symptoms uniquely.

As an example of the latter therapeutic bind, an exalcoholic patient in her fifties with a history of sedative abuse and severe insomnia developed tongue protrusion and chewing movements after a year on thioridazine for her insomnia and anxiety. Tricyclic antidepressants caused agitation, and sedative-hypnotics were ineffective even in large doses. After discussion of the alternatives, the patient is now emotionally stable and cheerful, sleeping well but with mild, barely visible dyskinesia after three months on 100 mg of chlorpromazine at bedtime, which seems, overall, the least bad of the available alternatives.

**Q. Can tardive dyskinesia be avoided in schizophrenic patients?**

A. We are not sure that it can. Although the occurrence of dyskinesia gets more frequent in patients with longer histories of illness and antipsychotic drug therapy, the relationship between total drug dose over the years and the presence of dyskinesia is only weakly positive [2,4]. Since records of past drug therapy in chronic schizophrenics in public facilities and in patients with multiple hospitalizations with multiple periods of drug therapy in aftercare are notoriously poor, it is hard to be sure whether better data would make the relationship between dosage and dyskinesia more compelling.

It seems reasonable to maintain schizophrenic patients on antipsychotic drugs only if they clearly are helped by them and to use the lowest dose consistent with stability and social adjustment. We are not sure that administrative devices such as drugless weekends do more than remind everyone of the problem and reduce nursing workloads on weekends.

The only therapies for schizophrenia that do not appear to cause dyskinesia are electroconvulsive therapy (ECT) and lithium. However, ECT history in drug-treated schizophrenics is sometimes positively correlated with the presence of dyskinesia. ECT is probably effective in treating schizophrenic excitements but probably does not prevent relapse or recurrence. Occasional schizo-affectives and nonaffective schizophrenics are helped by lithium [5], but response is neither reliable nor predictable. This use is not approved by the FDA.

**Q. Are any antipsychotic drugs safer than others with respect to dyskinesia?**

A. It seems reasonable that drugs with a low incidence of acute neurological side effects might be less likely to be associated with tardive dyskinesia. Clozapine, which may have a slightly different action on dopamine receptors than other antipsychotic drugs, has been on trial or on the market in Europe for several years and is alleged to "never" cause tardive dyskinesia. If it were marketed in this country, it might be the treatment choice in schizophrenics with dyskinesia. It is far too early to be sure about either suggestion [6,7]. Our one great clozapine success in a girl with severe treatment-emergent dyskinesia has been mentioned above. Two other patients with mild choreiform movements have continued to show these symptoms for their first month on clozapine.

Thioridazine sounds as though it should be a "safer" drug. Having personally seen two patients with clear dyskinesia after treatment only with thioridazine for a year (a depressed woman in her sixties and the postalcoholic patient cited above), we are convinced that the drug can elicit dyskinesia. It is currently impossible to tell whether thioridazine does elicit it less frequently. A recent Boston State Hospital study [4] showed total use over the years of non-piperazine phenothiazines (thioridazine and chlorpromazine in about equal amounts) was positively correlated with the current presence of dyskinesia, whereas total oral use of piperazine phenothiazines was not. These results could, of course, be a fluke, but they suggest that piperazine drugs, with a high incidence of neurological side effects, are not differentially associated with tardive dyskinesia. An important issue concerns the association between long-acting fluphenazine and tardive dyskinesia. Although it is true that patients maintained on injectable fluphenazine tend to receive lower milligram quantities of drug than patients maintained on oral antipsychotics, there is no evidence that injectable fluphenazine is less likely to induce tardive dyskinesia; in fact, the converse may be true [4].

Since newer drugs—loxapine and molindone—have not been associated, to date, with tardive dyskinesia, probably because they have not been in use long enough, a case could be made for their use in patients who are showing dyskinesia. One might be in a slightly better medicolegal position for obvious reasons, but we are not optimistic that this approach is really rational. Reserpine, a less effective antipsychotic agent, has, unfortunately, been reported to elicit tardive dyskinesia, as has haloperidol [2]. We have encountered cases of dyskinesia, after exposure only to thioridazine, haloperidol, thiothixene, chlorpromazine, fluphenazine, and trifluoperazine and infer that all classes of antipsychotic drugs share the same risk.


**Q. Do antiparkinsonian drugs cause or help dyskinesia?**

A. Dyskinetic movements are sometimes made worse by antiparkinsonian drugs [8]. However, a few patients with typical tardive dyskinesia are helped by them. In fact, amantadine, an effective antiparkinsonian drug, has been shown to alleviate cases of tardive dyskinesia. However, a controlled investigation failed to confirm its efficacy [9] in tardive dyskinesia.

Trial and error seems the only way to tell the effects of antiparkinsonian agents on individual patients.

This situation is probably a result of the heterogeneity of the syndrome we call tardive dyskinesia. Even though it is widely assumed that tardive dyskinesia is due to overstimulation of dopamine receptors in the basal ganglia, a patient was recently described whose severe dyskinesia only responded to apomorphine, a dopamine synapse stimulator [10].

A recent report by Gerlach [11] has complicated the situation. He writes that biperiden, an antiparkinsonian drug, increases the frequency of mouth openings and tongue protrusions in tardive dyskinesia patients, while alpha-methylparatyrosine, an inhibitor of dopamine synthesis, reduces the frequency but increases the duration of such movements.

Although it is possible that patients who require antiparkinsonian drugs because of neurologic side effects during antipsychotic drug therapy might be at greater risk of developing tardive dyskinesia, we have seen three patients with tardive dyskinesia who had never received an antiparkinsonian drug. Clarification of this possible relationship would require detailed complete drug histories on a large cohort of patients treated with antipsychotic drugs, some of whom also received antiparkinsonian drugs.

**Q. Are there any drug treatments useful in tardive dyskinesia?**

A. None are clearly useful in most patients. Antipsychotic drugs can suppress dyskinetic movements by blocking dopaminergic synapses, but it seems irrational to treat a condition with drugs strongly suspected of causing it. In rare instances, this may be the only way to relieve distress in patients with severe dyskinesia. The literature suggests that abnormal movements may "break through" such suppressant therapy. Kazamatsuri et al. [12] reviewed the earlier literature in this area in 1971.

More recent uncontrolled or partially controlled studies have suggested that unusual drugs such as deanol [13-22], lithium [23-25], papaverine [26,27], low-dose reserpine [28], tetrabenazine [12], and Periactin [29] may improve dyskinesia, but controlled studies are often negative, or the magnitude of the effects is often small (e.g., 10% to 20% reduction in movement severity [30-32]). Even benzodiazepines [33] may reduce movements, perhaps by reducing anxiety and tension; all neurological conditions, including tardive dyskinesia, may be more obvious when the patient is upset or anxious.

Currently, we are beginning a trial of clozapine in tardive dyskinesia and are considering studies of Periactin and a benzodiazepine.

Despite the plethora of negative studies, the situation is far from hopeless. One must not lose sight of the fact that each one of the promising therapeutic agents listed above tends to produce marked improvement in a few of the patients studied (which tends to be counterbalanced by adverse changes in others). The explanation probably lies in the heterogeneity of tardive dyskinesia. It is much more likely that one of a series of different drugs will help a given patient, than that any given compound will help a lot of patients. Therefore, a rational approach to treating an individual patient with dyskinesia might involve administering single doses of cholinergic and dopaminergic agents and their antagonists to obtain a pharmacological profile of the patient's dyskinesia and then selecting the appropriate pharmacological agent to induce similar long-term effects.

**Q. If a patient appears to have real tardive dyskinesia, what is the long-term prognosis?**

A. Having known chronic patients with obvious dyskinetic movements at Boston State Hospital for five years or more, we are impressed by the nonprogressive nature of the syndrome even when patients are on chronic antipsychotic drug therapy. Some patients are less dyskinetic now than they were a year or two ago, and none have shown steady worsening. The same is true of the three McLean Hospital patients with moderate dyskinesia—two are unchanged and one is clearly better after a course of ECT a year ago.

We sometimes think that the condition erupts for obscure reasons at some time in the course of a patient's chronic illness and then persists, with ups and downs, indefinitely thereafter.

Although occasional patients—often nonschizophrenics—are bothered by their movements, many chronic patients in good contact are either unaware of or untroubled by their movements. One has to point out, however, that stabilized chronic schizophrenics hardly ever complain about anything, not even about a major illness. In many chronic psychotics, the dyskinetic movements are far less of a problem than their residual psychotic symptoms and social ineffectiveness. Many such patients with dyskinesia are stable (on a low-maintenance antipsychotic drug dose), content, and adjusted in the community; one hesitates to pressure them into trying either a trial off antipsychotic drugs or a trial on a drug like deanol or Periactin that might cause new side effects.

**Q. What do current research efforts have to offer?**

A. No good animal model of tardive dyskinesia exists. The best currently available model is Klawans' guinea pig [34]. He finds that guinea pigs maintained on haloperidol for several weeks and then abruptly withdrawn from it show hypersensitivity to dopaminergic drugs (d-amphetamine, apomorphine). After haloperidol "sensitization," much lower doses of these drugs will elicit the stereotyped movements usually produced in lower mammals by these drugs. Klawans and Weiner have recently reported that lithium carbonate, given during and after the haloperidol exposure, prevents the dopaminergic hypersensitivity [35].

There is increasing evidence that the brain has several dopamine systems. In their recent excellent and detailed review, Meltzer and Stahl [36] suggest that the "parkinsonian" and the "schizophrenic" systems are probably separate. If drugs can be found that affect these systems differentially, perhaps an antipsychotic drug can be found which improves schizophrenia without producing either early neurological side effects or late dyskinesia.

Until such a drug emerges, research will probably focus on the well-known balance between cholinergic and dopaminergic systems in modulating parkinsonian and dyskinetic syndromes, hoping to find effective central cholinergic agents or unusual dopamine blockers, which will have clear and specific effectiveness in tardive dyskinesia. Other drugs with specific biochemical effects on other brain systems—gamma-aminobutyric acid, serotonin, norepinephrine, glycine—will be explored in the hope that modulating other systems could have some unpredictable effect on this disorder.

Although efforts continue to develop better methods for measuring dyskinetic movements, existing methods are certainly adequate to pick up small (10% to 20%) reductions in movements. We have been collaborating with George Simpson of Rockland State Hospital on standardizing his descriptive rating scale and have demonstrated good inter-rater reliability using earlier versions. Other, more elaborate, methods have been developed using polygraphic approaches, which are useful in focused research studies. If really effective drugs are developed for tardive dyskinesia, they can probably be distinguished from placebo even on relatively simple global rating scales. More complex instruments like the Simpson scale will be most useful in identifying drugs with more discrete effects or in identifying subgroups of dyskinetic patients likely to respond to a particular drug.

The other, potentially promising, approach to characterizing dyskinetic patients is the use of drugs as diagnostic tools. For example, Cogentin (2 mg) and physostigmine (1 mg) given intravenously can be used to examine the response of movements to cholinergic and anticholinergic drugs. Haloperidol or droperidol and L-dopa can be used to test movement response to dopamine receptor blockade and stimulation. Daniel Casey, now at the University of Oregon, has recently used this approach in six intensively studied patients to identify three deanol responders and three deanol nonresponders.

The vast maze of basic and clinical data reviewed by Meltzer and Stahl [36] gives one hope that our proliferating knowledge of brain systems is rapidly appproaching the point of real payoff. It is hoped that the next five years will find us able to diagnose and treat dyskinetic patients with precision and to find ways of preventing the emergence of these undesirable sequelae to the use of our only really effective treatments for schizophrenia.


**Commentary**


Tardive dyskinesia continues to be a major problem for psychiatry. Despite the passage of over three years and my continuing active involvement with both research and clinical consultation in this area, I cannot improve markedly on the positions Gardos and I took in this paper. The American Psychiatric Association (APA) appointed a task force on tardive dyskinesia headed by Dr. Ross Baldessarini of McLean Hospital. This group, of which we were members, has exhaustively and comprehensively reviewed the available information. The final report, with a massive bibliography, should be available from the APA late in 1980.

Epidemiological data continue to emerge from cross-sectional surveys. John Kane reported his analysis of this data at a recent meeting, giving prevalence figures of about 20% for 46 surveys involving 31,630 patients; it shall be noted that many of the surveys focused on chronic institutionalized patients, a group where one would expect the incidence to be higher [37]. Only increasing age was associated with a higher incidence of dyskinesia in more than 50% of the surveys that reported data on any specific risk factor. Even total duration of antipsychotic rug therapy and total cummulative dose of antipsychotic drugs were significantly associated with the presence of dyskinesia in less than 25% of the surveys that provided this information. This fits with my clinical impression that some unidentified biological vulnerability must account for the fact that some patients develop tardive dyskinesia after only weeks or months on a drug and others remain free of it for years. Several clinicians believe that depressed patients may develop dyskinesia after shorter exposure to antipsychotic drugs than do schizophrenics.

The whole issue of how much movement abnormality constitutes "real" tardive dyskinesia remains unclear. Cases with borderline, minor suggestions of dyskinesia are currently being systematically followed at several centers to determine the risk to the patient of evolving a more serious dyskinesia and patients with early clear dyskinesia are also being longitudinally followed to see if the condition is ever progressive and, if so, under what circumstances. At present, in my clinical judgment, brief or prolonged drug holidays may be as likely to aggravate as to improve matters, though no clear data is available, and permanent stopping of antipsychotic drugs is obviously the treatment of choice. Unfortunately, it is an unfeasible option in most chronic schizophrenics with clear dyskinesia.

At present, as will be detailed in the APA task force report, lecithin or choline may help some patients with dyskinesia, presumably by increasing brain acetylcholine. Benzodiazepines may ameliorate the condition a bit. Unfortunately, Rosenbaum has just reported the *emergence* or worsening of dyskinesia on benzodiazepines [38], and I have just seen a patient with mild dyskinesia who had been off antipsychotics for almost a year, in which shifting from clonazepam to diazepam led to sudden emergence of new dyskinetic symptoms, which were not suppressed when clonazepam was restarted. My limited personal experience with lecithin in six cases has not been overly encouraging; only two were somewhat improved.

The most intriguing new therapy, introduced by Friedhoff and Alpert at New York University, involves giving increasing doses of L-dopa up to the equivalent of 4 gm/day. This results in temporary worsening of the dyskinesia followed by an eventual marked drop in dyskinesia scores when the L-dopa is stopped. Eleven patients were discussed at a recent meeting [39]. Most were over 50% improved. The treatment is based on animal data, which show that chronic treatment with antipsychotic drugs leads to marked increase in the number of dopamine receptors in the brain. High-dose L-dopa therapy can cause a marked decrease in dopamine receptors. Thus, L-dopa therapy may markedly reduce the dopaminergic hyperactivity believed to be at the basis of tardive dyskinesia.

Despite some new knowledge and new therapies, the area of tardive dyskinesia is still confused. There is no clear and optimal way to either avoid the condition in schizophrenic patients or to treat or manage it once it has occurred. Luckily, the vast majority of cases I have seen have mild, barely noticeable movements that do not subjectively trouble the patients. Avoiding antipsychotic drugs in nonschizophrenics and using low-maintenance doses in schizophrenics who clearly benefit from the drugs and relapse when they are stopped seem the best courses to follow. In the current, increasingly hostile legal climate, drug effects and side effects need to be discussed early with both patients and family and such discussions need to be recorded in the patient's chart. In the absence of adequate knowledge, the best any clinician can do is to record the dimensions of the problem thoughtfully and justify clinically, as clearly as reality permits, the decision to continue with or to stop antipsychotic drugs.

**References**

1. Editorial: Neurological syndromes associated with antipsychotic drug use: A special report. Arch Gen Psychiat 28:463-467, 1976.

2. Marsden CD, Tarsy D, Baldessarini RJ: Spontaneous and drug-induced movement disorders in psychotic patients. *In* Psychiatric Aspects of Neurological Disease, Benson DF, Blumer D (eds). New York, Grune and Statton, 1975, pp 219-266.

3. Gardos G, Sokol M, Cole J, et al: Eye color and tardive dyskinesia. Psychopharm Bull 12(2):7-9, 1976.

4. Gardos G, Cole JO: Drug variables in the etiology of tardive dyskinesia. Application of discriminant function analysis. Presentation to Tenth Congress of the Collegium Internationale Neuro-psycho-pharmicologicum, Quebec, 1976.

5. Small JG, Kellams JJ, Milstein V, et al: A placebo-controlled study of lithium combined with neuroleptics in chronic schizophrenic patients. Am J Psychiat 132:1315-1317, 1975.

6. Cole JO, Swett C, Pope H: Agranulocytosis revisited. McLean Hosp J 1:37-39, 1976.

7. Simpson GM, Varga E: Clozapine: A new antipsychotic agent. Curr Therap Res 16:679-686, 1974.

8. Turek I, Kurland AA, Hanlon TE, et al: Tardive dyskinesia: Its relation to neuroleptic and antiparkinson drugs. Br J Psychiat 121:605-612, 1972.

9. Janowsky DS, Sekerke HJ, Davis JM: Differential effects of aman-tadine on pseudoparkinsonism and tardive dyskinesia. Psychopharm Bull 9(1):37-38, 1973.

10. Carroll BJ, Curtis GC, Feinberg M: Neurotransmitter mechanisms in dyskinesia. Paper delivered at Annual Meeting APA, 1976.

11. Gerlach J: The relationship between parkinsonism and tardive dyskinesia. Paper delivered at Annual Meeting APA, 1976.

12. Kazamatsuri H, Chien C, Cole JO: Therapeutic approaches to tardive dyskinesia. Arch Gen Psychiat 27:491-499, 1972.

13. Fann WE, Lake CR: Cholinergic suppression of tardive dyskinesia. Psychopharmacologia 37:101-107, 1974.

14. Miller EM: Deanol: A solution for tardive dyskinesia? N Engl J Med 291:796-797, 1974.

15. Casey DE, Denney D: Methylaminoethanol in tardive dyskinesia. N Engl J Med 291:797, 1974.

16. Casey DE, Denney D: Deanol in the treatment of tardive dyskinesia. Am J Psychiat 132:864-867, 1975.

17. Casey DE: Deanol for tardive dyskinesia (concluded). N Engl J Med 293-359, 1975.

18. Escobar JI, Kemp KF: Dimethylaminoethanol for tardive dyskinesia. N Engl J Med 292:317-318, 1975.

19. Fann WE, Sullivan JL, Miller RD: Deanol in tardive dyskinesia: A preliminary report. Psychopharmacologia 42:135-137, 1975.

20. Curran DJ, Nagaswami S, Mohan KJ: Treatment of phenothiazine induced bulbar persistent dyskinesia with deanol acetamidobenzoate. Dis Nerv Sys 36:71-73, 1975.

21. Crane GE: Deanol for tardive dyskinesia (cont.). N Engl J Med 292:926, 1975.

22. Laterre EC, Fortemps E: Deanol in spontaneous and induced dyskinesias. Lancet 1:1301, 1975.

23. Simpson GM: Letter to the editor. Tardive dyskinesia. Br J Psychiat 122:618, 1973.

24. Prange AR, Wilson IC, Morris CE, et al: Preliminary experience with tryptophan and lithium in the treatment of tardive dyskinesia. Psychopharmocol Bull 9:36-37, 1973.

25. Reda FA, Escobar JI, Scanlan JM: Lithium carbonate in the treatment of tardive dyskinesia. Am J Psychiat 132-560-562, 1975.

26. Gardos G, Cole JO: Papaverine for tardive dyskinesia? N Eng J Med 292:1355, 1975.

27. Gardos G, Cole JO, Sniffin C: An evaluation of papaverine in tardive dyskinesia. J Clin Pharmacol 16:304, 1976.

28. Crane GE: Mediocre effects of reserpine on tardive dyskinesia. N Engl J Med 288:104, 1973.

29. Goldman D: Periactin in tardive dyskinesia. Psychopharmacologia 47:271-272.

30. Gerlach J, Thorsen K, Munkvad I: Effect of lithium in neuroleptic-induced tardive dyskinesia compared with placebo in a double-blind crossover trial. Pharmakopsych 8:51-56, 1975.

31. Simpson GM, Branchey MH, Lee JH, et al: Lithium in tardive dyskinesia. Pharmakopsych 1976 (In press).

32. Cole JO, Gardos G, Granach RP: Drug evaluation in tardive dyskinesia, papaverine and deanol. Paper delivered at Annual Meeting APA, 1976.

33. Itil TM, Unverdi C, Mehta D: Clorazepate dipotassium in tardive dyskinesia. Am J Psychiat 131:1291, 1974.

34. Klawans H, Goetz C, Westheimer R: The pharmacology of schizophrenia. In Klawans HL (ed): Clinical Neuropharmacology, Vol 1. New York, Raven Press, 1976.

35. Klawans HL, Weiner WJ: The effect of lithium on an animal model of tardive dyskinesia. Paper presented at the Tenth Congress of the CINP, Quebec, 1976.

36. Meltzer HY, Stahl SM: The dopamine hypothesis of schizophrenia: A review. Schizophrenia Bull 2:19-76, 1976.

37. Kane J: Preliminary findings with regard to risk factors and the development of tardive dyskinesia. Paper presented at the 18th annual meeting of the American College of Neuropsychopharmacology, San Juan, December 13, 1979.

38. Rosenbaum A, De La Fuente J: Benzodiazepines and tardive dyskinesia. Lancet ii:900, 1979.

39. Alpert M: Treatment of tardive dyskinesia. Paper presented at the 18th annual meeting of the American College of Neuropsychopharmacology, San Juan, December 13, 1979.

# 11 Agranulocytosis Revisited

*Jonathan O. Cole, M.D.,*
*Chester Swett, Jr., M.D. and*
*Harrison G. Pope, Jr., M.D.*

There are a number of rare but serious drug-related conditions that worry psychiatrists—delirium, retinopathy, hepatotoxicity, hypertensive crisis, and agranulocytosis. Some of these—delirium with anticholinergic, antidepressant or antiparkinsonian agents, retinitis pigmentosa with thioridazine, hypertensive crisis with monoamine oxidase inhibitors—are pharmacologically foreseeable in the general sense, since they are related to dose of drug or to known drug interactions influenced, perhaps, by the special relative vulnerability of some patients.

Other conditions—chlorpromazine-induced jaundice and phenothiazine agranulocytosis—are much rarer and far less predictable. Agranulocytosis has long been assumed to be some kind of allergic or hypersensitive response because of its rare occurrence. Although psychiatrists are aware that patients on phenothiazines run a low risk of developing agranulocytosis, the extent to which such knowledge affects clinical behavior is not known. In most hospital admissions, white blood cell counts are regularly obtained, providing at least a baseline for reference should agranulocytosis occur. But how often do psychiatrists in private practice or working in public or private outpatient clinics obtain even *baseline* blood testing? We suspect that the logistic problems involved in obtaining specimens and sending them to the laboratory make such routine laboratory work rare unless the clinic or office is located in a general medical setting. How often are outpatients starting on antipsychotic drugs told of the possibility of agranulocytosis and told to report sore throats or fevers at once for at least the first three months on the drug? Again, nobody knows, but such warnings are very likely omitted. The next level of precaution, frequent monitoring of the patient's leukocyte count, must be far rarer and probably never occurs in clinic or office practice.

## Clozapine

Since most psychiatrists and psychiatric facilities have not actually encountered a case of drug-induced agranulocytosis in years, this side effect has seemed of mild academic interest; we have tended to feel secure if we occasionally reminded staff and patients of the potential problem and occasionally obtained white blood cell counts when a patient on phenothiazines spiked a fever.

In the last year, however, we have begun to study clozapine, an antipsychotic tricyclic drug, which is on the market in several European countries and is highly regarded because of its alleged freedom from neurological side effects (parkinsonism, akathisia, or dystonia) and its lack of association (to date, at least) with tardive dyskinesia [1,2,3,4]. Early in 1975, we started three patients on the drug. Two experienced severe akathisia on other antipsychotics but have responded very well to clozapine. One schizophrenic patient has been able to return to full-time professional work, apparently free of thought disorder for the first time in five years. The second patient has recovered from an acute psychotic illness of several months' duration. A third patient had developed severe persistent dyskinetic movements while on both chlorpromazine and haloperidol, but her dyskinesia is almost subliminal on clozapine, and her psychosis has cleared. It had not done so on the other drugs. As we were about to expand our study on this investigational drug, we were informed by the company (Sandoz) and by the Food and Drug Administration (FDA) that clozapine has caused a high incidence of agranulocytosis in Finland.

As reported in a published letter to Lancet [5], which is a bit lacking in detail, eight cases of fatal agranulocytosis had occurred in an estimated 1,500 to 2,000 patients exposed to clozapine during its initial six months on the market in Finland (nine other cases of unspecified blood disorder also had been observed in clozapine patients). In three of the fatal cases, clozapine was the only drug administered. The other patients received one or more additional drugs. The symptoms were first observed between 16 and 107 days after clozapine treatment was started. The eight fatal cases occurred in six (of 69) mental hospitals in Finland, located in one corner of the country (the south and southwest).

If clozapine were just another me-too drug with an unusual propensity for causing agranulocytosis, there would be no problem. One would stop all clinical studies on the drug without any particular regret. Clozapine, however, is the only drug with antipsychotic effects that appears likely to be really different from even thioridazine in causing little or no akathisia, parkinsonism, or dystonia and in failing to precipitate tardive dyskinesia. In our experience, persistent akathisia inadequately relieved by current antiparkinsonian drugs is a major problem in antipsychotic drug therapy. The problem has been well-described by Van Putten [6]; however, we lack his optimism that biperiden will always solve that problem. The literature alleges that thioridazine can cause tardive dyskinesia; locally we have seen one such case developing in an elderly woman after a year on the drug for the treatment of anxious depression. Even if clozapine fails to live up to the informal claims made for it, an antipsychotic drug that causes neither neurological side effects nor tardive dyskinesia is too important to be thrown automatically into the trash heap on the basis of serious toxicity reported in one country.

The ominous Finnish reports must be balanced against the larger experiences with the drug in Switzerland, Austria, and Germany where the drug is still on the market despite the Finnish problems. In the other three countries, the incidence of agranulocytosis is apparently low [4]. At the University Hospital in Munich, for example, 2,000 patients have been treated with clozapine over an eight-year period, and only a single case of agranulocytosis has been observed [7]. The hospital's experience with older drugs—thioridazine and chlorpromazine—is comparable.

Our three current clozapine patients were thoroughly briefed on the facts involved, given extra blood tests, and, with the FDA's approval, continued on the drug. All are currently outpatients, essentially symptom-free and well able to comprehend the issues involved. No evidence of any white blood cell abnormality has been noted under careful observation.

As of this writing, the FDA appears to agree with our decision at McLean Hospital. We are able to continue to use clozapine in patients who are unable to tolerate other antipsychotic drugs or who have developed tardive dyskinesia. Frequent white blood cell counts are, of course, mandatory.

**Agranulocytosis**

Our interest in clozapine led us to review the available literature on agranulocytosis associated with other antipsychotic drugs. The data on the incidence of agranulocytosis associated with other drugs are very limited. The American Medical Association (AMA) kept data on cases of agranulocytosis from 1957 to 1966. Over that period, there were 83 cases associated with chlorpromazine, 13 with mepazine (Pacatal), 6 with thioridazine, and 30 with promazine [8]. Occasional cases have been reported with the high-potency antipsychotics (perphenazine, prochlorperazine, haloperidol). Pisciotta, who has done most of the work in this area, believes that the higher dose drugs (e.g., chlorpromazine and thioridazine) are more likely to cause bone-marrow depression [8]. Simple leukopenia (white blood cell counts under 3,700) is relatively common and generally benign. When agranulocytosis occurs, it appears within a few days; in contrast, aminopyrine—an analgesic associated with the occurrence of agranulocytosis—causes an *abrupt* destruction of white cells and sudden fever [9]. The mechanism of phenothiazine-induced agranulocytosis seems to be due to the suppression of DNA synthesizing enzymes in bone-marrow cells which, in turn, blocks granulocyte production [10]. Patients developing agranulocytosis are believed to have a preexisting limitation in the cell-making potential of their bone marrows. In vitro examination confirms that, in patients with a history of chlorpromazine agranulocytosis, the capacity of bone marrow to make DNA can be decreased by chlorpromazine.

There are only two recent large series of psychiatric patients carefully screened for agranulocytosis with weekly blood counts. Pisciotta, at the University of Wisconsin Medical School at Milwaukee, obtained 37,400 leukocyte counts in 6,300 psychiatric inpatients and found five cases of agranulocytosis [8]. In the same sample, 2,000 patients showed benign leukopenia at one time or another on "high" doses of antipsychotics. Litvik and Kaelbling obtained 40,000 leukocyte counts in 11,407 patients at Ohio State University Hospital over a 15-year period and found only five patients with leukocyte counts of 2,000 or less [11]. Of these, only three developed fever and one of the three recovered before antibiotics could be started. They also identified 80 other asymptomatic patients with counts below 3,700. They carried out 40,000 white counts to find these patients.

In general, agranulocytosis is more likely to occur on antipsychotic drugs in patients over 40 and in women. There is still some confusion in the literature as to whether or not older women receive antipsychotic drugs more frequently than men or younger women. In general, they do receive more drugs of all sorts—they go to doctors' offices more than younger women or men, too—but it seems likely that antipsychotic drugs, in particular, are used in patients under 60 and in men at least as often as in older women.

A recent study has looked at the possible relationship between outpatient phenothiazine use and bone-marrow depression [12]. The study covered 1,048 psychiatric hospital admissions previously treated as outpatients as well as over 42,000 general medical hospital inpatient admissions. No cases of agranulocytosis were found in either sample, and the rates of leukopenia at admission observed for patients with histories of outpatient phenothiazine administration were similar to the rates of leukopenia in patients who had received other drugs prior to psychiatric hospital admission. Only rarely (twice) was a patient preferentially admitted to a general hospital because of phenothiazine-induced bone-marrow depression (leukopenia, not agranulocytosis).

What inferences can be drawn from all this with respect to the use of routine blood counts in psychiatric patients? It will probably warn everyone—nursing staff, patients and relatives—to report sore throats and fevers at once and then to get emergency white blood cell counts, particularly in the first few months of drug therapy. This is the best and most feasible way of preventing the serious consequences of agranulocytosis. If routine leukocyte counts are to be used at all, older patients receiving chlorpromazine and thioridazine might be selected for this relatively high-cost, low-yield prophylactic procedure during the first few months of their drug therapy. However, Litvik and Kaelbling argue that their routine practice of weekly leukocyte counts may have made their clinical personnel underalert to the sudden emergence of serious agranulocytosis [11]. The other possible argument is that, clinically, it is hard enough to get schizophrenic patients to continue taking antipsychotic medication under present circumstances. To expose them to weekly venipunctures at one's office or clinic may make drug taking even less popular. If the patient has to be sent to a distant clinical laboratory or hospital to have blood drawn, this dubious prophylactic routine becomes really unfeasible. For the interested reader, the two best review articles—neither of which offer specific recommendations on prevention—are by Pisciotta [10] and by Ebert and Shader [13].

To return briefly to the clozapine issue, until the Finnish experience is more thoroughly evaluated, weekly white counts are a requirement for patients receiving clozapine, if only to show due appreciation of the possible hazard; for patients who have failed to respond to safer drugs or who have experienced intolerable side effects on safer drugs, the inconvenience and risk may well be acceptable.

At the larger policy level, the ambiguous state of our knowledge about the risk of agranulocytosis on various antipsychotic drugs can only be remedied if a large, epidemiological system is created that relates the exact numbers of patients exposed to antipsychotic drugs to the development of documented adverse effects. Until that time, one cannot be sure whether chlorpromazine and thioridazine are more likely to cause agranulocytosis than other antipsychotic drugs or whether they were simply used more widely when the AMA was still collecting semisystematic data on blood dyscrasias.

**Commentary**

This paper was written because of our initial positive results in the use of clozapine, which appeared at the time to be a uniquely valuable drug in psychiatry. The drug's future was threatened by early reports of agranulocytosis associated with its use.

Since this paper was written clozapine has passed almost completely out of existence, mourned and not forgotten. Further reports of agranulocytosis associated with its use continued to appear, and a number of additional deaths occurred in Europe. I was given the opportunity to review these cases. Almost all of them occurred in patients whose blood counts were not being monitored at all, and several of the deaths might well have been prevented by earlier and more appropriate medical treatment. Nevertheless, the risk was real. We had one patient on clozapine at McLean Hospital whose white blood count dropped to 3,000. We stopped the drug and it rose again. Because she had a recurrent episode of mania and tardive dyskinesia, we started the drug again cautiously; however, the white count again began to sink, and this approach to her treatment had to be abandoned.

Sandoz Pharmaceuticals, the company responsible for marketing the drug in Europe and for supporting its clinical trials in the United States, stopped the study of all new patients in the spring of 1977 when one group of new cases of agranulocytosis was reported. It allowed resumption of clozapine in patients with tardive dyskinesia or severe intolerance to the neurological side effects of other antipsychotics in the late summer of 1977 but finally discontinued all marketing and new investigational use of clozapine in the winter of the same year. A few patients who had done well on clozapine have been allowed to stay on the drug ever since with weekly hematology being required.

Our experience with clozapine in 28 patients was generally positive. It was at least as effective as any prior antipsychotic medication in all patients and better than any prior drug in several patients. It caused no parkinsonism and did not aggravate preexisting tardive dyskinesia. Patients able to stay on the drug for more than a few months showed some general amelioration of their dyskinesia. Two patients developed some akathisia and two had transient tongue stiffness, which abated when the dose was lowered. This was perhaps a form of dystonia, though the symptoms came on after several weeks of therapy, an unusual time for dystonia to emerge. Clozapine caused tachycardia (usually asymptomatic), hypotension, drowsiness, and drooling. It was, therefore, not the ideal antipsychotic drug, but it was both effective in psychosis and unique in the virtual absence of neurological side effects.

I personally believe that clozapine should continue to be made available for use in selected patients with full informed consent and careful monitoring of blood counts (much as chloramphenicol is used in the antibiotic area) as a uniquely useful but dangerous drug where the benefit sometimes outweighs the risk, at least until a safer clozapine-like antipsychotic becomes available.

Unfortunately, Sandoz Pharmaceuticals was unwilling to accept this line of reasoning, being fearful, I imagine, of multimillion-dollar law suits whenever a patient died of agranulocytosis. A few clozapine patients (four at McLean Hospital and a handful at other sites where clozapine studies had been in progress) are still on the drug through the company's kindness and are doing reasonably well.

Even more unfortunately, no new antipsychotic with clozapine's unique properties is, to my knowledge, in clinical trial either in the United States or in Europe. The few potential candidates to replace clozapine have not fared well in clinical studies to date. Although my naive belief had been that, having found one clozapine, it would be easy to find other chemicals with identical properties, I appear to have been quite wrong. One may only hope.

## References

1. Gross H, Langer E: Das Neuroleptikum 100-129/HG-1854 (Clozapin) in der Psychiatrie. Int Pharmacopsychiat 4:220-230, 1970.

2. Matz R, Rick W, Oh D, Thompson H, Gershon S. Clozapine—a potential antipsychotic agent without extrapyramidal manifestations. Current Therap Res 16:687-695, 1974.

3. Simpson GM, Psych MRC, Varga E: Clozapine—a new antipsychotic agent. Current Therap Res 16:679-686, 1974.

4. Kline NS, Angst J: Side effects of psychotropic drugs. Psychiatr Ann 5:8-39, 1975.

5. Idänpään-Heikkila J, Alhava E, Olkinuora M, Palva I: Clozapine and agranulocytosis. Lancet: Sept 27, 1975.

6. Van Plutten T, Mutalipassi LR, Malkin MD: Phenothiazine-induced decompensation. Arch Gen Psychiat 30:102-105, 1974.

7. Klein H: Personal communication.

8. Pisciotta AV: Agranulocytosis induced by certain phenothiazine derivatives. JAMA 208:1862-1868, 1969.

9. The Medical Letter. Dipyrone and aminopyrine—for relief of fever. Issue 365: Jan 5, 1973 (Vol 15, No. 1).

10. Pisciotta AV: Mechanisms of phenothiazine-induced agranulocytosis. In Efron D (Ed.) Psychopharmacology: A Review of Progress, 1957-1967, pp 597-606. Public Health Service Publication No. 1836, GPO, Washington, D.C.

11. Litvak R, Raelbling R: Agranulocytosis, leukopenia and psychotropic drugs. Arch Gen Psychiat 24:265-267, 1971.

12. Swett C Jr: Outpatient phenothiazine use and bone marrow depression. Arch Gen Psychiat 32:1416-1420, 1975.

13. Ebert MH, Shader RI. Hematological Effects. In Shader RI, and DiMascio A (Eds.): Psychotropic Drug Side Effects. Baltimore, Williams and Wilkins, 1970.

# 12

# Lithium and the Kidney

*Jonathan O. Cole, M.D.*
*Richard I. Altesman, M.D.*
*Martin Ionescu-Pioggia, A.B.*
*Patricia M. Brewster, R.N., M.A.*

Lithium salts were first studied in the treatment of mania approximately 35 years ago. They have been widely used in this country for the treatment of affective disorders, usually as a maintenance therapy, since the late 1960s. They have been used extensively in European countries for a much longer period. Although lithium use has been associated with a variety of side effects—e.g., tremor, nausea, acneform rash, edema, goiter, dizziness, confusion, leukocytosis, and hypothyroidism—most of these are mild or occur only at nearly toxic serum levels. Acute lithium intoxication has always been recognized as a potentially serious medical emergency, but the other side effects have generally been considered relatively benign annoyances. In our clinical experience, the side effects most likely to limit lithium's acceptance by patients have been tremor, malcoordination, and general malaise. Occasional patients are seriously troubled by edema, weight gain, acne-like rash, or by polydipsia and polyuria [1,2]. Until 1977, these last-named side effects were viewed as undesirable but not potentially harmful in any permanent sense. Even marked polyuria was said to remit fairly rapidly when lithium was stopped. Patients whose recurrent affective episodes were not clearly and immediately responsive to lithium were still often maintained on lithium for one to three years in the hope that some gradual amelioration of the episodic illness might occur. Lithium achieved a certain éclat through television appearances of lithium-responsive manic-depressive celebrities and by the publication of popular books on the benefits of lithium in affective disorders [3,4].

This lithium-positive attitude on the part of psychiatrists received a blow in 1977 when Hestbach et al. from Aarhus in Denmark reported that 13 of 14 patients hospitalized for lithium intoxication or marked polyuria showed abnormalities of the kidney on renal biopsy [5]. These abnormalities included tubular atrophy, sclerotic glomeruli, and increased fibrous tissue characteristic of interstitial fibrosis. This finding has led to a series of studies of renal status in patients on lithium. The purpose of the present paper is to review the available studies and to evaluate the implications of the currently unsatisfactory status of our knowledge in regard to clinical treatment. Nephrologists knowledgeable in the lithium area point out that

173

the renal pathology caused by analgesics like phenacetin took many years to become well understood and accepted and that the changes alleged to be associated with lithium, although generally milder, are less clear [6,7]. It may, therefore, be far too early to expect a definitive appraisal of lithium's effects on the kidney, but a clinically oriented attempt seems necessary and desirable at this point.

## Tissue Pathology

There have now been 12 additional cases [8-11] showing the interstitial fibrosis and tubular atrophy described by Hestbach et al. Two of these are essentially individual case reports [10,11]. As far as can be determined, no patient on lithium for less than a year or so has shown these changes. However, Burrows et al. found other, perhaps earlier, changes mainly in the distal convoluted tubules and collecting ducts in the two patients on lithium for only four and five months, respectively [8]. An apparently similar set of tubular changes were found on the autopsy of a patient with marked polyuria who had been on lithium for a year or so and who had committed suicide by "presumed self-poisoning," not further explained [12].

To date, the only sample of renal biopsy specimens from lithium patients *not* selected for symptoms of kidney malfunction or other toxicity was reported by Rafaelson et al. in Copenhagen. They induced 50 of their 100 lithium clinic patients to agree to a two-week hospitalization for evaluation of renal function. They found only four patients with interstitial fibrosis of the sort described by Hestach (8%), and 15 additional patients (30%) had kidney biopsies "cautiously called borderline by the pathologist" [9].

There are at least three problems with these data. One is that the biopsy sections were probably not read "blind," a necessary control in such a charged area. Also, there seems little correlation between length of time on lithium and the extent of kidney abnormalities. Lithium studies in animals have shown changes in the distal convoluted tubules and collecting ducts but these too have not been uniformly well controlled [13]. Furthermore, other conditions, including anatomic abnormalities, analgesic abuse, hyperuricemia, nephrosclerosis and kidney stones, as well as antibiotic toxicity, have been identified as probable causes of interstitial nephritis [14,15].

## Polydipsia and Polyuria

The other approach to renal abnormalities in patients on lithium is via the symptoms of thirst, excessive drinking, and excessive urination. This has been recognized as a lithium effect for many years and has been the basis of several studies. No extensive data on the frequency of these side effects are available, but probably somewhere between 10% and 40% of patients on maintenance lithium have subjective awareness of increased thirst and urination, whereas a small proportion, perhaps 2% to 5%, have massive polyuria that interferes seriously with their functioning. Cases with 24-hour urine volumes comparable to those seen in diabetes insipidus (10 to 12 L/day) have been reported. Possible explanations for the voiding of large amounts of fluid in lithium-treated patients could include: (1) a direct central effect on thirst, causing increased water consumption; (2) a suppression of production of antidiuretic hormone (ADH) from the posterior pituitary, leading the kidney to be unable to concentrate urine (central diabetes insipidus); or (3) a reduced response of the distal tubules in the kidney to ADH (nephrogenic diabetes insipidus). On the basis of several studies of lithium patients with marked polyuria, it is clear that most such patients are unable to concentrate their urine adequately and show no improvement when given ADH parenterally. Occasionally patients do show some response to ADH. Patients on lithium with polyuria have also been shown to have elevated blood and urine levels of ADH, suggesting an ineffective compensatory response by the pituitary to the syndrome. As is the case in naturally occurring diabetes insipidus, urine concentration is paradoxically improved by thiazide diuretics and even by a low-sodium diet.

The specific studies supporting the above statements are not numerous. Singer et al. studied three polyuric lithium patients [16]. All three showed markedly reduced urinary osmolality after water deprivation. Only one of the three showed improved urinary concentration after vasopressin. Glomerular filtration was normal, however. Forrest et al. did a more extensive study, screening 96 consecutive lithium clinic patients for subjective complaints of polydipsia and polyuria [17]. Forty percent complained of polydipsia. Twelve percent excreted over 3 L/day of urine, while another 20% reported unmeasured increases in urine volume. Ten polyuric patients were studied under water deprivation with and without added vasopressin (ADH). Four patients showed marked urine concentration defect, while the other six showed clear but less severe defects. Two of the ten were able to concentrate better after vasopressin; the others had no response. Ten additional patients had their urine-concentrating ability studied before and after 10 to 12 weeks on lithium; they showed a significant decrease in urinary concentration from about 1,000 milliosmol/kg to about 850 milliosmol/kg. Three patients with severe polyuria (6 to 9 L/day) were treated with chlorthiazide, 500 to 1,000 mg/day; this caused a substantial reduction in urine volume and an increase in urine-concentrating ability. MacNeil et al. found three of five lithium patients to have decreased concentrating ability; only two had urine volumes over 3 L/day [18]. Seven patients on lithium showed increased urinary ADH excretion. Two patients with polyuria showed no response to treatment with a vasopressin analog; one showed some reduction in urine volume on a low-sodium diet and four showed a marked reduction in urine volume on a diuretic. Baylis and Heath studied 48 randomly selected lithium clinic patients under dehydration and compared them with 20 control subjects [19]. Seventeen of the 48 patients as a group showed elevated plasma ADH concentrations. Plasma osmolality was normal. The data suggest a gradual transition from normal to abnormal values in lithium patients rather than suggesting a clear demarcation between "normal" and "abnormal" patients. Padfield et al. studied 18 lithium clinic patients [20]. Seventy percent reported increased thirst and 61% reported increased urination. The patients as a group showed elevated plasma levels of ADH.

Bucht and Wahlin found mildly reduced urinary concentrating capacity (averaging 660 milliosmol/kg) in 19 clinic patients who had been on lithium alone and slightly lower values (averaging 620 milliosmol/kg) in 41 patients who had been on both lithium and antipsychotic drugs [21]. In both groups, concentrating ability was measured two months after lithium had been discontinued. Both groups were impaired relative to healthy controls (850 milliosmol/kg), while patients on antipsychotics only averaged about 810 milliosmol/kg. There was a correlation ($r = 0.33$) between the total amount of lithium ingested and impaired concentrating ability. On the other hand, Cattell et al. found only modest differences in total urine volume between lithium patients and patients not on lithium, even though the lithium patients averaged almost five years on the drug [22]. The patients were on sustained-release lithium.

The prevalence of polyuria in patients on maintenance lithium appears to vary substantially from series to series. Forrest et al. reported between 12% and 32% in a group of 96 patients, depending on whether the patients' subjective reports (reports not based on measurement) are included [17]. If urine volume of over 3 L/day is considered abnormal, then Cattell et al. found only three such "abnormal" patients in a series of 75 lithium patients [22]. Rafaelson et al. found 16 out of 40 patients with urine volume over 3 L/day (no clear relationship to years on lithium) [9]. In papers not available to us but summarized by Jenner [23], Hullin and Birch found nine of 111 patients with a volume of over 3 L/day [24]. Hansen et al. reported 18 of 110 patients in this range [25], but their paper is authored by the same group (from Aarhus in Denmark) who also reported "polyuria" in 58 out of 150 patients [26], which is hard to reconcile without seeing the papers. Thus, we have prevalence figures ranging from 4% to 39% in generally undescribed but probably representative samples of lithium-treated clinic patients.

## Lithium and Diuretics

The current package insert on lithium carbonate warns, with some reason, against the use of diuretics or low-sodium diets in patients on lithium. Adding diuretics, generally of the thiazide class, to lithium or restricting salt intake can produce a marked increase in serum lithium levels with associated toxicity [27,28]. We saw one patient, well controlled on lithium, who became markedly toxic after going on a 10-day total-starvation (and therefore very low-sodium) diet. On the other hand, several papers now have described the purposeful addition of diuretics to the treatment regimen of lithium patients with apparent benefit [29-33].

Thiazide diuretics have two reasonably clear effects in patients on lithium. First, they decrease the rate of lithium clearance by the kidney. Himmelhoch et al. presented data on 15 patients, five at each chlorthiazide dosage level, showing 500 mg/day reduces lithium clearance 40%; 750 mg/day reduces lithium 60%; and clearance 1,000 mg/day reduces lithium clearance by almost 70% [30]. Most, but not all, of these patients had polyuria and polydipsia, the exact proportion being unclear. Thiazide diuretics also can markedly suppress lithium-induced polyuria from levels resembling naturally occurring nephrogenic diabetes insipidus (10 to 12 L/day) to 2 L/day. In patients whose affective episodes are well controlled only by lithium but who have severe incapacitating polyuria, adding a thiazide diuretic can effectively relieve an intolerable side effect and permit continued control of the psychiatric disorder.

The mechanisms by which thiazide diuretics affect either the decrease in lithium clearance or the nephrogenic diabetes insipidus-like polyuria is not entirely clear. It is hypothesized that the thiazide blocks sodium reabsorption in the distal tubule and that this causes the kidney to attempt to retain sodium by reabsorbing more sodium in the proximal tubule. In the proximal tubule, both lithium and sodium are reabsorbed together, while in the distal tubule sodium but not lithium is reabsorbed. This explanation adequately explains the decreased lithium excretion caused by thiazide diuretics. However, it does not seem to explain the effects of thiazide diuretics in naturally occurring nephrogenic diabetes insipidus or in lithium-induced nephrogenic diabetes insipidus. In both conditions the distal tubule is unresponsive to ADH. It is hard to understand why a drug which normally blocks sodium reabsorption in the distal tubule should have the reverse effect in pathological situations. Nevertheless, the effects appear to be real and valuable [30,31].

At this point the picture becomes more complex. Himmelhoch et al. report that eight of 12 patients with mood disturbances on lithium showed clear clinical improvement after chlorthiazide was added to their regimen [34].  In this study, the patients had their serum lithium levels raised by the diuretic, sometimes with transient toxic side effects controlled by dosage reduction, making it unclear whether higher lithium dosages alone might have accomplished the same effect. However, most patients also had polyuria and several were said to be failing to develop adequate serum lithium levels despite high lithium dosage; the data presented, however, show only five patients on dosages as high as 1,800 mg/day and only one on 2,400 mg/day. In any event, the chlorthiazide, by blocking the polyuria, probably made the increased serum lithium levels more tolerable.

The situation is complicated by two studies which suggest that either a low-sodium diet or 50 mg/day of hydrochlorthiazide can produce clinical improvement in manic patients without a significant increase in serum lithium levels. In an early study, Demers and Heninger initially treated six manic patients with lithium who were on a low-sodium diet (70 to 90 mEq/day) [35].  After the patients had improved, they were shifted to a high-sodium diet (120 to 240 mEq/day). Lithium serum levels were generally comparable at the two regimens. On the high-sodium diet, patients showed a decrease in side effects and an increase in manic symptoms. In a recent study by Maletsky, manic patients unimproved after 14 days on lithium despite serum lithium levels of at least 1.2 mEq/L were placed in a 30-day study [36].  While remaining on lithium, the patients first were assigned to either 50 mg/day hydrochlorthiazide or to a low-sodium diet (2.5 gm/day of sodium) for 10 days; all patients were then on lithium alone for 10 days. Finally, patients were placed on the alternate therapy (e.g., low-sodium patients placed on hydrochlorthiazide) for 10 days. Mania-scale ratings dropped markedly during the low-salt or diuretic periods and rose almost to baseline levels during the middle 10-day period. Changes in clinical state appeared unrelated to serum lithium levels.

We, therefore, have some presumptions and some interesting possibilities about lithium, diuretics, and low-sodium diets! For example, (1) thiazide diuretics decrease lithium clearance in the kidney, raise serum levels, and may thus precipitate toxicity; (2) thiazide diuretics can relieve lithium-induced nephrogenic diabetes insipidus (while raising serum lithium levels); (3) thiazide diuretics may permit adequate serum lithium levels to be achieved in the occasional manic patient who fails to achieve adequate levels despite increasingly high daily lithium dosages in the absence of a diuretic; (4) it is possible, though not definitely proved, that patients not responding clinically to lithium may do better when a thiazide diuretic is added or when they are placed on a low-sodium diet, even if the serum lithium level is not much changed. Conversely, going from low to a high-sodium diet may worsen manic patients on lithium. The mechanism of these possible effects is unclear.

There are, of course, problems and risks in abruptly adding a thiazide diuretic in patients already on lithium. Patients will have substantial increases in serum level and can become toxic or at least show more side effects. If 500 mg/day of chlorthiazide were used, it would seem reasonable to decrease the lithium dose about 50% at the same time and then monitor serum lithium levels frequently and titrate the patient to the desired lithium level. Of course, in severe uncontrolled mania with polyuria and inadequate levels despite high oral doses, daily serum level monitoring after adding a thiazide without lowering the oral dose could be justified. Patients on thiazide diuretics may become potassium deficient and should be watched for this.

The same dose reductions could, of course, be employed if a patient maintained on lithium required a diuretic for other medical purposes (e.g., hypertension). Thus, patients already on a diuretic should be able to be started on lithium safely, with the dose being titrated in the usual way.

If a patient on lithium and a thiazide diuretic has the diuretic stopped, then a decrease in serum lithium level should be expected and adjusted for.

An important question concerns the effect of maintenance diuretic-lithium combination therapy in patients with lithium-induced marked polyuria. Does this pose any risk or any benefit compared with leaving the patient on lithium alone? Is more serious renal impairment—decreased glomerular function—more or less likely to occur? There seems to be no valid basis for predicting either benefit or harm. Therefore, if a patient clearly needs lithium and has marked polyuria, adding a thiazide diuretic seems clinically sensible. With or without an added diuretic, renal function would require regular monitoring.

Given the undesirable long-term effects of antipsychotic drugs, the number of patients with recurrent mania that is not prevented by maintenance lithium, and the patients with severe mania poorly responsive to antipsychotics and lithium, further study of the possibility that added thiazide diuretic could convert nonresponders to responders is indicated.

### Impaired Glomerular Function

Given that some patients on lithium show renal pathology on biopsy and a probably much larger proportion show urinary concentrating difficulty and polyuria, generally resembling mild to severe nephrogenic diabetes insipidus, do many lithium patients have serious abnormalities in the more crucial renal area of glomerular function? Are they at real risk for developing uremia? Impaired tubular water resorption alone does not necessarily lead to other serious problems beyond the polyuria if the patient has access to adequate fluid intake.

Schou, the international patron saint of lithium therapy with more than 20 years experience in the field, is reported as never having seen a lithium patient in terminal azotemia or requiring renal transplant [23]. However, Rafaelson et al. describe one patient identified by an elevated serum creatinine level of above 20 milliosmol/L (normal being < 0.15), who "is slowly progressing to uremia" [9] after lithium was stopped. The Aarhus group also describes a patient (with a history of kidney stones and hypertension) on lithium for three years [11]. His serum creatinine rose from 1.6 mg/100 ml to 5.7 mg/100 ml after lithium was stopped. His glomerular filtration rate also decreased to 13 ml/min. For the next nine months, kidney function remained stable without further progression. Both patients had severe interstitial nephritis on biopsy. Anecdotally, we have heard of two lithium patients in the Boston area with elevated blood urea nitrogen (BUN) levels who had to be taken off lithium. Gosenfeld, as reported by Ayd, had a patient who became toxic on lithium [10]; nine months later, "his creatinine clearance was one-third of normal." Simon et al. described a patient on lithium for six years who developed marked (7 L/day) polyuria and a concentration defect persisting at least 20 months after lithium was stopped [29]. Other aspects of renal function were not described.

If serious renal impairment *may* be associated with lithium use, the proper test for detecting damage is a measure of glomerular filtration. Creatinine clearance is the most widely used and standard test, though it requires a very accurate collection of 24-hour urine samples; loss of a part of the sample would cause the resulting computation to show impaired creatinine clearance when this might not, in fact, be the case. Other substances—insulin, ethylenediaminetetraacetic acid (EDTA)—are used, generally in research settings, to measure renal clearance over periods of a few hours.

Rafaelson et al. found impaired creatinine clearance (under 70 ml/min) in seven of 47 patients [9]. Hullin and Birch are reported to have found comparable impairment in 38 (33%) of 111 lithium patients but, most remarkably, found comparable defects in renal function in a control group of psychiatric patients with equal lengths of drug therapy but no exposure to lithium [24]. Two studies found decreased creatinine clearance in nine of 18 and 16 of 58 lithium patients with polyuria [21,25].

Two potentially more straightforward ways of measuring (or monitoring) renal function in lithium patients exist. One is the lithium dose necessary to maintain a desirable serum level and serum creatinine level. If renal function is impaired, then lithium will be cleared less efficiently by the kidney, and serum lithium levels should rise if oral daily lithium dose is held steady. This possibility has not been seriously examined. BUN, the old classic test of renal impairment, is influenced by nitrogen intake and is therefore only a crude indicator. Serum creatinine may well be the most useful; if muscle mass is constant, bodily creatinine production should stay constant. Therefore, serum creatinine should be highly correlated with creatinine clearance. If creatinine clearance is impaired, serum creatinine must rise. To date, only two studies have used elevated serum creatinine to identify patients with renal impairment. This approach has identified only a small proportion of the patients found to have impaired creatinine clearance by direct test. Hullin and Birch had three such patients among 38 with creatinine clearance under 70 ml/min [24]. Rafaelson found three such patients on routine examination but found none in 50 lithium patients volunteering for an extensive renal evaluation program [9].

It would be rational and helpful if concentrating difficulty as measured by a urine volume of over 3 L/day occurred first, followed by impaired creatinine clearance, but the four studies that determined both 24-hour urine volume and creatinine clearance leave the whole matter in doubt. Rafaelson had seven patients with impaired creatinine clearance and 16 with polyuria [9]. They may not have been the same patients. Hullin and Birch had 38 patients with impaired creatinine clearance but only nine with polyuria [24]. Hansen et al. reported impaired clearance in nine and polyuria in 18 [25]. To complicate matters, not all patients with marked polyuria show concentration difficulties on water deprivation.

**What to Do?**

It seems reasonably clear that lithium maintenance patients are at some risk for renal impairment. In general, polyuria seems more common than decreased creatinine clearance. Patients approaching uremia seem quite rare, indeed. The whole picture is complicated by the possibility that other conditions can cause renal impairment in lithium patients. There is even a suggestion, which clearly needs more study, that other drugs used in psychiatric patients particularly antipsychotic drugs, may impair renal function. Phenothiazines have been reported to suppress ADH production but not, to our knowledge, to produce clear renal damage.

One implication of these ambiguous but unpleasant findings is that prolonged maintenance lithium therapy should not be carried out in the absence of clear evidence that the patient's psychiatric condition is benefited. In the case of bipolar manic depressives, lithium is probably less troublesome, given monitoring of renal function, than prolonged use of antipsychotic drugs or the hazards of repeated hospitalization for mania. In patients with recurrent unipolar depressions only, tricyclic antidepressants, if effective in preventing depressions, may be safer in patients who tolerate these drugs well. In patients with less clear indications—treatment-resistant schizophrenia, serious impulse disorders, emotionally unstable character disorders—lithium should be clearly able to produce early and persistent symptomatic improvement, which disappears when the drug is withdrawn before maintenance treatment is seriously considered.

Given that maintenance lithium therapy is indicated and beneficial, how should the renal function of the patients be monitored? Our belief is that careful creatinine clearance tests are almost impossible to do accurately in outpatients and hard to do in most inpatient psychiatric settings. We therefore recommend this procedure only in patients with other evidence of renal impairment. We have shared with Rafaelson et al. [9] the idea that monitoring of serum creatinine levels periodically, watching for gradual increases over time even if the total level remains below local laboratory upper limits of normal, would be the simplest way to monitor renal function.

## A Survey of Current Lithium Patients

With this concept in mind, we have developed a lithium register of all McLean inpatients and partial hospital patients, which has now been maintained for 14 months. We initially included all patients then on lithium and have added all new admissions who either were already on lithium at the time of admission or who were started on lithium in the hospital. Old records were searched for prior serum creatinines. "New" patients to the register were tested for serum creatinine levels on three separate occasions within the first month on the register and then had serum creatinines done every three months, more often if values over 1.5 mg/100 ml were obtained, in which case the measure was repeated, usually within a week. Since we do not have a formal outpatient lithium clinic, longitudinal data are available only on patients with prior creatinine levels and patients who have been hospitalized or followed in our partial hospital program for prolonged periods. The current data from the register are provided in table 12-1 which presents mean creatinine levels for various time periods on lithium. It is obvious that there is no striking change in serum creatinine over time; none

## Table 12-1
## Creatinine Levels Over Time in Patients on McLean Lithium Register

| Time on Lithium (Months) | N | Mean | Standard Deviation | Paired t Test vs. Baseline |
|---|---|---|---|---|
| Baseline | 126 | 1.12 | .34 | — |
| 2-3 | 37 | 1.14 | .33 | ns |
| 4-6 | 38 | 1.11 | .50 | ns |
| 7-12 | 36 | 1.08 | .23 | ns |
| 13-36 | 38 | 1.04 | .19 | ns |
| Over 36 | 13 | 1.17 | .26 | ns |

of the differences between means at the baseline level and at any of the time points is statistically or clinically significant.

When one inspects variations in the level of serum creatinine over time for individual patients, no patients with persistent steady slight increases in creatinine levels are seen, although several patients have shown single abnormal serum creatinine levels of 1.5 mg/100 ml to 1.7 mg/100 ml, invariably followed by lower values at subsequent time points.

One patient had a creatinine level of 1.9 mg/100 ml when first tested, which has persisted unchanged. A second patient, one of the two in the Boston area with clear renal impairment while on lithium, ran levels of around 3.2 mg/100 ml before being transferred to a general hospital for medical evaluation.

We found a weakly positive correlation (Pearson r) of 0.26 between total time on lithium and the last available serum creatinine for all patients on the register. However, the correlation between time on lithium and last creatinine for the 13 patients on lithium longer than 36 months was negative (r = −0.12).

To date, our plan for monitoring renal function by regular serum creatinine determination has failed to detect any new patients developing progressive renal impairment on this measure, either because of the relative safety of lithium or the relative variability and insensitivity of the measure. The specific measure used in our routine clinical laboratory is based on the Jaffe reaction, as described by Taussky [37].

**Summary**

Overall, the available data indicate that lithium therapy can impair renal function. A small proportion of patients develop renal pathology characteristic of interstitial nephritis, often with associated polyuria and polydipsia, difficulty concentrating their urine and, sometimes, reduced creatinine clearance. Since other medical conditions can cause the same renal pathology, not all such cases are necessarily a result of lithium toxicity. On the other hand, a larger number of lithium patients can show a concentration defect, usually with some polyuria, and some patients develop a marked nephrogenic diabetes insipidus with severe polyuria and polydipsia. This seems more clearly a pharmacologic effect of lithium, even though many patients are asymptomatic.

Thiazide diuretics can improve renal concentration ability and lower urine volume in patients with lithium-induced polyuria. At the same time, the diuretic increases serum lithium levels and can induce general toxicity if the lithium dosage is not lowered and the serum level carefully monitored.

There is no evidence that adding a diuretic in lithium patients affects other aspects of kidney function favorably or unfavorably; the problem has not been studied. There is suggestive evidence that a thiazide diuretic (and probably low-sodium diet) could improve psychiatric status in some manic patients inadequately improved on lithium alone.

The implications of all this for clinical practice are as follows:

1. To date severe renal effects seem so rare that lithium treatment should be tried in clinically appropriate patients and responders can be continued on the drug for even prolonged periods with monitoring of renal function. However, patients with marginal or unclear clinical benefit should be taken off lithium and have their need for the drug reassessed. In general, patients with recurrent unipolar depressions without manic episodes, in whom prophylactic maintenance therapy is indicated, should be maintained on an antidepressant rather than on lithium if the antidepressant is effective and well tolerated.

2. Polyuria without other evidence of renal impairment in clear lithium responders can be treated with thiazide diuretics with appropriate reduction in lithium dosage.

3. Renal function in patients on maintenance lithium should be monitored. Measuring serum creatinine at three-month to six-month intervals at the time of lithium level determinations is the simplest approach but may lack sensitivity to modest decreases in renal clearance defects. Patients with persistently elevated serum creatinine levels should have medical evaluation by an internist or nephrologist. Probably moderate to marked polyuria (over 3 L/day) should also lead to medical reevaluation. If one wished to be more cautious, creatinine clearance could be measured at the beginning of treatment or at the next annual medical evaluation in patients already on lithium and repeated annually. Patients whose serum lithium gradually rises, despite constant lithium intake, should also be suspected of having developed renal impairment and be evaluated medically.

4. In patients with clear but mild renal impairment, the risks and benefits to the patient of continuing lithium therapy should be carefully assessed and a trial off lithium should be considered. Obviously, severe manic-depressive patients well controlled with lithium still pose the major problem. For patients whose severe, recurrent mania is controlled by lithium, but who have renal impairments, maintenance on antipsychotic medication, although not equivalent to lithium in efficacy, could be tried. However, such medication has its own drawbacks, not the least of which is tardive dyskinesia.

In summary, lithium probably does have adverse effects on the kidney, but patients with severe progressive impairment are, fortunately, still quite rare. The best way to identify such patients is not entirely clear, but a set of procedures are suggested. The whole area needs larger and more detailed studies. At present, the benefits of lithium clearly outweigh its risk in appropriate patients.


## Commentary

This area, I have just discovered, is also being more exhaustively reviewed by a task force of the American College of Neuropsychopharmacology, headed by Dr. Herbert Meltzer of the University of Chicago Department of Psychiatry. He appears to have contacted a large number of lithium clinics and may have access to more unpublished data. His group's final report and recommendations should be available in the latter part of 1980.


## References

1. Schou M: Lithium in psychiatric therapy and prophylaxis. J Psychiat Res 6:67-95, 1968.

2. Altesman RI, Cole JO: Lithium therapy: A practical review. McLean Hosp J 3:106-121, 1978.

3. Kline N: From Sad to Glad. New York, Putnam, 1974.

4. Fieve R: Moodswing. New York, Morrow, 1975.

5. Hestbach J, Hansen H, Amdisen A, et al: Chronic renal lesions following longterm treatment with lithium. Kidney Internat 12:205-213, 1977.

6. Coggins C: Personal communication.

7. Altesman RI: Summary of papers presented at the International Lithium Conference, New York City, June 5-9, 1978.

8. Burrows G, Davies B, Kincaid-Smith P: Unique tubular lesions after lithium. Lancet 1:1310, 1978.

9. Rafaelson O, Bolwig T, Brun C, et al: Lithium and the kidney. Paper read at the Annual Meeting of the American Psychiatric Association, Chicago, Illinois, May, 1979.

10. Ayd F (Ed): Lithium-induced nephrotoxicity: A further report. Internat Drug Newsletter 13:25-28, 1978.

11. Kestla J, Aurell M: Lithium-induced uremia. Lancet 1:212-213, 1979.

12. Lindop G, Padfield P: The renal pathology in a case of lithium-induced diabetes insipidus. J Clin Pathol 28:472-475, 1975.

13. Birch NJ: A note on animal and human studies of possible kidney damage caused by lithium. In Johnson FN, Johnson S (Eds): Lithium in Medical Practice. New York, Univ Park Press, 1978, pp. 265-266.

14. Murray T, Goldberg M: Chronic interstitial nephritis: Etiologic factors: Ann Int Med 82:453-459, 1975.

15. Editorial: Antibiotic damage to damaged kidneys. Lancet 1:558-559, 1978.

16. Singer I, Rotenberg D, Puschett J: Lithium-induced nephrogenic diabetes insipidus: In vivo and in vitro studies. J Clin Invest 51:1081-1091, 1972.

17. Forrest J, Cohen A, Torbetti J, et al: On the mechanisms of lithium-induced diabetes insipidus. J Clin Invest 53:1115-1123, 1974.

18. MacNeil S, Jennings G, Eastwood P, et al: Lithium and the antidiuretic hormone. Brit J Clin Pharmacol 3:305-313, 1976.

19. Baylis P, Heath D: Water disturbances in patients treated with oral lithium carbonate. Ann Int Med 88:607-609, 1978.

20. Padfield P, Park S, Morton J, et al: Plasma levels of anti-diuretic hormone in patients receiving prolonged lithium therapy. Brit J Psychiat 130:144-147, 1977.

21. Bucht G, Wahlin A: Impairment of renal concentrating capacity by lithium. Lancet 1:778-779, 1978.

22. Cattell W, Coppen A, Bailey J: Impairment of renal-concentrating capacity by lithium. Lancet 1:44-45, 1978.

23. Jenner F: Lithium and the question of renal damage. Arch Gen Psychiat 36:888-890, 1979.

24. Hullin RP, Birch NJ: Effects on renal and thyroid function and bone metabolism in long-term maintenance treatment with lithium salts. *In* Cooper TB, Gershon S, Kline N, et al (Eds): Lithium: Controversies and Unresolved Issues. Amsterdam, Excerpta Medica (in press).

25. Hansen HE, Hestbach V, Olsen S, et al: Renal function and renal pathology in patients with lithium-induced impairment of renal concentrating ability. Proc Eur Dial Transplant Assn 14:518-527, 1977.

26. Vestergaard P, Amdisen A, Hansen HE, et al: Lithium and the kidney. Paper read before the 11th Congress of the Collegium Internationale Neuro-Psychopharmacologicum (CINP), Vienna, Austria, July, 1978.

27. MacFie A: Lithium poisoning precipitated by diuretics. Br Med J 1:516, 1975.

28. Lutz E: Lithium toxicity precipitated by diuretics. J Med Soc New Jersey 72:439-440, 1975.

29. Simon N, Garber E, Arieff A: Persistent nephrogenic diabetes insipidus after lithium carbonate. Ann Int Med 86:440-447, 1977.

30. Himmelhoch J, Poust R, Mallinger A, et al: Adjustment of lithium dose during lithium-chlorthiazide therapy. Clin Pharmacol Ther 22:225-227, 1978.

31. Solomon K: Combined use of lithium and diuretics. Southern Med J 71:1098-1099, 1978.

32. MacNeil S, Hanson-Nortey E, Paschalis C, et al: Diuretics during lithium therapy. Lancet 1:1295-1296, 1975.

33. Price T, Beisswenger P: Lithium and diabetes insipidus. Ann Int Med 88:576-577, 1978.

34. Himmelhoch J, Forrest J, Neil J, et al: Thiazide-lithium synergy in refractory mood states. Am J Psychiat 134:149-152, 1977.

35. Demers R, Hininger G: Sodium intake and lithium treatment in mania. Am J Psychiat 128:100-104, 1971.

36. Maletsky B: Enhancing the efficacy of lithium treatment by combined use with diuretics and low-sodium diets. A preliminary report. J Clin Psychiat 40:317-322, 1979.

37. Taussky HH: Standard Methods of Clinical Chemistry, Vol. 3. New York, Academic Press, 1966, p 99.

# 13

# Memory Difficulty and Tricyclic Antidepressants

*Jonathan O. Cole, M.D.* and
*Alan F. Schatzberg, M.D.*

Ideally, a depressed patient who receives a tricyclic antidepressant experiences only a little sedation and dry mouth but feels a great deal better in a week or two. The physician may sympathetically acknowledge the discomfort of dry mouth but otherwise usually does not need to be unduly concerned. All our safest and most useful antidepressant drugs (imipramine, amitriptyline, desipramine, nortriptyline, doxepin, and protriptyline) have significant anticholinergic effects inextricably connected with their antidepressive action. In some patients, however, anticholinergic side effects may not be limited to dry mouth and perhaps blurred vision but may create more serious problems (e.g., urinary retention). It is fascinating that little attention has been paid to the nature or management of these side effects in the published literature [1]. One recent article [2] reports the use of bethanechol chloride (Urecholine) at a dosage of 25 mg t.i.d. as a peripheral cholinergic agent for both the prevention and the treatment of peripheral anticholinergic side effects of these drugs.

Tricyclic antidepressants also have central anticholinergic effects and can cause a full-blown toxic delirium similar to that seen with the more conventional anticholinergic drugs like atropine or scopolamine. The identifying characteristics of an anticholinergic delirium are "mydriasis, tachycardia, deep-red cutaneous flush, absent salivation and mucous secretions, anhydrosis, confusion, agitation, restlessness, picking motions and possible hyperreflexia and hallucinosis," to quote from Shader and Greenblatt's excellent review chapter [3]. In recent years, attention has been forcefully directed toward the dramatic ability of physostigmine (in doses of 1 to 2 mg/day parenterally) to reverse dramatically these manifestations of anticholinergic toxicity. It should be added that these effects, though dramatic, are relatively short-lived (one or two hours) and that most other cholinergic agents in general use (e.g., neostigmine) do not cross the blood-brain barrier and therefore do not affect the central actions of the atropine-like drugs.

It may be that knowledge of a potential treatment for a condition makes one more alert to its possible existence. While the occurrence of a frank delirium is relatively rare with routine doses of antidepressants, we

189

have been struck by the many spontaneous complaints of memory difficulty in patients who are otherwise generally pleased by the degree to which a tricyclic drug has alleviated their depression. Of course, not all treated patients complain of memory problems. Although we have not systematically probed for the symptoms, we estimate that about 20% of our recently treated patients have noted some difficulty with memory. Patients' experiences vary from a subjective sense of impairment, with perhaps little in the way of objective signs, to an objective impairment, primarily in functions of recent memory and storage. The following cases illustrate some clinical presentations of memory effects of the tricyclics.

## Case Examples

### Case 1.

A man in his mid-twenties had a history of recurrent unipolar depressive illness. He was hospitalized at McLean Hospital for a depressive episode characterized by lowered mood, sleep disturbance, decreased interest, and suicidal ideation. He had previously been treated with 150 mg/day of imipramine, which had precipitated an agitated perhaps hypomanic state; this caused him to be started on lithium carbonate. After admission, imipramine was discontinued and amitriptyline was instituted at 150 mg/day. On this dosage, he felt less depressed but had a vague feeling that he was unable to think as well as usual or to recall things as easily. However, his immediate recall of digits was excellent—eight digits forward and backward with no problems. In addition, he had a mild hand tremor. A reduction of amitriptyline to 100 mg/day resulted in disappearance of these symptoms. However, within ten days he felt depressed again. When the tricyclic was again increased to 150 mg/day, his depression again lifted. He did not, however, experience any problems with memory, although his tremor worsened; this resolved when the lithium carbonate was discontinued. It is interesting to speculate that this patient may have become acclimated to the central anticholinergic effects of the tricyclic.

### Case 2.

A woman in her mid-forties was admitted to McLean Hospital for a unipolar depression of approximately four months' duration. Major signs and symptoms included anorexia, sleep disturbance (middle and late insomnia), decreased interest in activities, diurnal variation, and lowered self-esteem. She had a history of gastrointestinal difficulties for which she took

60 mg/day of propantheline bromide (Pro-Banthine). At McLean Hospital, she was treated with amitriptyline, which was increased over approximately one month to 225 mg/day. On this dosage she felt considerably less depressed, and she showed improvement in vegetative signs. However, after she had been on tricyclics for a total of some eleven weeks, the nursing staff noted that she would forget whether or not she had taken her medication. On closer investigation, she exhibited difficulty in organizing herself, particularly in regard to processing and storing information. She appeared to have great difficulty with her memory although she could repeat, in a stumbling manner, six digits forward and six digits backward. Pro-Banthine was discontinued, and the patient was started on homatropine 20 mg/day because of its minimal central anticholinergic activity. Within four days, her memory difficulties abated. She could recall eight digits forward and backward with no difficulty, and she exhibited none of the behavioral signs the staff had noticed previously. It is unclear why the patient did not develop difficulties until she had been on the tricyclic and Pro-Banthine for some time. Anticholinergic agents, such as Pro-Banthine and amitriptyline, may potentiate each other and produce memory difficulties that would not have been caused by either drug alone.

*Case 3.*

A man in his forties was admitted to McLean Hospital for a depression of several years' duration. He had a variety of vegetative signs. He was treated with amitriptyline, which was increased gradually over five to six weeks to 300 mg/day. The patient felt relief from his depression on this dosage. However, within seven days of being on 300 mg/day he complained of difficulty remembering formulae he used regularly in his accounting work and figures he had used recently. Previously, while depressed, he had claimed some difficulty in memory, but on closer investigation, this appeared to reflect only psychomotor retardation. The effect with amitriptyline was subjectively different. Medication was adjusted downward to 200 mg/day. Memory impairment symptoms abated, and patient remained undepressed.

**Discussion**

Systematic research on memory function divides memory into (1) immediate recall (e.g., digits forward or backward); (2) storage processes, transferring information into memory; and (3) retrieval of information previously stored. As illustrated in the cases presented, spontaneous patient complaints tend to emphasize difficulty in recent memory, which probably involves difficulty in storage or, less likely, in retrieval. This may not be particularly evident when the patient's digit recall is tested, since this test chiefly assesses immediate recall.

A recent article by Sternberg and Jarvik [5] reports on a detailed study of memory function in depressed inpatients tested in a drug-free state and again after four weeks of treatment with imipramine or amitriptyline in doses ranging from 150 to 350 mg/day. They found depressed patients were less able than normal people to do immediate recall tasks but had no impairment in retaining learned material. After successful drug therapy, the problem with immediate recall cleared, but the most improved patients showed some impairment in ability to retain learned material. Although the authors do not make this association, it seems possible that the anticholinergic actions of the antidepressant drugs could have produced this impairment. The least improved patients did not show impairment of retention.

Another recent study [6] of a typical preanesthetic dose of scopolamine (8 ng/kg or about 0.6 mg) administered intramuscularly to normal subjects showed no impairment of immediate recall of short lists of items but marked impairment of delayed recall and retention of material learned while under the influence of scopolamine. Recall of material learned in the predrug period was not affected. Recognition was less affected than recall. Litjequist et al. [7], using "chronic" (two-week) administration of nortriptyline (20 mg t.i.d.) or chlorimipramine (25 mg t.i.d.) to normal volunteers, demonstrated that nortriptyline, as compared with placebo, impaired paired-associate learning but not the recall of digits, which fits the general thesis that anticholinergic drugs impair storage more than very short-term memory.

Ketchum et al. [8], in a much more elaborate and complex series of studies with higher doses of scopolamine and atropine, found more general impairment of both immediate and delayed recall, but their subjects were often too disorganized even to respond to questioning.

We are aware of no large-scale data on memory impairment as a drug side-effect in patients treated with antidepressants. Davies et al. [9] found confusional episodes, "characterized by impaired orientation or memory or other evidence of acute intellectual impairment" to occur in 35% of their 55 patients over age 40 treated with imipramine or amitriptyline; it occurred only once in their 95 patients younger than 40. Perhaps aging, which also interferes with retention of information rather than its immediate recall [10], also predisposes patients to anticholinergic confusion. Schulterbrandt et al. [1], however, report only three instances of confusional reactions out of 201 imipramine-treated depressed inpatients with a median age of 42.

In summary, we propose that varying degrees of central nervous system anticholinergic toxicity may be caused by tricyclic antidepressants, ranging from mild memory difficulty to full-blown delirium. It is possible that different tricyclic agents have varying effects on memory, which may be related to their relative anticholinergic potential. In addition, although the exact significance of doses and length of treatment is unclear, anticholinergic effects may be compounded by the concomitant administration of medication with anticholinergic activity—e.g., phenothiazines, antiparkinsonian drugs, and antispasmodics. Although physostigmine may be used as both a diagnostic and therapeutic agent in delirious states, physostigmine is probably too likely to cause cholinergic side effects to be used routinely in cases of mild subjective memory impairment. In any event, its effects would be too short-lived to permit its use as a treatment for tricyclic memory impairment. Lowering the dose of the tricyclic (or removing concurrently administered drugs like thioridazine, diphenhydramine, or those antispasmodics that penetrate the blood-brain barrier) is a more conservative approach. As a long-range solution, we note with interest that several newer antidepressants (e.g., trazodone) with negligible anticholinergic effects are in the market in Europe and are being tested in this country.

## Commentary

This brief paper was written to alert clinicians to the possibility that tricyclic antidepressants could impair memory to varying extents ranging from barely detectable impairments to full delirium. Since that time, we have reported in another journal on a tricyclic-related speech defect characterized mainly by an inability to complete sentences, a kind of speech blockage that seems to be another manifestation of the same basic difficulty [11].

I have continued to see occasional patients in whom mood response to tricyclics (and more rarely monoamine oxidase inhibitors) is complicated by memory difficulties of which the patient is often painfully aware and which disappear when the drug is stopped or the dose is reduced. I have sometimes been able to maintain mood elevation by shifting from a more anticholinergic tricyclic (e.g. amitriptyline) to the least anticholinergic tricyclic (desipramine), but I have seen patients develop memory problems on desipramine as well.

Recent work on the biochemistry of senile dementia has also stresed the role of cholinergic mechanisms in memory (see chapter 8).

Fortunately, a number of newer antidepressants are on the market in Europe and are well advanced in clinical evaluation in this country. These are not tricyclic and appear to be lacking in anticholinergic side effects and to show very little in the way of cardiac toxicity. Although several exist, the two with which I am most familiar are Trazodone, recently reviewed in detail by Ayd in his *International Drug Therapy Newsletter* [12], and mianserin, which has been the subject of two major published symposia [13,14]. Both drugs appear to be superior to placebo and equal to tricyclics in the treatment of depression. These and other newer drugs under development should provide the clinician with better alternatives for the treatment of depressed patients who tolerate older tricyclics badly. A controlled study comparing amitriptyline, mianserin and placebo in depressed elderly outpatients is nearing completion at the Geriatric Psychopharmacology Unit located at Boston State Hospital. A preliminary analysis of the data so far available suggests that both drugs improve depression but that mianserin improves cognitive functioning, while amitriptyline tends to impair it. I hope the completed study, on full analysis, will confirm these preliminary impressions.

## References

1. Schulterbrandt JG, Raskin A, Reatig N: True and apparent side effects in a controlled trial of chlorpromazine and imipramine in depression. Psychopharmacologia 38:303-317, 1974.

2. Everett HC; The use of bethanechol chloride with tricyclic antidepressants. Amer J Psychiat 132:1202-1204, 1975.

3. Shader R, Greenblatt DJ: Belladonna alkaloids and synthetic anticholinergics. *In* Psychiatric Complications of Medical Drugs. Shader R (Ed). New York, Raven Press, 1972.

4. Granacher RP, Baldessarini RJ: Physostigmine. Arch Gen Psychiat 32:375-380, 1975.

5. Sternberg DE, Jarvik ME: Memory function in depression. Arch Gen Psychiat 33:219-224, 1976.

6. Ghoneim MM, Mewaldt SP: Effects of diazepam and scopolamine on storage, retrieval and organizational processes in memory. Psychopharmacologia, 1976 (in press).

7. Litjequist R, Linnoila M, Mattila MJ: Effect of two weeks' treatment with chlorimipramine and nortriptyline, alone or in combination with alcohol, on learning and memory. Psychopharmacologia 39:181-186, 1974.

8. Ketchum JS, Sidell FR, Crowell EB Jr., et al: Atropine, scopolamine, and Ditran: comparative pharmacology and antagonists in man. Psychopharmacologia 28:121-145, 1973.

9. Davies RK, Tucker GJ, Harrow M, et al: Confusional episodes and antidepressant medication. Amer J Psychiat 128:95-99, 1971.

10. Isaacs B, Kennle AT: The set test as an aid to the detection of dementia in old people. Brit J Psychiat 123:467-470, 1973.

11. Schatzberg A, Cole J, Blumer D: Speech-blockage: a tricyclic side effect. Am J Psychiatry 135:600-601, 1978.

12. Ayd F: Trazadone: a unique new broad spectrum antidepressant. International Drug Therapy Newsletter 14:33-40, 1979.

13. Brogden R, Heel R, Speight T, Avery G: Mianserin: a review of its pharmacological properties and therapeutic efficacy in depressive illness. Drugs 16:273-301, 1978.

14. Drykoningen G, Rees W, Ruiz-Ogara C (Eds): Progress in the Pharmacotherapy of Depression: Mianserin HC1. Excerpta Medica, Amsterdam, 1979, 84 pp.